NIKOS A. SALINGAROS

ANTI-ARCHITECTURE AND DECONSTRUCTION

THIRD EDITION

WITH
CHRISTOPHER ALEXANDER, MICHAEL BLOWHARD,
JAMES STEVENS CURL, BRIAN HANSON, JAMES KALB,
MICHAEL MEHAFFY, TERRY M. MIKITEN,
HILLEL SCHOCKEN, AND LUCIEN STEIL

UMBAU-VERLAG

ACKNOWLEDGMENT

Grateful acknowledgment is made for permission to reprint the following material, which originally appeared in various journals, both printed and online. *"The Chessboard Model of Architectural Styles"* was originally published in Italian in *Il Covile, No. 320* (April 2006), English translation by the author. *"The Danger of Deconstructivism"* first appeared in Italian in *Temi di Stefano Borselli* (February 2003); English version in *2Blowhards* (March 2003). A much shortened version of *"Charles Jencks and the New Paradigm in Architecture"* appeared in *Chaos & Complexity Letters Volume 3* (2004); the present full version is previously unpublished. *"Deconstructing the Decons"* in *PLANetizen* (January 2003); shorter version in *The American Enterprise, Volume 13*, No. 2 (March 2003), page 13; Spanish version in *AMBIENTE Revista 90* (March 2003). *"Death, Life, and Libeskind"* published in *Architectural Record Online — In the Cause of Architecture* (February 2003); shortened version in *2Blowhards* (January 2003), reprinted with permission from *ArchitecturalRecord.com*. Postscripts are hitherto unpublished. Book review of Anthony Vidler's *"Warped Space. Art, Architecture, and Anxiety in Modern Culture"* in *Journal of Urban Design, Volume 6* (2001), pages 332-334, reprinted with permission from *Carfax Publishing, Taylor & Francis Ltd.* *"Twentieth-Century Architecture as a Cult"* in *INTBAU Volume 1*, Essay Number 3 (November 2002). Postscript is unpublished. *"Anti-architecture and Religion"* first appeared in Portuguese in *Brotéria (Lisbon) Volume 155* (November 2002), pages 381-388; English version in *Sacred Architecture, Issue 7* (Fall/Winter 2002), pages 11-13, reprinted with permission from *The Institute for Sacred Architecture*. *"Contemporary Church Architecture and Saint Augustine's 'The City of God'"* was originally published in Italian in *Il Covile, No. 300, Speciale Architettura Religiosa* (January 2006), English translation by the author. *"The Derrida Virus"* in *TELOS No. 126* (2003), pages 66-82. *"The New Ara Pacis Museum"* was originally published in Italian in *Il Covile, No. 329* (June 2006), English translation by the author. *"The New Acropolis Museum"* in *2blowhards* (February 2004); republished in *Temi di Stefano Borselli, No. 196* (March 2004), in *I Fileleftheri* (March 2004), and in *Archimagazine* (April 2004); *"Architectural Cannibalism in Athens"* originally published in Orthodoxy Today (November 2007); republished in Greek Architects (November 2007). *"Architectural Theory and the Work of Bernard Tschumi"* in *2blowhards* (April-May 2004). *"The Nature of Order: Christopher Alexander and the New Architecture"* appeared in *Vogue Hommes International 15* (Spring-Summer 2004), pages 116-119; French version in *Vogue Hommes International 15* (Printemps-Été 2004), pages 116-119. *"Aggression In Architectural Education: The 'Coup' In Viseu"* appeared in a shorter version in 2Blowhards (September 2004). *"Why Do We Have Horrible Inhuman Architecture?"* by James Kalb was originally published in three parts in *Turnabout* (January 2008).

SALINGAROS, NIKOS A.
"ANTI-ARCHITECTURE AND DECONSTRUCTION"
THIRD EDITION

ISBN 978-3937954-097

"More irritating than someone's actual stupidity is their mouthing a scientific vocabulary... One of the worst intellectual catastrophes is found in the appropriation of scientific concepts and vocabulary by mediocre intelligences."
— Nicolas Gomez-Davila, 1992

"In architectural and art schools, soulless dogma is still being taught; against reason, beauty, nature and man. Man is misused as a guinea pig for perverse, dogmatic, educational, architectural experiments... Young architects who still have dreams of a more beautiful and better world in their heads, these get their dreams taken away from them by force or else they don't receive their architectural diploma. Thus, only architects who have been brought into line become certified and so have the right to build."
— Friedrich Hundertwasser, 1993

"There grew around the modernists a class of critics and impresarios, who offered initiation into the modernist cult. This impresario class began to promote the incomprehensible and the outrageous as a matter of course, lest the public should regard its services as redundant. It owes much to state patronage, which is now the principal source of funding for high culture; it shares in the serene unanswerability of all bureaucracies with power to reward the "experts" appointed to oversee them... The new impresario surrounds himself with others of his kind, promoting them to all committees which are relevant to his status and expecting to be promoted in his turn."
— Roger Scruton, 2000

"The humanities have, in adopting jargon, tried to ape the sciences without grasping the actual nature of scientific thinking. In other respects, they have consciously and dogmatically rejected the scientific model altogether."
– Dennis Dutton, 2003

"One thing becomes ever clearer, however, and that is that schools of architecture, as presently constituted, should be closed down, and architectural education replaced by practical training, as was once the case. Certainly it is arguable that the resulting architecture was greatly superior to that produced after "architectural education" became a supposedly "academic" subject, with spurious degrees given to mark each hurdle jumped."
— James Stevens Curl, 2004

CONTENT
WITH ANNOTATIONS BY MICHAEL BLOWHARD

PART 1
THE CHESSBOARD MODEL OF ARCHITECTURAL STYLES
P. 26

One objection that inevitably arises to the Alexander-Salingaros approach is that it limits the artist's creativity. And aren't freedom and creativity always good, as well as signs of life? Shouldn't we always be looking to expand our sense of what's possible? Salingaros addresses these anxieties in a subtle but wide-ranging way. Why not conceive of architectural styles as a chessboard? A chessboard represents a very special kind of complexity: a variety of elements and rules that promote life. Beyond the chessboard is blankness, death — an infinity of combinations, via none of which life can come to fruition. In the name of creativity, Modernism and its descendents have steered us away from the chessboard and hurtled us out into cold wastelands where non-life is inevitably the result. Let's return then to what works. Constraints aren't deterministic; rules and patterns can enable creativity. Besides, the number of possible chess games — of life-giving moves and solutions — is infinite. Who should feel limited by this? And if we're to choose infinities, why shouldn't we opt for the one that confers life instead of death?

PART 2
THE DANGER OF DECONSTRUCTIVISM
P. 36

What is the relationship between intellect and emotion in art and architecture? Here Salingaros establishes the primacy of emotional experience in architecture. In his discussion, he also demonstrates something fundamental: that the exploration of emotional experience does not itself have to become a histrionic scene, but can in fact be a rational, civilized exercise.

PART 3
CHARLES JENCKS & THE NEW PARADIGM IN ARCHITECTURE
P. 41

Charles Jencks is a perceptive phrase maker and style tracker. In this review of some recent Jencks writing and thinking, Salingaros takes note of Jencks' use of scientific concepts to justify his contention that Deconstructivist architecture is an exciting and significant development. A man of science himself, Salingaros gently hints that Jencks' understanding of these concepts is, to be kind, superficial. In fact, Deconstructivist architecture represents no deep engagement at all with these ideas. Here it is simply fashion, a "look" that has been glamorized by clouds of fancy rhetoric.

PART 4
DECONSTRUCTING THE DECONS (WITH MICHAEL MEHAFFY)
P. 53

In this short essay, Salingaros lets himself begin to ask the question: what might Deconstructivism really represent? He doesn't hesitate, however modestly, to introduce a positive alternative to it, one that truly is based in the new science.

PART 5
DEATH, LIFE, AND LIBESKIND (WITH BRIAN HANSON)
P. 57

Salingaros turns his attention to a single, prominent Decon project, Daniel Libeskind's proposal for the rebuilding of the World Trade Center site. How to interpret this proposal? For one thing, how does it feel? Once again, a return to our basic emotional experience. What Salingaros shows convincingly is that for all the rhetoric surrounding this style the emotional experience and creative process itself of Decon is a negative one. We aren't set free; instead, we're brought down. We're led down gloomy and deterministic hallways. A humane man of the world, Salingaros asks not just if this morgue-like feeling is appropriate but also, can it be said to represent any unfolding of the human spirit at all?

PART 6
WARPED SPACE
P. 73

In this deceptively casual review of a book about Deconstructivism's treatment of space, Salingaros employs one of his most enjoyable strategies, which is to simply take them directly at their word, even to draw them out. We're left wondering: "What is this all about?" and "Who are those people talking to?" (Unstated but perfectly obvious answer: they're talking to each other, of course.)

PART 7
TWENTIETH-CENTURY ARCHITECTURE AS A CULT
P. 76

We have encountered Decon; we have opened our thinking to it. The time has come to tackle, as straightforwardly as possible, the question of what Deconstructivism as an architectural movement is, and what it represents. Some may find Salingaros' thesis shocking or facile; having had my own encounters with the Decon set I find it entirely convincing. A question stays with us after we've finished this essay: the leaders and stars of this movement — What are they getting out of it? And how is it serving them?

POSTSCRIPT: THE AUTHORITY OF THE GOSPELS P. 81

PART 8
AGGRESSION IN ARCHITECTURAL EDUCATION:
THE 'COUP' IN VISEU
P. 86

It's hard to believe but true: only a handful of architecture schools teach traditional architecture and urbanism — which means, in other words, that there are only a very few schools in the entire world that teach students how to create the built environments that most people find pleasing and rewarding. What a strange state of affairs, no? All the other schools are modernist enclaves, devoted to whatever's chic and hot: deconstruction, blobitecture... Once again, I find myself shaking my head over the bizarre and noxious schemes our elites are determined to put over on the rest of us. So it was heartbreaking to learn that one of the rare traditional architecture outposts was recently toppled.

PART 9
ANTI-ARCHITECTURE AND RELIGION
P. 92

Part of the strength and daring of the people in the alternative tradition I describe in my Introduction to this book lies in their willingness not just to raise some of the questions that art has dodged for over a hundred years now, but also to tackle these questions very directly. Perhaps the deepest of these questions is the relationship between art and religion. I can't begin to summarize Nikos' thinking here. But let me say that passages in this essay convey as much gravity and substance as any art criticism that I'm aware of. He writes at one point, "This indicates the transference of values from traditional symbols and rules (which could express religion) to an abstract ideal (which therefore competes with religion)" — that's saying an amazing lot.

PART 10
CONTEMPORARY CHURCH ARCHITECTURE AND SAINT AUGUSTINE'S 'THE CITY OF GOD'
P. 98

Why do collaborations between the Church and up-to-date architects seem to express the global marketplace more than the sacred? Fearing irrelevancy, Church fathers choose to project an image of contemporaneity. Yet the new churches they commission are the antithesis of what satisfying religious buildings need to be. Worshippers too often don't feel exalted or deepened; instead they're left feeling bereft and alone. Faith in God is thwarted, and spiritual yearnings are displaced onto blank forms and modern materials — onto the activity of abstract (if striking) image making — instead. By setting modernist procedures head to head with the fundamentals of being human Salingaros here brings the role of belief to the fore.

PART 11
THE DERRIDA VIRUS
P. 103

It has to be admitted that Decon has a unique kind of power: the ability to consume and destroy perfectly good brains. It goes that even one better, because it also fills that brain with feverish excitement, a kind of exhilaration at the spectacle of its own self-destruction. Here, Salingaros gives us an almost admiring appreciation of the distinctive power of Decon.

Now that the elements of Salingaros' perceptions and arguments have been established, the view broadens. Stepping back, we take in the overall structure. Here we begin to see how the deconstruction of Deconstructivism can become an act of creation.

Salingaros zeroes in on a recent real-life example — perfect in its scale and ironies — to crystallize his arguments: the Ara Pacis Museum in Rome, designed by the American uber-modernist and geometricist Richard Meier to house the remains of a 13 BCE altar memorializing the stability of the Roman Empire. (The Museum, which opened in April 2006, is the first work of modernist architecture to be built in the Historic Center of Rome since the 1930s, and it has been and continues to be controversial). The contrast between life and death is complete. The angles, planes, voids, surfaces, and blinding light of Meier's work convey nothing more than the sterile chic of an expensive dentist's waiting room. Meanwhile, the exquisite small classical building it shelters and dwarfs is as vital as ever, and still radiates an intense life. Sadly, Meier's new Museum represents something all too emblematic of our time: an intrusion into the living soul of a great city by a jet-setting global elite peddling nothing more than their own conviction that they know best. When will the rest of us wake up to what is being done to us?

What a test case: Decon in the person of Bernard Tschumi is invited to make his mark on the foundations of Western civilization — Athens, Greece. The generative past meets a destructive present.

PART 15
ARCHITECTURAL THEORY & THE WORK OF BERNARD TSCHUMI
P. 149

What is meant by Theory anyway? While addressing this question in a sober, substantial way — one based in history and science — Salingaros displays his sly side as well. Numerous unasked (but perfectly apparent) questions float up as we read this essay; numerous unstated (but perfectly apparent) answers arise too. What are these people really up to? If they aren't trying to accomplish something worthwhile, what are they doing? Their version of architectural theory couldn't be; well, a cosmetic smokescreen for an anti-civilizational enterprise, could it? Are we to sacrifice our own well-being so their stars might burn brighter?

PART 16
CHRISTOPHER ALEXANDER & THE NEW ARCHITECTURE
(INCLUDES AN INTERVIEW WITH CHRISTOPHER ALEXANDER)
P. 173

In arriving at the end, having made our way through thorny thickets, having dug them up by the roots, we arrive at the field's true starting gate. With this review of Christopher Alexander's magnum opus "The Nature of Order", and with a discussion with Alexander himself, we're given a substantial taste of the positive thing that architecture (as well as architectural theory) can be. Our wrestle with Decon leads us back to the thought that Decon is devoted to obscuring: that building and urbanism can be activities that contribute to human wellbeing.

AUTHOR'S PREFACE

This book offers a critical analysis of deconstructivist architecture and its underlying philosophy. I have felt strongly enough about this topic to write a series of essays, previously published in a variety of online and paper journals. Some first appeared in different languages — the present compilation brings them together in English for the first time. In the absence of any other book that is sufficiently analytical so as to make an impact on today's infatuation with this peculiar building style, I present instead this collection of essays.

The second edition includes three new essays originally written and published in Italian and a Postscript to Part 7. Michael Mehaffy contributed an Endnote for the Second Edition. Although only three years separate the First and Second editions, a lot has happened that is worth noting. This book has been unexpectedly influential, and its impact is growing. I am gratified that it received very positive and prominent reviews and was praised by many people, but — perhaps more significant — it has provoked a remarkably hostile over-reaction among some in the current architectural establishment. It seems to have struck a nerve.

The book began modestly as a collection of essays severely critical of the most fashionable and esteemed contemporary architects, published in English by a small architectural press in Germany. The book was unknown to general readers, since the major American and British bookstores (including the online ones) did not sell it. One prominent architectural bookstore in the US did carry it, but astonishingly, condemned it on its website! When my publisher complained that this did not make good sense for promoting sales, the bookstore in question promptly dropped the book. Despite such obstacles, the book has been translated into French, Italian, Persian, Portuguese, and Spanish, and the first edition has now sold out.

Consistent with its original purpose, the book seems to have been quietly embraced by a number of influential people. I am gratified to have heard from architects, architectural historians, philosophers, scientists, and journalists who have adopted some of my ideas. A few of them have thanked me for providing what they consider a useful framework for discussing architectural and social topics. Others, whom I don't know personally, picked up key concepts from this book (or from the individual articles as they originally appeared before being collected into the book). All in all, many people have found here a convenient rubric for analysis.

At least the vocabulary I introduced has caught on. On the Internet, in books, in newspapers, and in journals, the most offensive contemporary "star" architects are increasingly described as "anti-architects", the paradoxical proliferation of inhuman buildings is explained in terms of viral methods of infection, and monstrous new forms are analyzed with reference to their willful non-adaptivity. People started noticing that some built forms and spaces create anxiety and symptoms of physiological distress in the user, but this connection is denied by the architect (and by architectural critics who promote that architect). I expect that the first litigations over architecture-induced sickness will settle the matter quite soon, and this book may even be used in evidence.

The architectural debate is starting to take place outside architecture altogether, in an open forum where these fundamental questions can be freely discussed. In the twentieth century, architecture assumed a wholly unjustified role of authority (characterized by some as a substitute religion, complete with proselytizing and grandiose self-delusions), yet this key aspect is hardly discussed within architecture itself. Many people projected and continue to project their aspirations onto architecture, which thus acquired lofty ideals. Those excited by new and strange shapes seek a thrill in man-made forms. Nevertheless, this sort of visceral pleasure gets mixed up with defunct religious yearnings, and subsequently assumes aspects of a religious cult open only to the initiated. At the same time, its adherents celebrate a geometry that denies the generative experience of life in the world.

Ordinary citizens have suddenly discovered that their own intuitive feelings about architectural form are not aberrations, but have a basis in scientifically-comprehensible conditions. What looks and feels ugly, monstrous, and evil is in fact bad architecture from a user's point of view. Confused and disoriented by the peculiar discourse of our prominent architectural critics, illustrious schools, and the international media, they finally found a group of people (i.e., my circle of friends and co-authors) who validate their own deeply-felt frustrations. Theirs are normal responses to the perceived decline of the built environment, and the irresponsibility of our architectural leadership. I am incredibly gratified to have been able to help people stand on their convictions against the onslaught of media propaganda and specialist conditioning, supported and promoted by powerful institutions.

As far as the practice and teaching of architecture are concerned, the situation is more complicated. Everyday architects go on as usual, oblivious to the polarization of their discipline. Most of them continue to believe the delusional assumption that ordinary citizens "just don't get" architecture. The profession is not self-governing, and as a result, the public is not protected from professionals who abuse or damage nature's delicate geometry. Accusations about the inability or unwillingness of the architectural profession to adapt to human sensibilities and the ecosphere are answered by superficial gloss and a lot of hype. The debate on contemporary architecture's failure to adapt to biological forms and processes has only just begun, and will soon get more intense.

Architectural education remains isolated from the rest of the world, its very future in question (although those in control either don't know it, or don't wish to consider the possibility). I lecture at various architecture schools around the world, where I am confronted by the fundamental disconnect between living forms, on the one hand, and what is promoted as the nihilist standard of avant-garde art by professors, required course books, magazines, and the global media on the other. Students don't see the extent of the deception going on in architectural academia; otherwise they might get locked into a destructive struggle with their teachers, and thus never get to finish their degree. It's better that they discover this when they can stand on their own two feet (either upon entering graduate architecture school, or after they begin to practice).

I have found more sympathetic recognition from colleagues within Classical and Traditional Architecture, Landscape Architecture, Sustainable and Biophilic Architecture — all respected communities that are currently somewhat peripheral to the world of iconic architecture. Those disciplines are gaining in influence, however, and may eventually supply our future architects. As the agenda of sustainability and human wellbeing becomes paramount, iconic architects are beginning to find themselves isolated, and on the defensive. Quite aside from analyses like this one, it becomes more and more difficult for iconic architects to pretend to embrace sustainable urban concepts, without anyone noticing an incompatibility with their fundamentally destructive approach to the built environment.

As a welcome and positive development, a small number of architectural educators increasingly embrace my writings as offering opportunities for innovation. Those individuals are not aligned with any particular ideology or power structure. They genuinely want their students to become better architects — and make this their priority over and above political games. It is a challenge for me to help them try and work out future directions for architectural education from within the system. Even if only a handful of academics and practicing architects (and they are so far in the minority) are willing to make a change for the better, that can surely be accomplished, although it goes against established tradition. My writings help stir up a healthy debate in schools of architecture, a process encouraged in some places. Although most architecture schools advertise an open approach to the topic, they will not go so far as to include my views!

I have actually been careful not to foment any more controversy than is strictly necessary. For instance, I recently had to sit through a lecture by the Dean of one of the world's premier architecture schools, in which he presented the three greatest architectural thinkers of all time as Vitruvius, Palladio, and Libeskind. I kept quiet, not wishing to upset the conference's organizers who had also invited me. At the same conference, I befriended the Dean of another prominent architecture school, who had given a reasonably good talk on urbanism. I later sent him this book as a gift. He sent it right back! Now that's odd — Deans receive all sorts of books they don't particularly want, and they donate them to the school library. Clearly, he didn't want this book available in his school's library. He could have tossed it in the trash instead of paying return postage, but he must have found it remarkably provocative — so much so that he felt it necessary to distance himself from it in no uncertain terms.

The deepening crisis in which iconic architecture finds itself is of its own making — aided and abetted by a commodity culture that is only too happy to package up nihilistic kitsch. The present period of nihilistic expression continues for the time being, creating an alternative reality of seductive, translucent images offered for public consumption. Its corrupt support by vested interests might yet be superseded by a wonderful flowering of emotionally-nourishing, enduring buildings. It is with this goal in mind — a naïve wish that people will eventually rediscover simple, living architecture — that I hope this book will continue to provide inspiration to readers.

Two new parts are included in the third edition: a second essay on the New Acropolis Museum; and a description of the takeover of the Architecture School in Viseu, Portugal, written just after that architectural coup d'état took place. My original comments against the museum in Athens were published in several languages, and became known all around the world — except in Greece. That was not for lack of me trying, however. The outcome I predicted for the New Acropolis Museum turned out to be far worse than I could ever have anticipated. A successful propaganda campaign for starchitecture was carried out with consummate skill and efficiency. It destroyed, and is still threatening, part of Athens's historical urban fabric. The public was brainwashed using methods I had outlined in this book (but not learned from me!). Those who thought my warnings were exaggerated should look to Athens, where the methods were actually put into practice.

The second focus is on architectural education. We cannot hope to train humanistic architects in our existing architecture schools without a radically new type of educational program. The architectural establishment correctly perceives this as a major threat to its continued ideological domination. The ruthless takeover of one architecture school that introduced a humanistic design curriculum was a terrible setback for world architecture. Nevertheless, I believe that a lesson can be learned here. A single historic defeat can eventually become a rallying cry leading to eventual victory.

James Kalb rejoined the battle with three recent postings on his website. He was kind enough to let me use them here as a new endnote, entitled 'Why do we have Horrible Inhuman Architecture'. James raises profound questions about the religious implications of contemporary architectural styles, a discussion that Christopher Alexander is currently engaged in as well.

Co-opting the recent movement towards humanistic architecture by those who have suppressed it for the past several decades is a very worrying development. In the Postscript to Part 7 of this book, entitled 'The Authority of the Gospels', I mention how proponents of an inhuman architecture have now adopted a scientific vocabulary, and make up plausible-sounding but false arguments to promote their bizarre forms. This is simply an attempt to maintain their hegemony on the discipline — one more pretense in a long line of deceptive practices used to hold onto power. Students are easily fooled, however, since they are faced with new books containing attractive organic illustrations, in which deceptively sincere architectural theorists talk about exactly the same things I talk about: but twisting them to promote the worst sort of absurd anti-architecture. The arguments rely on the most superficial analogies with biological forms, betraying a fundamental lack of scientific understanding (which is unfortunately not evident to architects and students).

I must admit that this recent propaganda campaign is very cleverly done! Titles of the new books promoting a new direction in design all include the catchy words "Biological", "Green", "Landscape", or "Nature". Their authors (and publishers) have abandoned their usual sadistic architectural style of using a too small sans-serif font in a light gray ink, with blurry, grainy photographs; and have instead adopted a nice large serif font in solid black, with sharp, detailed photos of biological forms. There are also paragraph breaks for the first time in decades! Those books could be mistaken for the writings of my friends, not only for their superficial content, but also for their "look and feel". That, I'm afraid, is the intention: to marginalize us yet one more time by stealing our own vocabulary. Remember when the old totalitarian political regimes finally fell? Those who had worked for the secret police presented themselves as resistance fighters and moved quickly to take over the new democratic governments. It's the old trick all over again.

FOREWORD

BY JAMES STEVENS CURL

This book should be required reading in every institution concerned with the teaching of architecture, planning, and all other aspects of the built environment. It should also be read by every person claiming to be an architect.

That, however, is a forlorn hope, as most architects seldom read at all: they only look at seductive pictures and absorb slogans. There are a very few honorable exceptions; these are those rare individuals who conserve and restore old buildings, add to them or adapt them with sensitivity and scholarship. It includes those who can still design buildings that delight and enhance life rather than threaten it, and who understand the nature of the materials used in their buildings without having to call in engineers and contortionists to enable their designs to be realized.

The rise of Deconstructivism and its adherents can partly be explained by the spread of the contagion Salingaros, in this essential and timely book, calls "The Derrida Virus", and partly by the Imprimatur given to the style (for that is what it is) by Philip Johnson. Before the 1939-1945 War, Johnson had also encouraged the pandemic of the International Style with the exhibition he and H. R. Hitchcock organized in New York City. Now, Deconstructivism has been hailed as a "New Paradigm" by those who ought to know better, and the cult is being forced on students in those breeding grounds of the ugly and the unworkable, namely the Schools of Architecture. (In my opinion, they ought to be properly renamed "Schools for the Destruction of the Environment", and, in any reasonable society, closed down because of the menace they pose for the future).

This excellent and thoughtful book dismantles the flimsy codification known as Deconstructivism, showing how the ill-educated have been fooled by obfuscation, which they have mistaken for profundity. It also warns of the wholly negative nature of Deconstructivism. How many more of these so-called "iconic" buildings, with their jagged forms and uncomfortable spaces, their grotesquely impractical corners, their expense, and their disregard for context, can be sustained? Already, *LAUS DEO*, there are rumblings of discontent, and certain projects are being called into question as support falls away. Despite the pseudo-intellectual apologies for this cult/style, buildings resembling crumpled boxes, or with fronts looking as though they are sliding off in shards, cannot be justified, even using obfuscatory non-language. Nor can all the glossy pages of the journals that purport to be "architectural" (but are nothing of the sort) justify them, raising questions about trades descriptions.

"The Emperor Has No Clothes" is an old adage, but, in the sad case of Deconstructivism, it is absolutely appropriate, as the style is really nothing more than Modernism in a new guise. Modernists, notably the Bauhäusler, aimed for the clean slate — the *tabula rasa* — jettisoning everything that went before. Yet, at times, they claimed links with antecedents such as the Parthenon (Jeanneret-Gris alias Le Corbusier, and company), the English Arts-and-Crafts Movement (Pevsner *et. al.*), and Prussian Neo-Classicism (Mies van der Rohe) to give a spurious historical ancestry to their aims and creations. Now all sorts of barmy links and precedents are being claimed for the works of Deconstructivists by Deconstructivist architects and their supporters.

As this book points out, "architects and architectural critics have become expertly adept at fancy wordplay, sounding impressive while promoting the deconstructivist style's unnatural qualities. This linguistic dance is used to justify a meaningless architecture of fashion." Quite so, except that to some of us, blessed with a Classical education, it does not even sound impressive. We know it is simply empty jargon, meaningless pseudo-language, and ranting drivel of the worst sort. Cults invent their own liturgies and fraudulent language. Deconstructivism is a perfect example of this.

Deconstructivism is just another phase in the creation of the inhuman world dreamed of by Modernists. That world of uninhabitable cities, incessant noise, violent and pornographic "entertainment", destruction of natural resources, an uncivilized, dangerous, selfish population, and all other attendant horrors, is rapidly becoming a nightmare of the most ghastly kind, in which even the buildings are distorted, misshapen, and menacing.

Architects are trained nowadays to destroy: they are brainwashed into killing off living organisms such as cities, and have no feeling for old buildings other than to wreck them too. They are also trained to worship, starry-eyed, the few "star" architects who have gained favor with the arbiters of taste — the journals — so that when the stars go out or fall from the firmament, they have nothing left to worship. What is to become of them? They cannot do anything expect ape the once-fashionable and that which is *passé*, so (empty-headed and unskilled as they are) they really ought to be retrained to do something useful in a completely different field. Probably a mindless job — which seems to be the most common these days, and one for which the products of most architectural schools are eminently suited — is appropriate.

This book is the beginning of a long-overdue counterattack.

Professor James Stevens Curl is one of the world's leading architectural historians, and the author of "The Oxford Dictionary of Architecture" (1999).

"SOME THOUGHTS ON CULPABILITY"

BY JAMES KALB

The obvious method of dealing with the virus of deconstruction in architecture, as Professor Salingaros describes it, is no doubt intellectual hygiene: sunshine, fresh air, and a change in theoretical and aesthetic scenery. Get rid of the cultishness, accept the possibility of rational discussion with whoever has relevant knowledge, and open the doors to what people need and what actually works. A further necessity, as the author points out, is "stop[ping] its modes of informational transmission." Presumably, that would mostly be a matter of the normal practices of education and serious discussion. Intellectual influence depends on reputation, so recognizing the problem is the greater part of exorcizing it. Every field has standard examples of disasters to analyze and avoid, and in architecture deconstruction should be one such example.

Still, something further is needed to contain and cure the infection. Anything as complex as architecture requires mutual trust, cooperation, and a degree of subordination, so it is difficult for those working in the field, and for the general public, to deal with highly-placed authorities who promote irrationality on principle. Leading deconstructivists are skilled at manipulation, and their theories and actions are designed to disable rational criticism. When a major figure in deconstruction is able to respond to criticism with the assertion that all third-person indicative statements about his work are inadmissible something very odd is going on, and when thereafter his prestige only grows the situation is evidently one that requires clarity and vigor.

Clarity and vigor means that the issue of culpability must be addressed. As described in this book, deconstruction seems less a style or theory of architecture or anything else than an attempt to disorder fundamental aspects of human life. It is viral warfare carried on against any possible intellectual order, and thus a crime against humanity. Since deconstruction is a wrong as well as a disaster in the making, one cannot understand and respond to it adequately without considering the question of responsibility. Formal legal penalties are not at issue. While there is evidently wrongful intent, and the damage is potentially immense, the crime is too general, and involves the participation of too many respected people, to treat like an ordinary confidence game or sale of adulterated goods. As Edmund Burke suggests, it is difficult to draw up an indictment against a whole people — or even the dominant group in a profession or intellectual class. Extent, numbers and social position obscure blame and confer impunity.

Justice is never perfect. An 18th century Englishman comments:

"The law doth punish man or woman
Who steals the goose from off the common,
But lets the greater felon loose,
Who steals the common from the goose."

Human culture — which includes the implicit connections and implications that make coherent thought and action possible — is the greatest of all commons. It is the field in which all life, thought, and social cooperation play themselves out. An attempt to disrupt and destroy something so basic to what we are should be viewed as a crime. Nonetheless, a crime perpetrated by designing and propagating toxic memes to be embodied *(inter alia)* in the built environment and thus forced on the whole society seems too abstract to define and prosecute. Perpetrators infected by the virus they spread may not be fully responsible for their actions. Those not infected are likely to be adroit enough to adjust their conduct and avoid any system of legal liability. And if disordering of thought is the problem, prosecutors and judges may themselves be unreliable. With all that in mind, how does one sort out the blame, and what does one do about it?

The author touches on the issue, but does not develop it at any length. The most culpable, in his view, are the few theoreticians of deconstruction who act with a clear understanding of what they are doing and what is at stake. If the author's description is correct, such people cannot be accepted as participants in intellectual life. The organized thought of an intellectual community is vulnerable to fraud, abuse and vandalism, and it will be degraded unless such actions and those who engage in them are identified, confronted, resisted, and condemned. Such policing must be primarily the responsibility of the malefactor's fellow professionals. If they do not act, and the case seems egregious, the rest of us must form our own conclusions, both as to the specific acts and the degree of respect owed an intellectual community that tolerates them.

The culpability of others whose subjective purposes and degree of consciousness are more obscure is less clear. Perhaps they should be protected from blame by the principle that "theoretical investigations should be free and each should say what he thinks," or perhaps there are grounds to condemn individual architects who leave their meaning obscure but interweave their work with sadistic images of violation in what looks like a game of psychosocial manipulation. It is difficult to pursue such issues closely in the case of most individual theoreticians, who may only be presenting their thoughts for public consideration, or at worst attempting to provoke.

The officials, educators and institutions that promote bogus or harmful theories and back them with their authority are, as the author observes, a different matter. Those bearing practical responsibility for the built environment should be expected to exercise good or at least conscientious judgment. When they fail to do so they should be held responsible and suffer professional consequences. Those who push forward thinkers and projects that are at best modish and at worst toxic have the same culpability as anyone in a responsible position who adopts plainly destructive policies on account of stupidity, laziness, cowardice, frivolity, opportunism, or implicit sympathy with evil. The culpability of such people should be publicly recognized, and they should suffer the consequences accruing to any official whose willfulness or gross negligence brings on disaster. The same can be said of intellectual gatekeepers like architectural critics and those who sit on prize juries.

But what about everybody else — working architects, who must do the best they can in a professional world they did not create, and members of the intellectual and lay public in general? Here each must look to himself and herself. We get the leaders and the public arts we deserve. The inhumanity of contemporary architecture could not have been perpetrated without the support, cooperation or acquiescence of a great many people at many levels of society. How has it been possible for outrageous or incomprehensible claims to be accepted and inhuman buildings built, acclaimed and imitated for so many years? Modern life pushes us all toward subordinating our duty of independent judgment to the pretensions of certified or self-defined experts who claim the exclusive right to determine what can be thought and said. That tendency opens the way for endless abuse and fraud and must be resisted for the sake of our humanity. To the extent we submit to it, we become accessories to our own victimization. If we are to consider culpability for conduct leading to something as pervasive as the current built environment, we should consider and correct our own as well as that of the most obvious evil-doers.

INTRODUCTION
by Michael Blowhard

Too often it seems that posted prominently on the doorway to the arts is a sign that reads, "Abandon all rational thought, O ye who enter here."

But why must the arts — the activities of making and experiencing, as well as discussing and thinking about them — always be such a murky realm? What, after all, do attitude and jargon really signify? And of what help is mystification? Broadening our experience of the arts, looking for guidance, we're given to understand that there are levels of significance that — once having been initiated into the cognoscenti — we might gain access to. What a stirring privilege that would be!

We're being sold, in Thomas Sowell's great phrase, "the vision of the anointed".

In fact, and although it's much too little known, there's an alternative view of the arts abroad. It's a way of seeing and doing art that's reasonable; that doesn't defy common sense or plain experience; that's based in what's tried and true; that embraces the lessons of science and history; and that does all this not in any way that discourages or impedes the imagination, but that instead enhances and enables it.

The development of this view has been one of the most exciting and heartening developments in the arts in the last thirty years. It has also been one of the least-reported and most-unknown. Arriving in the arts-and-media worlds in the mid-'70s and being cursed with a certain kind of brain, I first marveled at the nonsense that was being spouted about the arts — it simply didn't match what I was encountering. Then I went in search of people, writers and thinkers, who made more sense.

What I discovered during the years since was a cast of brilliant, heterodox iconoclasts: Christopher Alexander, Ellen Dissanayake, Frederick Turner, Denis Dutton, Léon Krier, Mark Turner, Philip Langdon, James Howard Kunstler, and many others, none of them well-enough known — artists, critics, scientists and philosophers who were taking advantage of the crackup of Late Modernism to give art itself a thorough re-think. What they seemed to share was the curiosity, honesty, and imagination to wonder: if the arts have taken leave of their senses, how might they reconnect?

The book you have in your hands is one of the most urbane and convincing examples of this approach that I know of. A professor of mathematics and physics at the University of Texas, Nikos Salingaros grew interested in architecture through his friendship with the great architectural theorist Christopher Alexander.

As his involvement in architecture has broadened and deepened, so has his engagement with the really substantial art questions. To read his work and accompany his mind is to sense art finding its footing. But why bother taking on Deconstruction? Isn't it the silliest of movements, condemned already by virtue of its ingrown solipsism to vanish soon without a trace?

I'm sorry to report that the above questions, correct though they are, are the kinds of things a down-to-earth person might ask — not someone, in other words, with much chance to make sense of the mind-warping hall of mirrors that is the contemporary academic avant-garde architecture world.

In point of fact, architectural discourse (and much architectural practice) is dictated by a small number of players. Many of these are well-situated — in academia, on boards, in the editorial offices of newspapers and magazines. And although a public art should get a good public discussion, the discussion of architecture is by and large dictated from above by an interlocking cabal of insiders.

This group, currently devoted to the style known as Deconstructivism, is genuinely dangerous. They're dangerous in the first place to the art they practice. To see what Deconstruction can do to a field, all we need do is look at countless English Departments, transformed by French-derived philosophical vogues into politically-correct wastelands. When the *Atlantic Unbound* asked the critic and professor Harold Bloom why the Theory people carry on as they do in the literary world, he answered: "These are ideologues, dear. They don't care about poetry." Should similar consequences be tolerated in architecture, let alone desired?

More important are the practical, built consequences. *The New York Times'* absurd architecture critic may have resigned, but the projects and architects he (and others) did public relations for will be with us for decades. Because of their positions at the controls of the public conversation, the Decon crowd is having an impact on our shared built environment far beyond their numbers. They're also training further generations of students to go do likewise. The basic fact that needs remembering is that architecture isn't just any art. After all, what does one more Theory-driven poem really matter? It's easily overlooked or ignored. But a bad building can ruin a block; it can even ruin a neighborhood. If enough such buildings accumulate, they can help bring about the ruin of an entire city.

What's it like to co-exist with these structures? In a comment on a recent weblog posting about a much-praised new Deconstructivist building, a man who had spent an afternoon in the building wrote about the feelings of vertigo and disorientation he'd experienced.

Being sentenced to live, work in, or pass by a Theory-driven, Deconstructed building can have an unpleasantly disorienting impact on the lives of hundreds, even thousands, of people for many years.

Dream though we may about letting the theorists and practitioners of Decon simply pass away, this is a trend that needs to be faced. But how? One doesn't want to contribute to the destructiveness, after all. And tactics are a challenge.

As everyone has discovered who has tried to engage a true-believing Decon partisan in direct conversation, once you admit any of their terms, it's almost impossible to avoid vanishing with them down a rabbit hole of illogic.

(Once again: this is the vertigo experience that the Decon crowd thinks is so important.) When you shake your head clear, it's only to be greeted by the spectacle of your opponent doing a victory dance. What to you seems like definitive proof that the Decons are up to pointless no-good seems to them like vindication.

With his articles, his website, and his books, Nikos A. Salingaros has become a senior partner in this alternative crowd. It's been a pleasure and a privilege to publish some of his writing on my website, *2Blowhards.com*, and to introduce his mind and his writing to new readers. This collection of articles and essays is direct and substantial; I've read few attacks on fashionable nonsense so devastating.

Dr. Salingaros was born in Perth, Australia. He grew up in Greece and the Bahamas, got degrees from the University of Miami and the State University of New York at Stony Brook, and has been teaching at the University of Texas since 1983. He lives in San Antonio with his physician wife, Dr. Marielle Blum, and their two daughters. He painted professionally — portraits, landscapes — as a young man, and is also an avid classical music buff.

Twenty years ago he met the architect and theorist Christopher Alexander, best known for his books *"A Pattern Language"* and *"The Timeless Way of Building"*. They became friends and colleagues. Dr. Salingaros has worked with Alexander since on the editing and shaping of Alexander's long-brewing, long-awaited *"The Nature of Order"*, a four-volume work on art, science, nature and beauty.

Over the years, Dr. Salingaros found himself more and more preoccupied with architecture, building, living form, and the foolishness of Modernism. About nine years ago he began publishing his own papers on these topics.

You'll forgive me for a moment if my inner aesthete takes over. I can't resist expressing the reading pleasure this book has given me. I love Nikos' dry and deadpan humor. I'm dazzled by his courage and straightforwardness, and impressed and moved by the power of his brain. I think I recognize most of his sly rhetorical strategies, and many of them have made me laugh out loud with admiration and delight. It's a brilliant book in many ways, not least of which is Nikos' way with a telling phrase. *"Geometrical Fundamentalism"* — which to my mind takes care of Modernism in a scant two words — is only one of the many beauties Nikos has coined.

Although it consists of a variety of essays and reviews, Salingaros' book has its own dramatic structure. Let me hint for a second, without making too much of it, at how the way this book works parallels the phenomenon of "emergent form" — the way that certain kinds of open-ended, unfolding processes result in wholes that are greater than their parts. On one level, the reader accompanies Salingaros' mind as his engagement with his subject deepens. There's a sense at the beginning of the book that Nikos feels that Deconstruction might be an honorable opponent that can be met head-on in straightforward battle.

But like some digital special-effect, Decon keeps coming back. Hit it though you may with a perfectly-placed and powerful swinging punch, it morphs into a new form. By the book's end, Salingaros has developed a canny respect for Decon's survival abilities; he's like a medical researcher who has learned to admire the tenacity and resourcefulness of the disease he's hoping to conquer. (It's fascinating and telling that the image of the virus starts to crop up in Salingaros's analysis.)

He's also developed his own strategies; they've deepened. Like a great diagnostician, he develops a theory of Theory: where it comes from; how it propagates itself; what its allure is. By the end of the book, his own theory is complete. He moves on first to address individual outbreaks of Deconstruction, and finally to offer a creative vision of his own. On another level, the book is also the story of Salingaros' own increasing involvement in architecture itself. As a humanist with a deep grounding in science and culture, he's offended — morally, aesthetically, intellectually — that an important field that deserves to be dealt with and discussed openly is being over-controlled.

Architecture should, after all, evolve and develop by trial, inspiration, response and error; it should be making a contribution to human welfare.

What he finds instead is a field that is being dictated from on high, and that is delivering unwanted and even poisonous goods — even while the field's stars and propagandists carry on as though they're up to something of artistic moment. Salingaros can't stay away from this spectacle; his own feelings about beauty and service rise to the fore.

I'm full of admiration for Salingaros' humor, brains, and courage. I'm amused and entertained by his urbane bemusement, as well as impressed and convinced by the depth of knowledge and conviction that underlie his discussions and observations.

One more bit of book-appreciation: Nikos' analysis of the psychology of cults and his discussion of the relations between art and religion strike me as a major contribution to the psychology of art.

Though Modernism has been a tragedy in so many ways — and I agree completely with Salingaros that Decon is simply Modernism's latest zigzaggy manifestation — we may owe something wonderful to it. Without its pervasiveness and persistence, would any of these great alternative thinkers have been driven to formulate their responses and ideas so completely and so beautifully?

What emerges in this work is a new and welcome vision of the place of intellect in art and in life. In this view, the intellect isn't there to dictate; instead, it is one participant in a larger conversation over which no one has ultimate control. It's a stirringly modest vision — helpful yet visionary, pluralistic yet realistic.

Talking about Salingaros' mind has got me thinking about the computer, by the way. Its qualities and characteristics are laid claim to by the Deconstructivists, whose bent-and-folded work is certainly unimaginable without digital technology. Yet the computer may well help bring them down; if Decon is a poison pill for culture generally, perhaps the computer is a poison pill for Decon specifically. After all, the computer doesn't just make possible new forms of design stunts. New connections get made; new networks take form. Closed, deterministic, on-high structures collapse of their own weight as new open-ended processes take form. The unanticipated occurs.

Computers and the Web have already enabled Nikos A. Salingaros to reach many new minds with his voice of reason and sense. May this new book enable him to reach many more.

PART 1

THE CHESSBOARD MODEL OF ARCHITECTURAL STYLES

This essay offers a geometrical model of visualizing different architectural styles together. It helps one to perceive relationships among them, and to better understand how one style evolved from another. Following what is done in science, representing the phenomenon of interest helps enormously in exploring its structure and qualities. Representation is the first step towards a classification, which eventually unites different facts into an organized model, and which permits a more complete conceptualization. This simple model is inspired by discussions with Christopher Alexander, who estimated the astronomically high ratio of possible non-living structures as compared to living structures (Alexander, 2005; pages 688-693). For the first time, a discussion of the relative numbers of distinct architectural styles and their adaptive properties dissolves all the old and misleading arguments about "architectural creativity".

1. A DEBATE ON ARCHITECTURAL STYLES.

After having followed a long and inconclusive debate on architectural styles, I wanted to try and clear up a few things. This is an argument permeated with many contradictions, and recognizing its true constituent elements becomes a problem. It is not even easy to identify a continuous line of thought in what is really important. Some of those who took part in the debate, even if they showed clear thinking about one particular argument, were confused on another point that is actually rather close. If the experts are confused, how can we possibly offer an understanding of the subject matter to interested citizens?

We are not facing here questions of purely academic interest: the debate on architectural styles grows in importance every day. It addresses the design of notable new buildings such as museums, university buildings, concert halls, railway stations, airports, and churches. The latter are definitely of primary importance, because the recent debate was ignited by asking: *"Are churches in contemporary architectural styles truly adapted to their sacred use?"* (Part 10). This question forces us to evaluate the relationship between forms and spaces constructed by people, and the connection between human beings with God. This is not a trivial question; nor is it limited to aesthetic issues, but goes right to the foundations of how human beings are able to transcend the physical world (or, instead, their stubborn refusal to do so). Christopher Alexander (2004) has devoted much thought to this topic, uncovering important truths.

Although these questions are too difficult to resolve fully, I can at least propose a model that allows us to visualize different styles and the relationship among them. The stylistic debate can then be played out on this model with a clarity that gets lost if one continues to employ the old way of thinking about these things. Here is the model I propose: *"The Chessboard of Architectural Styles"*.

2. THE MODEL OF THE CHESSBOARD IN THE PARKING LOT.

Let us imagine a chessboard placed on the ground in a large (empty) open parking lot, like the one of the local "Big-Box-Mart" (when the store is closed). I wish to emphasize the relative size of the chessboard compared with the area of asphalt paving defining the parking lot. On the scale of the parking lot the chessboard is negligible; it is lost in the immense surface of the surrounding void. In statistical terms it does not even exist, because it is so small. But in terms of organized information content, it is perhaps the only part of the parking lot that concentrates geometrical order. The rest of the lot is a black empty space, whereas our chessboard forms 64 beautiful squares contrasting among themselves.

In the model proposed here, the chessboard collects and represents architectural styles that are alive: those that can generate buildings which contain life within the organized complexity of their forms. Every square corresponds to a distinct architectural style, evolved by traditional societies over time. Architectural "life" is a mathematically measurable quality: an ordered complexity that helps to connect shapes, spaces, and surfaces to our perceptive system. Here I am speaking about something deeper than a superficial visual connectivity (Alexander, 2002). Every form, either alive or dead, evokes a response from the human spirit, originating half from our perceptive neuronal system (eye, ear, etc.) and half from our cerebral neuronal system (memory, innate conception of the world, etc.) (Part 5). Together, these mechanisms act to connect external forms to a human being.

Those architectural styles that *have* life and that *give* life are few, but are still infinite in number. How can we explain this contradiction in ordinary language … few but infinite …? Look at the chessboard. We can place all the living architectural styles on the chessboard — the number 64 of the squares does not really matter, it is only for a game. We assign every square to an architectural style adapted to human life and to human sensibility. Begin with the Classical style (just for the sake of argument). Then add the Romanesque style, Buddhist, Chinese, Byzantine, Armenian-Syrian, Catalan, Gothic, Early Muslim, Hindu, Seljuk, Khmer, Aztec, Late Muslim and Ottoman styles, etc., filling up other squares. We suppose that we can assign half of the chessboard to styles already explored by humanity during its history. The other half of the chessboard remains empty until now, waiting for us to invent new living styles to add to the classification.

Every style, every single square of the chessboard, represents an infinity of possible constructions. This infinite possibility, but still within the limits of the chessboard, does not end with the known traditional styles. There remains a wealth of unexpected, innovative, and unknown architectural styles; we only need the imagination of some talented young architects in order to discover them and build them.

3. ARCHITECTURAL STYLES OUTSIDE THE CHESSBOARD.

Maybe even contemporary architects can be in agreement with the model up to this point in the argument. I'm sorry to have to part company from them, but it is an unavoidable consequence of stating my thesis: contemporary architectural styles are not on the chessboard, but are situated instead in places far away, in some distant part of the parking lot.

The reason is as follows. The majority of more recent architectural styles, from Early Modernism to those showing themselves off in today's trendy architecture magazines, do not express life. They are unrelated to the intrinsic (mathematical) qualities of life. These topics are treated in the magisterial book by Christopher Alexander: *"The Nature of Order"* (2002-2005). I also discuss this in my book *"A Theory of the Architecture"* (2006). I cannot repeat the discussion here, because it is far too lengthy.

If the reader is following our model, it should be obvious that an infinite number of architectural styles do not deserve to be on the chessboard. This is true in spite of the most fervent desires of contemporary architects, their supporters in academia (our architecture schools), and the architectural media (critics, newspapers, television, boards of architecture prizes). Architects imagine that they are continuing the historical practice of architecture. They would like to believe that they are filling in the chessboard with new styles, but they are mistaken: their styles are lost in the empty, alien, inhuman space outside. This error is moreover founded on pride, because those architects do not understand in which way they are mistaken. They are unable to realize even the fact that they are mistaken. They act under a quasi-religious conviction, certain of promoting a future freed from the chains of the past. Instead, theirs is only a future disconnected from life.

4. ANALOGY BETWEEN THE CHESSBOARD AND THE EARTH.

The chessboard can also be used to represent our Earth situated in space. A tiny piece of matter (since only the surface of the Earth is inhabited) is alive in the vast expanses of astronomical space. We do not know of life elsewhere;

perhaps it does not exist in any other part of the universe. Up to today we must suppose that our chessboard (excuse me, our Earth) is the only place in the universe that supports life. Perhaps tomorrow we might discover radio signals coming from a form of intelligent life on the planet Arcturus situated in the constellation of Andromeda, but that has still not happened.

Why does life not exist in other places in the universe? Quite simply, the conditions of organized complexity necessary to generate and support life don't occur. It is too cold in empty space, there is not enough chemical concentration, no rich mixture of the right chemicals, nor is there a sufficiently high density of matter. In other planets of our solar system we find enough matter and chemical compounds, but water, atmosphere, or other elements essential for life are lacking. Or, more important still, sometimes the presence of toxic chemical compounds or extreme physical conditions do not allow the chemical development that leads to organic molecule formation complex enough for life processes.

We return to the architectural analogy. Minimalism corresponds to the extreme conditions in empty space. There is nothing there. There is certainly no life. The so-called "poetry" of pure, minimalist forms is a poetry without words; and is therefore empty of meaning. Minimalism is dead because it was never alive. It is the death corresponding to extreme cold — the cold of interstellar space. Other non-minimalist architectural styles may nevertheless lack some essential component of architectural life. They lack organization, complexity, visual and tactile richness in their surfaces, or something that is analogous to these qualities.

Many contemporary styles are not empty, but they contain elements that are noxious and hostile to life. I explain this in the rest of this book. It is not enough to have complexity: it must be organized in a very special manner before life emerges. Therefore, all of today's fashionable styles reside, in our model, outside the chessboard. Those styles are part of the empty parking lot, in analogy with the empty space of the physical universe without life. The dead region is infinite, but this time it is truly without limit.

5. THE TERROR OF ARCHITECTURAL CREATIVITY.

The model of the chessboard in the parking lot can help clear up some points in the architectural debate. Many architects interested in a living architecture have adopted elements of traditional styles, like the Classical style. This is a style that has been successful for millennia. In our times, a few architects like Léon Krier build beautiful new buildings that are similar to those of the past. Facing an extremely hostile attack from academic architects, the new Classicists find in the methods of the past, adapted to new materials, a useful instrument to create a more human built environment. This has not been done for decades.

Nevertheless, we are concentrating here only on a single square of the chessboard. Classicism is only one style, therefore one square in our model. There are so many other styles, many known are many others still unexplored, with which a human world can be constructed. People who do not like Classicism are sometimes terrorized because they believe falsely that the only alternatives left are the contemporary architectural styles. That assumption is not true. It represents a fundamental misunderstanding, a false dichotomy stated as "Classicism *versus* Contemporary Styles". In reality we don't have an opposition between two styles, but rather a classification of an infinite number of different styles. The important difference is that Classicism remains on the chessboard, whereas the fashionable Contemporary Styles are situated outside it.

The Classical style does not have to please everybody. It is only one of many living architectural styles. The essential point is recognizing the qualities of life in the Classical style, so they can be applied to the built environment (the living qualities, and not necessarily the typology of Classical architecture). Can we use new materials in order to simulate and reinforce the Classical style? Why not? It is not obligatory that we construct buildings only out of stone and wood, even if they are beautiful. I do not propose counterfeiting building materials. Once an architect deeply understands the complexity of living structure, he or she can use all materials in innovative ways, with every material in its proper setting.

The feeling of terror manifests itself in yet another way. After decades of indoctrination from modernist architects, we have been primed to react in a subconscious manner against any application of historical typologies. The chessboard as a collection of living architectural styles has been prohibited as a source of methods for constructing today. Yes, it sounds ridiculous, but we must face a severely negative reaction if we wish to erect a building that resembles something built in the pre-modernist past. If we do, it is automatically assumed that we are not being "contemporary", and that we are therefore putting at risk all our technological and social development. An architect who dares to do this is condemned by his or her colleagues as an apostate, a "traitor" to the cult. It is absurd to tie technological development to architectural images, however. Human development was not generated by buildings in the modernist style: those buildings are simply a toxic byproduct of industrially developed societies, just like pollution and the despoliation of the environment.

Modernist architects succeeded in introducing a fictitious link between progress and a temporal one-dimensional model of architectural styles. It was an ingenious trick. That simplistic model lines up all styles, ordering them in a sequence according to their time of invention. Those who profit from this model declare that human development works in exactly the same way, in a linear fashion. It is really a simple hence attractive image, but it carries a false, hidden, almost diabolical message. According to this one-dimensional model, old styles are *passé*, unusable, like our old and used clothes that we no longer want. People do not realize that this common conception of how architectural styles evolved is based on a prejudice, because it is influenced by a terribly deceptive model. The one-dimensional model, fixed as a cognitive framework in our subconscious, determines our general interpretation of architecture. Sad, but true.

Finally, one must not confuse inhuman contemporary styles with innovative human styles. They exist in clearly separated spaces. Innovation leads in many directions: either towards life or away from life. The chessboard classification follows mathematical characteristics, and has nothing to do with aesthetics. All styles adapted to human sensitivity are found on the chessboard, whereas inhuman styles are found outside it, in the parking lot, in an empty space devoid of life.

6. ARCHITECTURE AGAINST HUMANITY.

With our present scientific knowledge we are ready to construct a new world, which will be beautiful and human. The only problem is that today's architects cannot do it. Nearly all of them are trained to follow the cult of contemporaneity (Part 7). They are lacking in scientific knowledge and have no connection with the human soul. Their academic training was oriented towards constructing abstract shapes, without any reference to human beings, to our neuronal system, or to our biological make-up. Those architects don't think like us; not like other normal people.

In an unfortunate development, architects who have picked up some scientific knowledge are now applying it in order to destroy the environment even more effectively. They pretend to justify their monstrous buildings and designs with scientific and mathematical words (Part 3). People swallow all this because it sounds good and appears to have deep meaning. But, as I have demonstrated in my writings, this is just a great scam perpetrated on society. All of those fashionable designs are far from living architecture (they are outside the chessboard). They lack the essential qualities of buildings that possess life and which can connect with human beings. The buildings constructed according to supposed (but misunderstood) biological theories are always situated in the parking lot of our architectural model, in a sterile emptiness. They do not belong to living structure. But how can it be that a building founded on an analogy with biological shapes can be dead?

I know that the reader may find it difficult to believe that a celebrated architect, when he or she speaks about buildings that mimic biological forms, often speaks nonsense. In fact, that architect usually understands nothing about Biology, invoking only a superficial visual similarity. Those architects were not taught the structure of biological and complex systems. They did not get an advanced degree in Biology, but only saw some images in Biology textbooks. Their training in architecture school was visual, consisting solely of looking at pictures without understanding their underlying structure. A person trained exclusively through visual images, media images, consequently turns into a person that has lost contact with reality. Architecture faculties train their students to become persons disconnected from life, instilling in them at the same time the arrogance of the cult.

Now those architects wish to impose their unreality upon us.

7. NEUROPHYSIOLOGY MOLDS TRADITIONAL ARCHITECTURE.

According to some architects, the weak aspect of our model is that it makes us seem to be prohibiting so many innovative styles. One might therefore turn our own argument against us, declaring that we are the bad ones, because we are forbidding architectural innovation. Presumably, we are hindering the free exploration of the unknown solution space of future architectonic styles.

To understand the situation better, we must follow the birth and historical emergence of traditional styles. How did they evolve to represent such visual and structural complexity? Ornament is not necessary from a strictly utilitarian point of view, but it is necessary in order to define a living architecture. Humankind has developed design techniques and typologies by constructing its surroundings based upon our neurophysiology. We have always sought to construct forms and surfaces that make us feel better, and not the opposite (at least until recent decades). Our body and our senses recognize adaptive structures, which show a fundamental similarity with our own structure. Physiological and psychological wellbeing are based upon a kinship with the environment. Such an affinity is possible only in an environment structured according to a very special type of complexity. This complexity is a common quality of all traditional and vernacular architectural styles — all the styles that are situated on the chessboard.

It is only with the advent of industrialization that certain new directions opened, provoked by new industrial products and materials. It is not widely known how modernist architecture and its follow-ups were motivated and spurred by the production of industrial materials. This was a movement whose primary goal was to promote industrial consumption and therefore to boost the entire industry.

8. BIOPHILIA AND HEALTH.

The American scientist Edward Wilson is deeply convinced that human beings are tied to other living forms through their common genetic material. Wilson introduces the term "biophilia" to denote the close tie between us and our natural environment (Wilson, 1984). If we examine the human body as it has been formed in the prehistoric past, it is clear that the geometry of those ancient places in which we evolved is conserved in our hereditary memory. It has shaped what we are today, by forging the mechanisms for interacting with our environment. We therefore try unconsciously to reproduce those environments in our contemporary surroundings.

The quality of our original primordial environment — that is, a savanna with separated trees — is mathematically complex in a very precise sense. This is the same fractal complexity that is found in biological structures (for example, in the lung). We recognize the same complexity, or its absence, in the structures we build. Where this particular complexity exists, we feel well; and where it is absent, we feel badly. An entirely alien environment lacking in this complexity contributes to human pathology by lowering our resistance through increased stress, which in turn weakens our immune system. Dead environments literally make us sick.

We can connect with that which is alive. The same mechanism connects us to inanimate systems that possess the same organized complexity as living systems. In our chessboard model, the squares of the chessboard (which represent living styles) are privileged points in the abstract space of all architectural styles.

9. LIFE AS THE CENTER OF THE UNIVERSE.

The chessboard model implies a very special importance for life, and for us. Throughout the infinite universe, we know that only the surface of a small planet nourishes life. Some scientists consider the Earth as a giant living organism: the "Gaia" hypothesis. The Earth itself is alive.

By analogy, among the infinite possible architectural styles, only those on the chessboard support human life in a complete sense. Every other style is alien to human beings, and therefore hostile to life. Looking for innovation is a good thing, above all for an architect, but to seek it in dead regions does not help humanity. You have to look for it on the chessboard. This is defined to be a fundamental center, a central point of our universe. Losing the center means losing our foundation — losing our attachment to the world.

Without intentionally wishing to do so, this analysis has developed in a philosophical and ecological direction, even a religious one. Living structure defines the center of the universe, at least for us. The universe is not relative as far as life is concerned. The role of humankind is truly something very special in the infinite universe. The role of living architecture — the traditional and vernacular architecture of every country and every culture — plays the same role in the built environment. This is something sacred. One should never proclaim that it is "out of style", and that it can be destroyed so as to construct more modern-looking buildings. Modernity does not have to be a pestilence that annihilates all it touches.

In this way of thinking, the Earth is special. We have the responsibility to maintain life on the Earth, because there is no other place in the universe harboring life. Modernity does not create life, so we should be very careful not to replace life with death in our mad pursuit of modernity. We do not have the right to ruin the planet, to sacrifice species of animals and plants to the altar of the Money God. We do not have the right to destroy old buildings, old churches, whose value sometimes we cannot understand with our available knowledge today. Tomorrow, when we wake up, it will be too late.

10. CONCLUSION: REPRESENTING STYLES.

I have outlined here a geometric model in which every architectural style is situated on a two-dimensional plane within an abstract space. In order to illustrate my results, I have simplified a model developed previously in my book *A Theory of Architecture* (Salingaros, 2006). The model represents a visual way of thinking about the diversity of architectural styles. There is also a metric in the space of our model, because one can judge which styles are "near" and which are "far" from each other, and which styles have evolved from other older styles. The most important lesson is that non-living styles far outnumber the number of possible living styles (Alexander, 2005).

Even if the reader is not in complete agreement with my conclusions about architectural styles — that is, which styles have qualities of "life" and which do not — the idea of a model that represents styles in an easily-visualizable abstract geometry remains. This is certainly useful for analysis.

I believe that the problem of confronting and relating different styles can be resolved in this manner. Using a geometric model exposes the great imposture: that modernism and its derivatives defining contemporary styles are an unavoidable progress, and that all traditional styles are assigned to the trash heap. Finally, the chessboard model answers the widespread propaganda from the media and from architectural academia about "architectural innovation". Especially, we must convince everyday citizens that it was all a colossal deceit. In spite of everything, perhaps the evil is too immense, too ugly, and too alarming for the truth to be accepted.

How it is possible that we even arrived here? We the educated, who have advanced in so many sciences and technologies? We, who have developed the thermonuclear bomb and have read the DNA code of humans? Is it possible that architects operating in our society (and I am not speaking about a few; I mean the majority) destroy the qualities of life, dismantling the essential characteristics of living structure? Who destroy forms; destroy the coherence of matter itself, in order then to reconstruct their nightmares representing death. And how come our greatest experts accept all of this destruction as wonderful progress? And even the Church finances (with obvious self satisfaction) the construction of dead buildings in which one looks in vain for some sign of a God who we imagine gives life to humankind.

There is a simple explanation. I can remember other dark times in which terrible events have occurred, with the majority of the people being in agreement. Always in those instances, clever hustlers proclaim a society's supposed development and a "liberation" from the suffocating past. Their purpose is to make us accept evil, condemnation, prejudice, and violent death as a necessity. Only after the society (or the country, or the continent) has been more or less destroyed, do we realize that the words of our presumed saviors, and their seductive promises, were horrible lies. And we allowed ourselves to be manipulated like stupid beasts! It is so easy to believe in swindles.

PART 2

THE DANGER OF DECONSTRUCTIVISM

The following essay was motivated indirectly by an article I coauthored with Michael Mehaffy entitled "Geometrical Fundamentalism" (Mehaffy & Salingaros, 2002). Dr. Carlo Poggiali wrote an appreciative essay after reading the Italian version, using subtlety and irony to make points against modernist architecture. Poggiali suggests that we need to experience different buildings emotionally, so as to appreciate the truth of criticisms I make on the intellectual plane. Poggiali argues that the emotional impact of architectural style is better felt while one is relaxed and unhurried; otherwise in the hustle and bustle of everyday life, one cannot notice the environment sufficiently to make critical judgments. As an experiment, he suggests a vacation/conference in the Tyrolean region of Northern Italy, spending one week in each of two nearby hotels that he knows — the earlier one built in traditional vernacular style, and the other an early modernist "masterpiece" (Poggiali, 2002).

While very pleased and flattered by his essay, I felt the need to correct the possibly misleading impression that I am neglecting the emotional dimension of architecture. The following insights and ideas came out during a conversation with another friend, Terry Mikiten (coauthor of "Darwinian Processes and Memes in Architecture" (Salingaros & Mikiten, 2002)), and amply demonstrate my thinking about emotion as a central component of contemporary architecture. In "Geometrical Fundamentalism", I criticize modernism for originally disregarding our senses so as to concentrate on pure geometrical volumes and surfaces. Architects have since moved on to deconstructivism, which presents us with visual disorder. This is a style that abuses our sense of order. Even worse, it makes false claims of scientific legitimacy. I cannot, as a scientist, allow this to stand uncorrected. I also wanted to inject a sense of urgency to counteract Poggiali's relaxed approach, which I feel misses the seriousness and white-hot intensity of the contemporary architectural debate.

Dear Stefano,

I read the letter of Doctor Poggiali, published in number 119 of your Newsletter. As it refers to my own researches on architecture and urbanism, I wanted to answer personally. Carlo Poggiali distinguishes between two factors influencing the effect architecture has on people — emotional perception, and an analysis carried out on the intellectual plane. He suggests that we can understand the difference through specific experiences of being confronted with buildings having very different architectural character. Of course I agree.

It is necessary to develop a corpus of scientific knowledge, founded on the scientific method, and independent of any bias due to personal opinion (which could be negative and compromising). With this, we can face the future armed with a knowledge of architecture much deeper than that in the past, and especially that of the modernist 20th century. Architecture and urbanism cannot follow ephemeral tastes; they cannot be based on trivial images like those of today, which are fruits of a fantasy that creates frightening and alien things.

However, Poggiali is entirely too confident that I always remain on a strictly intellectual plane. In fact, only a few days ago, I met my friend Terry Mikiten for lunch in an Indian restaurant (an establishment that encourages long and relaxed conversations, interspersed with pauses to take new plates from the buffet). We discussed the architect Daniel Libeskind and the plans for the reconstruction of Manhattan. After a few minutes, Mikiten told me: "You have changed fundamentally. You are no longer the disinterested scientist that you were; now you are very passionate and speak almost like a fanatic!" I answered that the topic has seized me completely, and that I see things so darkly as to feel responsible for alerting the world to an extremely serious danger. I explained that we face the introduction of a new vision of the world, a destructive vision, which, if allowed to proliferate, can eliminate all that mankind has patiently constructed during centuries, during millennia. It represents a new philosophy of order that wants to replace knowledge with lies.

Architecture arises from our conception of the world, and the brain mechanisms that determine how we understand physical structure and the structure of the universe at that particular moment.

From the monumentality of the buildings of ancient civilizations, to the decorative details present in all vernacular architectures, the human spirit expresses itself creatively in the constructed realm. The man-made world represents our spirit, our mind and our heart — these are reflected in our buildings.

Deconstructivist architecture presents us with the vision of a world destroyed, of a universe reduced to fragments, shards of glass. This particular group of architects (greatly in fashion today) uses the term "fractal", but in a completely mistaken sense.

I happen to know what a fractal is, and I assure you that it is not that. In design projects and in architectural texts they speak about "chaos", "nonlinear systems", and "complexity" without having any idea of what these things mean. But for them, this ignorance is not a cause for shame, because it serves to promote their projects and themselves, rather than any scientific truth.

In fact, we find ourselves confronted with a mystical cult that uses scientific terminology just like magical words — whose effect is due only to their sound. The cult intentionally ignores scientific meaning. This works because most people have no scientific background, and because scientists (who should be the ones to expose this fraud) are closed in their own narrow world of research. It is an irony of our times that such a cult, founded on ignorance, survives and blossoms, and has taken control of the media and the Architecture Schools. Today, fractals are discussed in university departments of Science and Mathematics, while in departments of Architecture (situated in the next building) people say nonsense about fractals without anyone noticing.

The danger is this — every architectural style defines a model of the universe, and this includes human society. More than from the written word, we learn what order is from built prototypes and natural examples. This is how we became human through our evolutionary development. If we adopt the deconstructivist model, we abandon our fundamental connections — the ties among human beings, between persons and the built environment, and among the various threads that together weave the city into one urban fabric. We brutally cancel the interconnections and coherence that define human society and our civilization. And why? In order to make some architects rich and famous? To satisfy clients (among them the Church and Government) that must absolutely have the latest fashion in architecture? Or is it to subsidize those architecture journals that cater to the avant-garde?

When I explained all this to my friend Mikiten, he answered: "Now I understand your analytical thought, with an almost mathematical logic, and the conclusion is truly disturbing. When I first saw them, I thought that the models for the reconstruction of Manhattan represented new shapes, weird and unusual ones, perhaps ridiculous, but I never thought they could be dangerous. Now I believe that it is indeed so. There exists a coherence in every system, a central repository of information that needs to be protected. We have a central nucleus that is vulnerable — without which the system can be destroyed. The coherence of shapes is one of the foundations of the way we think, and this cannot be put at risk. It is much too important and fragile, like the DNA in the nucleus of cells."

At least I convinced Mikiten that I have not abandoned the scientific method. Indeed, it is almost unavoidable for me to have become so passionate about my discovery because of its grave consequences. Doctor Mikiten is the Associate Graduate Dean of the University Biomedical School, Professor of Physiology, and also an expert in artificial intelligence. In short, he's a "tough cookie". It is not easy to change his mind, but once that is accomplished, it's like having all of Science supporting you.

We agreed that a faith in observed structure is fundamental for human existence. As human beings, we use our understanding of the coherence and stability of structures, obtained through the physiology of our senses, in order to interpret the structures with which we are confronted in life. Science is nothing other than a search for the understanding of structure. We develop belief systems that are based on the mechanism of understanding physical systems. Such cognitive and intellectual bases influence our understanding of human and social systems, and actually form the basis for human intuition.

Deconstructivism challenges all the above ideas. A challenge, however, that does not replace those ideas with any coherent alternative. It is something fundamentally destructive. It destroys our communion with natural structures without supplying any explanatory value to take its place. Moreover, deconstructivism is arrogant because it does not need the participation of human beings in a dialogue with our surroundings. It does not require us because it is an entirely alien construction. It is an artistic trick picked up in the search for visual novelty, but which now threatens our ability to understand the universe.

Later on we spoke about the deconstructivist French philosophers. Mikiten knew their names — Derrida, Foucault, etc. . . . but told me that he had never understood their arguments. He kindly offered to read them again. I advised him not to lose his time, because they are intrinsically incomprehensible. And after all, it is not worth the effort. Contemporary architecture proclaims in a loud voice that it is founded on deconstructivist philosophy, but, like all its declarations, this one also has strictly propaganda value. Mikiten asked me if I am willing to take on this group of philosophers. I answered modestly that I am not ready to do that, because I am not a philosopher, and because they are much too powerful. The distinguished British philosopher Roger Scruton criticized them, and consequently lost his university professorship. He now lives on a farm in England.

I return finally to Poggiali to explain that, in my criticism of contemporary architecture, I refer not only to observations on an intellectual plane. I find it to be a deliberate aggression on our senses, which abuses the human perceptive mechanism in order to generate physical anxiety and discomfort. This is in my opinion quite intentional and is neither accidental, nor due to ignorance. At times I am astonished that so few people perceive these extremely important things. In an era of the globalization of information systems and media, it is disinformation that propagates best. The truth remains hidden without arousing people's interest.

Truth does not sell well, unlike the strange images of an architecture that no one understands. On the contrary, the latter have an enormous commercial value for the world of publicity in which we live today.

I don't agree with too much unhurried reasoning and discussion, drawn out during relaxed conversations among friends. The situation demands immediate action, and, furthermore, we (the few who know the unpleasant truth) find ourselves in a weak position. All the most beautiful cities of the world, including Rome "the Eternal City", are being destroyed by the alien images of a self-proclaimed "contemporary" architecture. This willful destruction, which seems necessary for the Cult of Contemporaneity, is doing more damage than all of the barbarian invasions. We have no time to waste vacationing in the Italian Tyrol.

PART 3

CHARLES JENCKS AND THE NEW PARADIGM IN ARCHITECTURE

Charles Jencks wishes to promote the architecture of Peter Eisenman, Frank Gehry, and Daniel Libeskind by proclaiming it "The New Paradigm in Architecture". Supposedly, their buildings are based on the New Sciences such as complexity, fractals, emergence, self-organization, and self-similarity. I disprove Jencks's claim, and show that it is founded on elementary misunderstandings. There is a New Paradigm architecture, and it is indeed based on the New Sciences, but it does not include deconstructivist buildings. Instead, it encompasses the innovative, humane architecture of Christopher Alexander, the traditional humane architecture of Léon Krier, and much, much more.

1. INTRODUCTION.

In a recent article, Charles Jencks, the well-known architectural commentator, proclaims *"The New Paradigm in Architecture"* (Jencks, 2002a). This was publicized at an address to the Royal Institute of British Architects in London on June 11, 2002. According to Jencks, the new paradigm consists of deconstructivist buildings, typified by the Guggenheim Museum for Modern Art in Bilbao, Spain, by Frank Gehry, and including other work and unbuilt projects by Peter Eisenman, Daniel Libeskind, and Zaha Hadid. Jencks has just revised his popular book *"The Language of Post-Modern Architecture"*, and has ambitiously re-titled it to mirror the above paper (Jencks, 2002b).

Jencks bases his proposed new paradigm on what he thinks are the theoretical foundations of those buildings he champions. He claims that they arise from, and can be understood with reference to applications of the new science; namely, complexity theory, self-organizing systems, fractals, non-linear dynamics, emergence, and self-similarity. In my own work, I have used results from science and mathematics to show that vernacular and classical architectures satisfy structural rules that coincide with the new science (Salingaros, 2006). Christopher Alexander's architecture relies on precisely the same new science (Alexander, 2002-2005), and crucially, Alexander is also a scientist.

Jencks became famous for his observation that modernism had ended, back in the first edition of *"The Language of Post-Modern Architecture"*. His announcement was based on, and signaled by the 1972 demolition (by Government agencies) of the award-winning Pruitt-Igoe housing in St. Louis, Missouri, by architect Minoru Yamasaki. If we count the enormous number of modernist buildings built around the world since then, Jencks's conclusive assessment was not fulfilled. On the other hand, Michael Mehaffy and I made a somewhat later prediction for the end of modernism, triggered by the 2001 demolition (by Al-Qaeda terrorists) of another Yamasaki project: the twin towers of New York's World Trade Center (Mehaffy & Salingaros, 2001).

Considering his failed (or at least premature) proclamation of the end of modernism, we might be justified in regarding Jencks's claim this time with a great deal of skepticism. He claims a new paradigm with the opposite characteristics of living structure. That's not what one expects from the new science, which helps to explain biological form. Trying to get a perspective on this contradiction leads one to a witches' brew of confused concepts and statements. I will show that Jencks does not provide a theoretical basis to support his claim of a new paradigm. An architecture that arises from the new science represents the antithesis of the deconstructivist buildings that are praised by Jencks. Clearly, we cannot have totally opposite and contradictory styles arising from the same theoretical basis.

2. SCIENTIFIC QUALIFICATIONS OF THE PARTICIPANTS.

Before I examine the topic, I need to review the scientific qualifications of the parties involved. Is there any scientific expertise to support Jencks's claims? Jencks admits to not being a scientist, but considering he makes such bold claims that might eventually determine how the world looks, he surely needs some support from professionals. On the other side, we have Christopher Alexander, who studied Mathematics and Physics at Cambridge. Alexander participated in the first conferences on complex systems along with the topic's founder, Herbert Simon. The American Institute of Architects awarded him a gold medal in 1972 for his mathematical work in *"Notes on the Synthesis of Form"* (Alexander, 1964).

Alexander has consistently used scientific methods in architecture, and his latest work, summarizing thirty years of effort and entitled *"The Nature of Order"*, flows directly out of his scientific training (Alexander, 2002-2005). Most architects don't know that Alexander is considered a theoretical visionary in Computer Science today for the concepts originally developed in *"A Pattern Language"* (Alexander *et. al.*, 1977; Gabriel, 1996). One of the world's leading computer scientists, Richard Gabriel, says of Alexander's forthcoming book *"The Nature of Order"* that volume 2 alone is likely to change the whole field of Computer Science. That is because, much more than just applying complexity theory to architecture, Alexander has developed fundamental results in complexity theory itself.

As a scientist who has taken an interest in architecture, I play a not insignificant role in this. I know Alexander's work intimately, having helped to edit *"The Nature of Order"* over the past twenty years. His insights have inspired and influenced my own research on architecture. Whenever I have coauthored a paper in architecture or urbanism, I have most frequently chosen as coauthors scientists and mathematicians, some of them very eminent. Alexander's work is an important and integral part of the new science. Our contributions to architecture are an extension of science into the field of architecture, beyond mere scientific analogies. The deconstructivists belong outside science altogether, and, despite their claims, do not come anywhere near to establishing a link with the new science. Instead, the deconstructivist architects draw their support from the French deconstructivist philosophers. Here we have two monumental problems:

(1) Deconstruction is rabidly anti-science, as its stated intention is to replace and ultimately erase the scientific way of thinking; and
(2) The spurious logic of French deconstructivist philosophers was exposed with devastating effect by the two physicists Alan Sokal and Jean Bricmont.

"We show that famous intellectuals such as Lacan, Kristeva, Irigaray, Baudrillard and Deleuze have repeatedly abused scientific concepts and terminology: either using scientific ideas totally out of context, without giving the slightest justification ... or throwing around scientific jargon in front of their non-scientist readers without any regard for its relevance or even its meaning" (Sokal & Bricmont, 1998). How can we therefore accept claims for a new paradigm in architecture, based on science, if it is supported by charlatans who moreover are anti-science? (Dawkins, 1998). A critical investigation into the pervasive and destructive influence of anti-scientific thought in contemporary culture is now underway, in what is known as the "Science Wars".

3. SUPERFICIAL COPYING VERSUS FUNDAMENTAL PROCESSES.

It turns out that there is a basic confusion in contemporary architectural discourse between processes, and final appearances. Scientists study how complex forms arise from processes that are guided by fractal growth, emergence, adaptation, and self-organization. All of these act for a reason. Jencks and the deconstructivist architects, on the other hand, see only the end result of such processes and impose those images onto buildings (see Part 5). But this is frivolous and without reason. They could equally well take images from another discipline, for this superficial application has nothing to do with science. To add further confusion, Jencks insists on talking about cosmogenesis as a process of continual unfolding, an emergence that is always reaching new levels of self-organization.

These are absolutely correct descriptors of how form arises in the universe, and precisely what Christopher Alexander has spent his life getting a handle on. Any hope that Jencks understands these processes is dampened, however, when he then presents the work of Eisenman and Libeskind as exemplars of the application of these ideas of emergence to buildings. None of those buildings appears as a result of unfolding, representing instead the exception, forms so disjointed that no generative process could ever give rise to them.

It appears that perhaps the deconstructivist buildings Jencks likes so much are the intentional products of *interrupting* the process of continual unfolding. They inhabit the outer limits of architectural design space, which cannot be reached by a natural evolution. We have here an interesting example of genetic modification. Just like in the analogous cases where embryonic unfolding is sabotaged either by damage to the DNA, or by teratogenic chemicals in the environment, the result is a fluke and most often dysfunctional.

Should we consider those buildings to be the freaks, monsters, and mutants of the architectural universe? Hasn't the public been fascinated with monsters and the unnatural throughout recorded history as ephemeral entertainment?

The key here is adaptation. I have looked into how Darwinian processes act in architecture on many distinct levels (Salingaros, 2006). A process of design that generates something like a deconstructivist building must have a very special set of selection criteria. No one has yet spelled out those criteria. What is obvious, however, is that they are not adaptive to human needs, being governed instead by strictly formal concerns. Some factors responsible for the high degree of disorganized complexity in such buildings are:

(1) a willful break with traditional architecture of all kinds;
(2) an expression of geometrical randomness and disequilibrium; and
(3) ironic statements or "jokes".

Trying to avoid the region of design space inhabited by traditional solutions, which are adaptive, pushes one out towards novel but non-adapted forms.

4. FRACTALS AND BROKEN FORMS.

By employing scientific terms in an extremely loose manner Jencks erodes his scientific credibility. As an example, he talks of "twenty-six self-similar flower shapes" used by Gehry in the Bilbao Museum (Jencks, 2002a). As far as I can see, there are no self-similar shapes used in that building. As to resembling flowers, they don't, because flowers adapt to specific functions by developing color, texture, and form, all within an overall coherence which is absent here. There is a tremendous difference between a mere visual and a functional appreciation of fractals. The Guggenheim is disjoint and metallic, and as far removed from any flower as I can imagine. Jencks then refers to these non-self-similar shapes as "fluid fractals". I have no idea what this term means, as it is not used in mathematics. A third term he uses for the same figures is "fractal curves". Again, those perfectly smooth curves are not fractal.

I was puzzled to read an entire chapter in Jencks's book (2002b) entitled *"Fractal Architecture"* without hardly seeing a fractal (the possible exceptions being decorative tiles). I can only conclude that Jencks is misusing the word "fractal" to mean "broken, or jagged" — even though he refers to the work of Benoît Mandelbrot, he has apparently missed the central idea of fractals, which is their recursiveness generating a nested hierarchy of internal connections. A fractal line is an exceedingly fine-grained structure. It's not just zigzagged; it is broken everywhere and on every scale (i. e. at every magnification), and is nowhere smooth. Jencks himself admits that: "The intention is not so much to create fractals per se as to respond to these forces, and give them dynamic expression" (2002b). What does this mean? He refers to a building that has a superficial pattern based on Penrose tiles, and calls it an "exuberant fractal". Nevertheless, the Penrose aperiodic pattern exists precisely on a single scale, and is therefore not fractal.

Jencks discusses with admiration unrealized projects by Peter Eisenman, which both claim are based on fractals. But then, Jencks adds revealingly: "Eisenman appears to take his borrowings from science only half-seriously" (Jencks, 2002a). Science, however, cannot be taken only half-seriously; one can only surmise that we are dealing with a superficial understanding of scientific concepts that allows someone to treat fundamental truths so cavalierly. Jencks cites Eisenman's Architecture Building for the University of Cincinnati as an example of what he proposes as new paradigm architecture.

However, from a mathematician's perspective, there is no evident structure there that shows any of the essential concepts of self-similarity, self-organization, fractal structure, or emergence. All I find is intentional disarray.

5. EMERGENCE VERSUS DECONSTRUCTION.

As is admitted by its practitioners, de(con)struction aims to take form apart — to degrade connections, symmetries, and coherence. This is exactly the opposite of self-organization in complex systems, a process that builds internal networks via connectivity. Extra binding energy is required to hold components together. Natural morphogenesis unites matter, establishing multiple connections on different scales and increasing the system's overall coherence; whereas deconstruction undoes all of this, mimicking the decay and disintegration of form.

For this reason, deconstructivist buildings resemble the severe structural damage such as dislocation, internal tearing and melting suffered after a hurricane, earthquake, internal explosion, fire, or (in an eerie toying with fate) nuclear war.

Complex systems are irreducible, in the sense that they represent much more than the sum of their components. The network of connections linking their components together establishes the crucial organizational structure that makes the system work. A complex system cannot be understood by looking at its components alone, and its separation into components destroys it. The word "emergence" is used to denote this property. When components are joined together to form a complex system, properties emerge that cannot be explained except by reference to the functioning whole. Actually the connectivity drives the system: in order to create the whole, the connections grow and proliferate, using the components as anchoring nodes for a coherent network.

Architecture and urbanism are prime examples of fields with emergent phenomena. Cities and buildings with life have this property of incredible interconnectedness, which cannot be reduced to building or design components. Every component, from the large-scale structural members, to the smallest ornament, unites into an overall coherence that creates a vastly greater whole. Deconstructivist buildings, however, show the opposite characteristics where each component degrades the whole instead of intensifying the whole. This is easy to see. Does a structural piece intensify the other pieces around it? Is the total coherence diminished if it were removed? The answer is YES in a great Cathedral, but NO in a deconstructivist building. I think that everyone will agree with me that each portion of today's fashionable deconstructivist buildings detracts from and conflicts with every other portion, which is the opposite of emergence.

6. THE REAL NEW PARADIGM.

Stephen Grabow published a book in 1983 entitled *"Christopher Alexander: The Search for a New Paradigm in Architecture"* (Grabow, 1983). The earlier new paradigm referred to the architecture of Alexander and his colleagues, developing upon the Pattern Language method of design that was first presented in 1977. This architectural movement sought to apply scientific methods to the problem of architectural form, believing that the most fully human architecture is first and foremost well adapted to human needs. This encompasses styles that are visually and structurally the opposite of what Jencks proposes twenty years later. Jencks never mentions this, although he knows Alexander's work.

Before one can claim a new paradigm in architecture, one needs to demonstrate that a drastically improved description of architectonics is being offered. Here, I think Stephen Grabow did an excellent job of explaining how Christopher Alexander's work unifies all of architecture — new, and traditional — that possesses human qualities into a group. "What distinguishes his work from that of his architectural predecessors is the unprecedented linguistic and mathematical system which he has built around the ancient ideas of differentiating space in order to create a new type of building" (Grabow, 1983). My own research enables us to appreciate traditional architectures, not merely from their historical/aesthetic advantage, but as a result of their mathematical complexity (Salingaros, 2006). Building traditions from around the world, and from all pre-modernist periods of history, share an essential and common mathematical structure.

A paradigm shift occurs in science when a description of nature, or the explanation of a particular phenomenon, undergoes a drastic revision. More than just replacing a theory, a paradigm shift means an entirely new way of looking at the world (Kuhn, 1970). We are now beginning to understand structural coherence as a cooperation among the different components of form in a building, and among the buildings in a city. A city is an emergent phenomenon, linking forces and networks on every different scale. A building is itself a coherent result of elements cooperating on many different scales, from the overall size of the building, down to the ornament and details in the materials (Salingaros, 2006). The real new paradigm in architecture is contained in the method for understanding and generating complexity developed by Alexander (2002-2005).

One reason this new paradigm was not adopted is because it produces emotionally comfortable buildings. Traditional architects such as Léon Krier and others have been using timeless methods for organizing complexity, and attribute their results to knowledge derived in the past (Krier, 1998).

It is only very recently that we have managed to join two disparate traditions:

(1) strands of various architectures evolved over millennia, and
(2) theoretical rules for architecture derived from a drastically improved understanding of nature.

The new paradigm is a revolutionary understanding of form, whereas the forms themselves tend to look familiar precisely because they adapt to human sensibilities. Most architects, on the other hand, wrongly expected a new paradigm to generate strange and unexpected forms, which is the reason they were fooled by the deconstructivists.

Ironically, the first edition of Jencks's highly influential *"The Language of Post-Modern Architecture"* coincided with the publication of Alexander's *"A Pattern Language"*. The ideas behind the two competing new paradigms thus have a 25-year history.

The confused and incoherent notions of the postmodernists were unsuccessful in totally displacing human architectural and urban sensibilities during that quarter-century, however, while at the same time failing to overturn a deeply entrenched Modernism. Now the time is finally ripe for an important architectural development. As I believe that Modernism ended in 2001 (and not in 1972, as Jencks had claimed), we are now seeing the real new paradigm in architecture beginning to take its place in our civilization.

7. POSTMODERNIST AND DECONSTRUCTIVIST STYLES.

Modernist, postmodernist, and deconstructivist buildings are distinguished by their low degree of organized complexity. The buildings that Jencks prefers all have a high degree of *disorganized* complexity. This quality is arrived at via design methods mentioned previously. One can also include the use of high-tech materials for a certain effect, which is carefully manipulated to achieve a negative psychological impact on the user. This last feature is best expressed by Jencks himself in describing a paradigmatic building: "It is a threatening frenzy meant, as in some of Eisenman's work, to destabilize the viewer . . ." (Jencks, 2002b). I don't think that anyone is going to consider the common theme of disorganized complexity as constituting sufficient grounds for claiming a new paradigm.

Jencks would have us believe that the old architectural paradigm (modernism) has been, or is being displaced with a new paradigm, defined by the examples of buildings he illustrates in his book (Jencks, 2002b). The beginning assumption is already problematic, as many people around the world never accepted modernism as an architectural paradigm. As to Jencks's current claim, if one considers the jumble of styles that postmodernism is supposed to consist of, one is hard put to see any unifying conception of architectonics contained in that contradictory ensemble of work. If anything, modernism (putting aside its fundamental unsuitability to accommodate human activities) was an intellectually more compact style than either postmodernism or deconstructivism. The shock is definitely there in the newer styles (intentionally so), but what about an improved conception of structure?

Jencks searches for a unifying theme upon which to declare a new architectural paradigm, which could somehow include all the buildings that he has always championed since the first edition of his book (Jencks, 2002b). That would neatly tie-up and help salvage the idea of a postmodernist architecture as a definable entity, something that has fallen apart (or, according to some, was always a myth). By saying that the buildings he illustrates in his book are united in their relationship to the new science, which demonstrably isn't true, he is in fact tying one fashion with another. What is known as the "new science" is simply a collection of scientific results that happen to have come to the public's attention recently, through the popular science press and the media.

8. SCIENCE, TECHNOLOGY, AND MATERIALS.

Jencks and the deconstructivist architects love certain buildings. They clearly derive a kind of thrill from their creations, and I can't deny that fact. I do, however, suspect a basic confusion between science and technology. The use of advanced computer modeling in design and production leads to intellectual satisfaction for some, and Jencks points to this factor as one of the hallmarks of the new paradigm he claims. There is also a fetish with high-tech materials. Nonscientists notoriously confuse science with its specific applications. This is dangerous because, whereas science gives us an understanding of the physical world, technology is merely a tool that can be applied either to create, or to destroy.

Stephen Grabow correctly summarized this conceptual error: "The popular image of the architecture of the future — the space-age fantasies of Hollywood, comic strips, and science fiction — is fundamentally incorrect, a misuse of science. A truly scientific (as opposed to technological) theory of architecture would be much more concerned with unlocking the creative processes that produce buildings than in the application of scientific technologies to buildings already produced" (Grabow, 1983).

Jencks suggests that we are supposed to get excited because a computer program that is used to design French fighter jets is then applied to model the Bilbao Guggenheim. We are also expected to value blobs (which mimic 19C spiritualists' ectoplasm) as relevant architectural forms simply because they are computer-generated.

This fascination with technology is inherited from the modernists (who misused it terribly). When the technology is powerful enough, one may be misled into thinking that the underlying science can be ignored altogether. Most informed people know that one can model any desired shape on a computer; it is no different than sketching with pencil on paper. Just because something is created on a computer screen does not validate it, regardless of the complexity of the program used to produce it. One has to ask: what are the generative processes that produced this form, and are they relevant to architecture?

We stand at the threshold of a design revolution; when generative rules can be programmed to evolve in an electronic form, then cut materials directly. There exists an extraordinary potential of computerized design and building production. Architects such as Frank Gehry do that with existing software, but so far, no fashionable architect knows the fundamental rules that generate living structure. A few of us, following the lead of Alexander, are discovering those rules, and we eventually hope to program them. Others working within traditional architecture have always known rules for generating living structure; now they are ready to generalize them beyond a specific style. When the scientific rules of architecture are universally adopted, the products will surprise everyone by their innovation combined with an intense degree of life not seen for at least one hundred years.

As far as materials are concerned, there is nothing wrong with high-tech materials when they are used within the context of creating an architecture that connects to human sensibilities. In general, the materials themselves affect the nature of the generative rules, since surface properties define the smallest scale of a building's structural hierarchy. The nature of the materials offers, via their different characteristics and properties, a range of different generative possibilities within the wholeness of the architectural process. The architecture of the future will employ all available materials in their proper place. Using exclusively high-tech materials can only define a restricted architecture because it constrains the set of generative rules, something that is not generally understood today.

9. PROMOTING ARCHITECTURAL AGENDAS.

Much of what I have said has already been voiced by critics of deconstructivism. And yet, like some mythical monsters, deconstructivist buildings are sprouting up around the world. Their clients, consisting of powerful individuals, corporations, foundations, and governments, absolutely want one of them as a status symbol. The media publicity surrounding deconstruction reinforces an attractive commercial image. I admit that the confused attempts at a theoretical justification, misusing scientific terms and concepts haphazardly, succeed after all in validating this style in the public's eye. It appears that something is clearly working to market deconstructivism, and Jencks's efforts help towards this promotion.

A paradigm shift is supposed to achieve a unification, not the separation that Jencks attempts. By initially dividing architecture into modernism and postmodernism, everything else is by implication irrelevant.

When deconstructivists eventually react within this false duality, they will return to Bauhaus modernism. What about the vast majority of the world's buildings? Does Jencks's proposed architectural paradigm explain how traditional architecture fits into a grand scheme? No. He actually polarizes the situation further by claiming a fundamental discontinuity in society itself, which would conveniently support his choice of architectural style: "If there is a new paradigm, or way of thinking in any field such as architecture, then it obviously stems from a larger cultural shift, a change in worldview, in religion, perhaps politics and certainly science" (Jencks, 2002b).

I am particularly bothered by the attempt to use religion in order to promote an architectural agenda. Jencks declares that: "On the one hand, there is a deterioration of previous cultural formations. Christianity and Modernism, the two reigning worldviews . . . are both . . . just hanging on" (Jencks, 2002b). "Post-Christianity and Late-Modernism may drag on for another hundred years . . ." (Jencks, 2002a).

I don't want to comment on these statements here, but would like to know the reaction of billions of devoutly religious people, Christians and others, from around the world, who are not only dismissed offhand, but even worse, are classed together with the anti-religious modernists. Jencks holds a fashionable philosophical position, which explains a decomposing, fragmented architecture by saying it is an expression of a decomposing, fragmented society. This is as pessimistic as it is unsupported, and the opposite of what the new science describes.

The contemporary Flemish philosophical school debunks such nihilistic sentiments: "Our opinion is that modernism cannot be surpassed simply by neglecting its ideals, as a certain interpretation of postmodernism would have us believe. The result would be an evolution towards a completely fragmented world, without any sense of direction and purpose. To the contrary, we believe that the ideal of a free and rational humanity is not dead, but has not yet been realized" (Aerts et. al., 1994).

By selecting deconstructivism and ignoring the rest, Jencks casually severs his stylistic preference from mankind's architectural heritage of four thousand years. In choosing a few fashionable buildings as models to follow, other styles are consigned to the scrap heap of history. The extreme narrowness of Jencks's most recent proposal serves to impose his formal prejudices on others. Jencks makes an incredible promise for deconstructivism: "Will it produce a more convivial, sensuous and articulate environment than before? I think so" (Jencks, 2002b). After the preceding analysis of how deconstructivist forms rely on randomness and fragmentation, and a denial of traditional emotional needs, this statement comes as a surprise.

Everything makes sense when it is viewed purely as a tactic for propagating a stylistic preference. This was successfully played once before, in the 1920s, to usher in another so-called new paradigm in architecture. Le Corbusier copied the latest technology consisting of sports cars, airplanes, ocean liners, and concrete grain elevators to define a new architecture. The trick was to create forms that looked nothing like what was around. The high-tech machine metaphor caught on. About twenty years later, Sigfried Giedion produced a voluminous but nonsensical explanation for why this new architecture was based on the new science of the day, namely relativity and space-time. This propaganda worked brilliantly. In the current re-run, deconstructivist architects expect the same method to work again.

10. CONCLUSION.

Architects today are told that the new science supports and provides a theoretical foundation for deconstructivist architecture. Nothing appears to justify this claim. On the contrary, I believe the evidence shows that there does exist a new paradigm in architecture, and it is supported by the new science. Charles Jencks is in part correct (though strictly by coincidence, since his own proposal for a new paradigm is based on misunderstandings). The new science leads inexorably to a new paradigm in architecture. Nevertheless, this new paradigm architecture does not include deconstructivist buildings. The new paradigm encompasses the innovative, humane architecture of Christopher Alexander, the traditional, humane architecture of Léon Krier, and much, much more.

PART 4

DECONSTRUCTING THE DECONS:

THE WORLD TRADE CENTER PROJECT SPOTLIGHTS THE EMPIRE'S NEWEST CLOTHES

By Nikos A. Salingaros and Michael Mehaffy

The proposals for the World Trade Center site unveiled in September 2002 by some of the world's leading architects reveal a curious state of affairs — the architecture profession's avant-garde is hopelessly mired in a failed past. This is not the creative past that New York Times architecture critic Herbert Muschamp contemptuously dismisses as "ye olde towne planning" — the past in which New York's complex urban fabric grew over time to define one of the earth's magnificent cities. This is instead a past of failed ideas and logical fallacies, of misapplied science and outmoded early 20th-century technology.

1. DECONSTRUCTING MANHATTAN?

Almost all of the new proposals for the World Trade Center (WTC) reconstruction come out of the currently fashionable design movement known as "Deconstruction" (Muschamp, 2002). As implied by its name, the Decon style breaks forms apart into jagged, unbalanced fragments. The stated intention is to create a new architecture that is bold and innovative, exciting and provocative. But public reaction — as distinct from what Decon architects and some architectural critics say — has been mostly to regard the products as frightening. The public wonders why architects are consistently designing such ugly buildings. Are non-architects perhaps too ignorant and unsophisticated to recognize the empire's newest finery?

Not really. Trendy architects are perversely going against the rules for putting matter together. Rules for structural coherence are built into the human animal, in an adaptive process that is essential for survival on this earth. Violating these rules triggers anxiety in our minds and stress in our bodies — hence the cries of outrage against the latest architectural conceptions. Nevertheless, our latest scientific insights are intentionally reversed for the sake of novelty and spectacle.

A look at many leading architecture schools confirms the pattern. Students are trained to ignore their intuitive feelings, and to instead pursue the latest fashionable form of technological novelty — blobitecture, crinkled napkins; whatever. As their grades depend on grasping the magnificence of the Emperor's clothes, they quickly catch on. After such desensitization training, architects simply pursue design novelty into unexplored territory without recognizing the inherent dangers. Followers of the Decon school lack the scientific background to comprehend that their audacious, thrilling designs are literally toxic — that they can cause enormous damage to the urban fabric and the quality of human life. In the end, these are not just playful sculptures. For better or worse, these structures will powerfully shape everyday human life for generations to come.

2. THE COMPLEXITY OF THE UNIVERSE.

Deconstructivism makes broad political and scientific claims, originating in the trendy "Post-Structuralist" French philosophers that include Foucault and Derrida, among others. They, and their Decon adherents in the design world, begin with a great truth — that the universe is a complex, intricate structure. But they go on to make one of the great fallacious conclusions of Western history — that the universe is nothing more than a collection of parts. Therefore, disassembly, or Deconstruction, of complex wholes such as buildings, cities, institutions, ideas, and traditions is essential to solving today's problems.

Almost any scientist will tell you that this premise is the sheerest nonsense. If science has revealed anything in the last 100 years, it is the coherent character of the universe, in which wholes are greater than the sum of their parts. Physical, chemical, biological, and ecological systems cannot possibly be understood as mere collections of fragments — indeed, no system can. Interactive field effects are just as important as constituents. Life can only be envisioned through a sequence of patterns defining coherent entities on larger and larger scales. Life emerges out of minute adaptive processes, each responding cumulatively to all the others before it. This process of generating complex wholes is repeated from the scale of atoms, to that of the organism and beyond, to societies of people and their creations.

Applied to cities, the point is that urban zones are not mechanical collections of abstract forms. They are living contextual fabrics that evolve over time. This fundamental scientific understanding of reality is absent from Decon philosophy. The allegedly most "modern" design movement of 2000 is rooted more in the scientific worldview of 1900 than in that of its own day.

But how can this be when, according to its promoters, Deconstructivism aspires to embrace "complexity" and "new science"? Alas, the Decons embrace not the genuine process, but only a misleading frozen image of it — and worse than that, one that gets all the important details totally wrong.

In place of complex adaptation, the Decons continue to impose the 1920's "machine aesthetic" from the Bauhaus — but now twisted and morphed at a grotesque scale. In place of fractal complexity, they impose massive jumbles of elementary crystalline forms.

This is absurd. It is also destructive of the urban fabric of human life. Apologists for this deception, strongly supported by the media and by our most powerful institutions, urge us to erect monstrous totems to such ignorance. These unfortunate symbols only advertise a gullible nation, driven by images and mindless fashions, and one that has turned against the genuine scientific knowledge that made it great. The damage to the urban fabric is far worse. In place of the slowly adaptive richness of the human city, the Decons impose only another modernist geometrical fundamentalism — a new metallic confection to replace the failed geometrical fundamentalism of the fallen towers.

3. NIHILISM AS POLITICAL IDEOLOGY.

But no matter — there is nothing less than a political ideology at stake here. For the Decon philosophers and their followers, all meaning is merely "socially constructed", i. e. a matter of opinion. Thus, any view of the world is as valid as any other, and only the privileged opinion of "elites" — in particular, the discoveries of scientists — is to be rejected. Any consistent attempt to commemorate a particular meaning — including anything with the slightest whiff of "tradition" or "history" — must be rejected as an imposition by "reactionary" bourgeois forces.

The Decons contradict the progressive, historically cumulative nature of science. (For a remarkable exposé of this absurdity, see the book *"Fashionable Nonsense"*, by Alan Sokal and Jean Bricmont (1998). It describes a spoof paper consisting of jargon-filled gibberish, which was eagerly published by a fashionable Post-Structuralist journal.)

This is the illogical, self-serving belief at the core of the Decons' power grab, which is disguised as "liberation". For what are the Decons themselves, if not self-appointed "elites"? Are they not worried about the hypocrisy of rejecting the valuations at the heart of science, while at the same time loudly claiming to embrace the latest scientific advances? Apparently not.

This clever political trick could have profound consequences for the shaping of our cities in the 21st century, as vividly illustrated in the latest WTC proposals. For in the Decons' future, the enduring values of tradition, historical continuity, and commemoration of American democratic ideals — all the things one would hope a post-9/11 monument should embody —

are mere social constructions, to be eschewed and even attacked. According to the Decons, monuments to 9/11 must only celebrate nihilism, despair, and the futility of existence.

4. AFTER THE DECONS:
AN ARCHITECTURE OF "RECONSTRUCTION"?

This project may indeed be "ground zero" for a self-pitying movement, built on an antiquated scientific worldview, and a modern philosophical fallacy. After the momentary fascination with the Decons has passed, we will be left to pick up the pieces and try again to erect a built environment worthy of our humanity. Far from justifying despair, the new science gives us fertile materials with which to reconstruct, and great optimism about what is possible in our technological age.

Strong evidence suggests that a genuine, "new" architecture is imminent — call it "Reconstructivism" — supported by the new sciences, and energized by a profound understanding of complexity, life, and wholeness.

This philosophical movement, together with its practical applications to reconstruct our severely damaged world, represents the opposite of the Decons' nihilism. It will reflect the past, but not slavishly copy it. It will be as modern and as timeless as any new species in nature, evolved from and reflecting its environment and its history.

Before our society can adopt this creative goal, however, the thinking public must learn to dismiss ignorant architectural commentators who brand everything containing life as "reactionary". Just as all living forms have fundamental structural similarities, so every living architectural form must have a commonality with — though not necessarily copy — the great architectural achievements of the past. Like blinders on a mule, the Decons have prevented a whole generation from seeing the basic qualities of living structure.

With the new enlightenment, honest buildings — connecting to human legacy and history — can again be proudly commissioned around the world. Meanwhile, in the mass hysteria to be "contemporary", the metropolis must see that it is in danger of betraying both its past and its future.

PART 5

DEATH, LIFE, AND LIBESKIND

By Brian Hanson and Nikos A. Salingaros

We contrast two distinct threads in the architecture of Daniel Libeskind —
the geometry employed in his Holocaust Memorials, and the geometry of those
buildings whose purpose is life and regeneration. We find no difference whatsoev-
er between the two types, thus concluding that Libeskind's buildings cannot serve
to bring architecture to life.

1. INTRODUCTION.

Daniel Libeskind's inclusion on the short list of architects who have
been asked to propose designs for rebuilding the World Trade Center (WTC)
site and the region around it represents for him a great leap forward. His
skewed, dismembered WTC design has been vehemently criticized for its
intentional shock-effect, but it is this very quality that endears it to the
avant-garde. We wish to find a reasonable basis for analysis that bypasses
the usual terms of debate on architectural deconstruction. That so far only
generates polemics without hope of sensible resolution. Towards this end,
it is necessary to dig deeper than superficial style.

Libeskind's participation in the WTC project symbolizes a jump from
buildings that crystallize a particularly horrific experience, but do not seek
to move on from it — such as his Jewish Museum in Berlin — into buildings that are meant to symbolize, even contribute to "regeneration". Nevertheless, there is essentially no difference between what he believes commemorates death, and what commemorates life, for the simple reason that
he gives them exactly the same geometrical properties. Whatever life he
thinks he is injecting into his "regenerative" work is no more than the artificial appearance of life, as in a Golem, or Frankenstein monster — terms
that will recur later in this essay.

There is indeed an enormous difference between structures that embody "life", and those that embody "death" — it is just that the currently
fashionable architects don't seem to be aware of that difference, or at least
of how to reflect it in their buildings. It suffices to look at Libeskind's World
Trade Center proposal to see what we mean. A tall, unbalanced form with
protruding, menacing components is supposed to be his answer to building on the memorial space while satisfying both the spirit of remembrance
for the victims of the tragedy, and rekindling the life of the region through
a regenerated urban fabric. We agree entirely with Libeskind when he says

that "Architecture is an act of optimism; the site can't turn into a funerary area". Nevertheless, we are convinced that his intervention would endow the site with neither life, nor optimism.

2. AN ARCHITECTURE OF DEATH.

Daniel Libeskind is one of a very few contemporary architects whose work constitutes a recognizable "brand". The brand consists of sharp, angular, metallic shards, with gravity-defying walls, and conveys the unmistakable thrill of transgression. The building most often used to illustrate these qualities is his Jewish Museum in Berlin. Physically impenetrable except via an underground route through a baroque courthouse, this building embodies completely in its architecture the various fates suffered in the 1930s and '40s by German Citizens who were Jewish, or who had some Jewish ancestry. The introduction into it of mundane exhibits, some time after its opening, was undertaken with fear and trembling. While the objects collected by the Museum strive to paint a portrait of Jewish LIFE — stretching over a period of one and a half millennia no less — the building that houses them is preoccupied by the DEATHS visited upon the Jewish people of Europe during the first half of the last century.

It is a testament to Libeskind's achievement that he reproduces the visceral revulsion of the Extermination Camps — not by copying their insipid, industrial Bauhaus style, but by using high-tech materials to define a specific geometry. This geometry succeeds in making us anxious and physically ill, and recreates the terrible purpose behind the camps — a rekindling of unspeakable evil, the human spirit's darkest and most horrible forces — by triggering our memory and senses strictly through form, space, and surface. A visitor to the Berlin Museum may well feel sick and depressed after going through the Jewish Department Extension, and this, we believe, is an appropriate experience.

In those of Libeskind's buildings which speak above all of despair, exile, and annihilation, there is a deliberate "geometry of death" at work — one so powerfully present that it threatens to suffocate any tokens of life that dare occupy its spaces. At the same time, we would expect to see, in those buildings that speak of regeneration, a corresponding "geometry of life". For a building to participate in regeneration there surely must be something generative about it, something life-giving in its very forms. However, search his work as you will, the "geometry of life" is nowhere to be found. Despite Libeskind's words, it is the "geometry of death" which predominates in his forms, and which ultimately compromises those of his works through which he hopes to effect reconnection or reconciliation.

These phrases, "the geometry of death" and "the geometry of life" are not used loosely here, or by way of analogy, but with the very specific meaning they have acquired over the last two decades, in scientific studies of life processes and living complexity — a body of work to which Libeskind will occasionally pay lip-service. Human beings demonstrate more affinity with buildings and environments which are shaped by processes like those that give rise to life, than those which are not, or which choose for some special reason to deploy a geometry deliberately counter to living processes. This emphasis on process is crucial, because so much of what has been deemed to be "organic" in twentieth century architecture — whether it be Frank Lloyd Wright's Guggenheim spiral in New York or the double-helix megastructures of Kisho Kurokawa's New Tokyo — has been merely a formal analogy of life, rather than life itself.

3. GOLEM AND FRANKENSTEIN.

Libeskind seems to have inherited some of the attitudes of the strange early Twentieth-Century organic tradition, that first cousin of expressionism. As a result, when he must confront the issue of life, as opposed to death, in a building like his Jewish Museum in San Francisco (the working title of which was L'Chaim — "To Life") rather than ask questions of life itself, he reaches for the formal analogy offered by the Hebrew alphabet. The phenomenologist in him accepts no distinction between a "real" object such as, for example, the fine, classically-composed substation façade which will be the frontispiece for this new museum space, and the "irreal" strokes of the scribe's pen, to which he makes appeal.

There could, intriguingly, be more to it than this. Libeskind has confessed on occasion to his attraction to the Cabalistic dimension of Jewish thought. One of the most famous Cabalistic myths — originating in 16th century Central Europe, the place where Libeskind himself was born — is that of the Golem given life by Rabbi Judah Loew ben Bezalel of Prague. The Hebrew word golem means "shapeless mass" — a description one might in any case apply to Libeskind's contribution to the new San Francisco Museum.

In myths like that of Rabbi Loew, a lifeless effigy is animated by the agency of a sacred word placed under its tongue. Libeskind's own account of how he generated the form for the San Francisco Museum uncannily recalls the Golem myth. He took the two Hebrew letters of *chai* — which he says are "literally the life source and the form of the museum" — and translated these strokes on paper into concrete forms in three dimensions, so as to bring "life" to the Yerba Buena district of San Francisco. (Ironically, our friend the architect Isaac A. Meir says of Libeskind's transformation of letters to building form that the letter *heth* has been drawn/redrawn inaccurately — or, at least, in a very "personalized" form — and the final building form is unlikely to remind anyone of a special Hebrew letter, let alone a word).

The Golem of Rabbi Loew — intended to be a perfect servant of his master, a protector of the race — turned out to be a destroyer, which its creator had in turn to destroy, to prevent it desecrating the Sabbath. Yes, the Prague tale is the earliest version of the Frankenstein story, and Libeskind's San Francisco Museum a literal example, therefore, of that "Frankenstein architecture" which the critics of modernism have often warned of. There is no better illustration of the profound contrast between what Libeskind means when he speaks of investing buildings with "life", and what most people would appreciate as living environments.

4. GEOMETRICAL DETERMINISM.

There is another, related point. A paradox of Libeskind's work is that an architect who claims to be so in thrall to the chaotic, the complex, the open-ended, and the democratic, should produce buildings so deterministic, and which leave so little to chance and personal choice. One should be wary of drawing conclusions from Libeskind's own words, because he is a master at producing a veritable fog of words on demand. Boaz Ben Manasseh (2001) observed that: "It is astonishing that Daniel Libeskind can write so much nonsense without endangering his reputation". But the architect has made it clear that he expects his buildings to communicate even to those who are unfamiliar with the apologies he provides for them.

The first of his buildings ever to be completed — the museum in Osnabrück devoted to the works of the local Jewish painter and Holocaust victim Felix Nussbaum — offers the same deterministic experience as the Berlin museum. Like the Berlin exhibits, Nussbaum's paintings are effectively stripped of their intrinsic, timeless qualities by the building they occupy. The paintings serve as little more than supporting documentation for the story that the architect has deemed more important — that of a flame being snuffed out.

Both these buildings display an arbitrary kind of determinism. For example, in Berlin there is a long rising staircase, offering one of three routes out of the underground passage (the only real route in fact, two of them being dead ends). This semantic confusion is matched by an approach to planning which, while intent on driving visitors along a particular route, nevertheless robs them of any sense of direction. This failure is made even worse by the architect's apparent indifference to the effect on circulation of merely practical elements such as fire doors in the Nussbaum Haus. Perhaps this disorientating dissonance is the point of such architecture. Both museums speak of death by having their galleries violated in some way.

Everywhere in Libeskind we find the rule that disallows contingent life its expression through either multiple connectivity or the processes that develop connections; and that therefore excludes spontaneity and emergence. Instead, he offers THE ANSWER, allowing no possibility of alternative interpretations. Libeskind's buildings, wrought with finality and closure, provide an urgency that will not allow life the leisure to unfold, and which are not sufficiently in touch with life as lived to be able to learn from it. It could well be possible to prove, with reference to living processes, that a classical museum by John Russell Pope (the architect of the Jefferson Memorial in Washington), which offers such variety within such apparent unity, is more truly alive in most, if not all, respects than one of Libeskind's deconstructivist essays.

5. REJECTION OF THE SACRED.

In one of the most lucid and revealing of his lectures — dealing with the Bauhaus, and delivered in Weimar in 1998 — Libeskind expressed his admiration for the Bauhaus model of an "architecture permanently displaced", which rejected outright the lure of the sacred. It was, he went on with growing admiration, "here, in the domain of the sacred, that the Bauhaus declared war and wrought havoc ... Gods were toppled, orders broken, walls smashed, the center removed". And, in the most revealing passage of all, he dismissed the whole notion of the sacred as being "no more ... than the empty ritual, a formalism ... the evil of senseless habits, the purpose of which is to deprecate reality in the name of convention so it may become fulfilled through an image" (Libeskind, 2001). These bleak words contain the essential generator of Libeskind's brand of architecture. His architecture revels in dissonance, is the *ne plus ultra* of theoreticism, and regards as antithetical any ritual that might promise a return to wholeness. It thus exiles itself from its primordial relationship with nature.

6. APPEALS TO SCIENCE.

Libeskind is not the first architect of the last century to have been inspired by popular science to make formal analogies with the natural world. This has led him into statements every bit as convoluted as those so mischievously exposed among post-Structuralist french philosophers by Alan Sokal and Jean Bricmont (1998). In Libeskind's texts, references to chaos and complexity, including fractals, conceal an approach to spatial organization which, as we have seen, is highly deterministic, and almost entirely lacking in the adaptive, stochastic processes which give rise to life-forms that exhibit such features naturally.

The jolt of novelty and strangeness one gets from Libeskind's designs is apt to blind one at first to their ultimate shallowness. They are no more truly scientific than those early twentieth-century buildings in which the search for geometrical novelty manifested itself through (non-fractal) forms that mimicked crystalline structure — forms entirely irrelevant to the manifold functions of such buildings.

Libeskind's employment of fractals (as a tiling design on so-called fractiles devised by the engineer Cecil Balmond) on the proposed "Spiral" extension to the Victoria and Albert (V&A) Museum is a case in point. These tiles represent nothing more than surface decoration, utterly at odds with both the overall massing, and the lines formed by the building's edges. This gives predominance to these aggressive edges, and creates a caesura between architectural form and decoration typical of Modernism, and which over the last century has served to reduce ornament to being either unnecessary, or "ironical". We have here a misapplication of the self-similar fractal geometry found in natural forms.

Libeskind's claim that his tiles are engaged in some kind of "dialogue" with Owen Jones's *"Grammar of Ornament"* (1982) ignores what successful ornament actually does. There is a world of difference between the arborescent nature of the ornament Jones catalogued, which could unite the broad masses with the fine tooling of historic buildings, and the fractals with which Libeskind merely distresses the sloping walls of the V&A "Spiral". This addition would therefore exist in isolation not only from the rest of the building, but also — because his fractal tiles occupy a self-contained world of mathematical perfection, insulated from truly living processes — the rest of the universe. Even in their details, therefore, Libeskind's buildings are deterministic rather than adaptive, and it is well known that adaptive natural structure is the source of life, non-adaptation leading only to death.

7. CONFUSING LIFE WITH DEATH.

If one examines carefully Libeskind's body of (mostly unbuilt) work, it can be seen to exhibit two distinct strands, with a few works attempting to combine aspects of both. On the one hand, his buildings (like Berlin [1988-99], and Osnabrück [1995-98]) view history and tradition in general, and civic culture in particular, as marked for all time by the awful scissure of the Holocaust, the Shoah. On the other, in a group of ongoing designs (the Jewish Museum in San Francisco [1996-2004], the Art Museum in Denver [2000-05], and the extension for the Victoria and Albert Museum in London [1996-?]), Libeskind says he wants to reunite the frayed ends of a city's history and culture. The first strand of work is desperately pessimistic, whereas the second is brimming with optimism. Between these extremes we have the recently-completed Imperial War Museum of the North, in Manchester [1997-2002], whose characteristic shards represent the brokenness of war, but which, at the same time, is intended to contribute to urban regeneration. In fact, Libeskind's architecture, as seen in the Jewish Museum or the Nussbaum Haus, seeks explicitly to embody an extinction on a massive scale — namely the Holocaust.

In Berlin the "geometry of death" which results from this might be accepted, on account of the fact that we must not turn away from, and forget, the awful events that building symbolizes; but it cannot be excused in buildings which pretend not only to participate in the life of the city, but even to enhance it in some way. Is the "geometry of death", which justifiably gives form to this class of building, transformed by Libeskind, and if so how? Do those of his buildings that seek instead to connect and give life obey a more appropriately generative geometry, a recognizable "geometry of life"? There is as yet no final agreement among scientists as to what life is, but there is a growing measure of consensus about what the nature of the processes might be that underlie it. Some characteristic properties are:

(1) Life has connectivity and pattern at its heart.
(2) Life is "organized complexity", a potent mixture of rule and contingency, order and spontaneity.
(3) Life is not definable through traditional mathematical equations which purport to give "an answer", but is more of an unfolding, comparable to the action of a computer program.
(4) Life is a genetic algorithm that evolves and develops complexities as it learns.
(5) And life is not just complex, but — even more mysteriously, perhaps — it is ordered, displaying an incredible range of symmetries.

Not one of these characteristics of organic life finds a parallel in the forms of Libeskind's architecture, but only occasionally in the words that accompany his projects. It is difficult to see how they could do so, in an architecture that is based on an utter rejection of the sacred, and that condemns those patterns of activity — for him only "senseless habits" after all — which inevitably accompany a sense of the sacred. Libeskind merely represents the latest stage in the profession's determined rejection of the knowledge and the representation of life, in favor of abstract, supposedly more architectonic means of expression.

8. EXPRESSING DEATH BY USING GEOMETRY.

A "geometry of death" reverses the properties of living structure, while at the same time suppressing the mechanisms by which human beings connect to the world. The first component recognizes death outside of us — its rules are summarized as an absence of the organized complexity found in organisms, and the presence of structural disorganization that marks their death and decomposition. This definition encompasses not only formerly living structures in the process of decomposing, but also structures that could never have been alive in the first place — what are commonly recognized as "alien" forms. An alien structure threatens us, making us anxious.

Such structures do exert an undeniable fascination — this is the fascination that children and adolescents have for things that scare them. The second component of the "geometry of death" recognizes death within us. It indicates (or mimics) a failure of our cognitive mechanisms that is characteristic of the onset of our own death.

Its purpose is to reduce our physical experience of the world by providing insufficient information to understand our environment. The method of achieving this is to create spaces and surfaces that frustrate our sensory embedding within our surroundings. For human beings to be fully alive means more than just to metabolize and reproduce — it presupposes our sensing and understanding the world. If we are confronted with obvious physical structures around us, which we see but to which we cannot connect, such an environment threatens our conscious existence as embodied beings. The anxiety we feel reflects this loss of connectivity.

These two components suggest specific techniques for simulating the geometrical presence of "death" in buildings:

(1) Dehumanizing structures and spaces — either too small or too large for a human being to relate to, built deliberately without a connective scaling hierarchy.
(2) Shapes that stand out from nature by lacking connective symmetries and attachment to the gravitational axis.
(3) Random, geometrically disconnected units that have no obvious means of support.
(4) Corners and sharp edges projecting toward us.
(5) Sheer, empty surfaces without internal differentiations, which shift our perceptual attention to their edge — surfaces unresponsive or intentionally repulsive to our visual and tactile senses, and which can be drab and colorless, smooth or rough, or made of sleek materials such a shiny metal and glass.

A third component of the "geometry of death" is to mimic the disorientation that comes about when we lose our ability for spatial navigation. Part psychological, part physiological, we possess a complex of senses that position us in the physical world and permit our locomotion. To deny this sense means to cut us off from our circulation realms. This is achieved via the techniques we have already mentioned, such as stairs that lead to nowhere; corridors that are arbitrarily cut; entrances or exits that are impossible to find; and, most of all, a deliberate circulation constrained by built structures that force us to walk in a direction different to what seems natural to us.

Although not the only architect working with the above rules to define a strikingly noticeable "style", Libeskind is certainly one of its most brilliant exponents. Of course, these rules are a well-kept trade secret, and have never, to our knowledge, been written down. They are applied with such confidence and deliberate intention that we find it hard to suppose that this is accidental, or that they could in any way be confused with their antithetical, "life-giving" rules.

9. "LIFE" IN ARTIFACTS.

In the case of the Victoria and Albert Museum, those who fail to see the presence of the "geometry of death" in Libeskind's proposed extension also clearly fail to appreciate what it is that this Museum houses. We have in this unparalleled collection a group of objects that embodies "life" to the greatest extent possible — the products of artistic, religious, and technical traditions that aim to capture mathematical life (as defined by contemporary complexity theorists) using only human intuition and humble materials. Those artisans and craftsmen did not have our latest scientific insights to help them, but relied instead on lessons learned over millennia of human ingenuity.

If we were to search the world over for man-made objects that best reflect the properties of what we now understand to be a "geometry of life", and which most closely capture the spirit (though not necessarily the form) of natural and biological structures, then we would come up with something like the catalogue of the V&A's collection — Chinese Shang bronzes; Byzantine miniatures; European Mediaeval sculptures; Seljuk Minai bowls; Iznik tiles; oriental carpets; Japanese sword guards; etc. This is discussed at length in Christopher Alexander's *"The Nature of Order"* (2002).

It is only appropriate that such objects — the prime representatives of a "geometry of life" applied to create artifacts that connect to the living beings that see and use them — be housed in a building with those very same qualities. If not, the structure will become locked in combat with these products of traditional crafts, representing a variety of sacred traditions, in the same way that the museums in Osnabrück and Berlin are in tension with their contents. Since Libeskind's design is, unlike almost all the objects in the museum, nihilistic, its effect would be to drain objects of their essential spiritual value.

Significantly, the V&A "Spiral" which Libeskind proposes is not a true spiral — i. e. a mathematical helix like Frank Lloyd Wright's Guggenheim. He is in fact coining a new term, the "contemporary spiral" lacking an axis, and thus continuing the task the Bauhaus began — to see "Gods ... toppled, orders broken, walls smashed, the center removed". All the symmetries of a helix that contribute to its coherence are removed. The V&A project is actually composed of lopsided, intersecting cubes, and bears an uncanny resemblance to the 1919 "Würfel (Dice) Komposition" by the Bauhaus's Johannes Itten (Marchetti & Rossi Costa, 2002).

10. CONCLUSION.

If one looks beyond mere formal analogies of life to the mathematical patterns and processes which scientists are now pointing to as the source of life itself, then Libeskind's buildings are invariably dead. All his attempts to transfer a geometry appropriate to Holocaust Memorials (which, in that context, is restrictive of freedom) to buildings which are intended to celebrate, if not engender life, have failed, as they must inevitably continue to do so.

What about the relationship of Libeskind's buildings to their surroundings? The life of traditional environments is not just seen in the forms themselves, but contains the seeds of its own dissemination. As is well known, the structure of DNA is such that the information it contains can be replicated and passed on. Lacking life in their forms, Libeskind's buildings lack also (some would say, thankfully) the ability to reproduce. They stand as sterile objects within the city, the most they can hope for being to be "cloned", by some one or another camp-follower of deconstruction. While traditional architecture both lived and reproduced, by dint of its origins in relatively simple human activities, the architecture Libeskind provides would serve to propagate only an avant-garde elite which, for all its talk of openness, thrives on a new form of mystification.

11. POSTSCRIPT: A FATE WORSE THAN DEATH?
(July, 2004)

This article appeared in February of 2003, only a few days before Daniel Libeskind managed to win the commission for the World Trade Center (WTC) reconstruction. After that, he was universally referred to — at least in the mainstream architectural media — as "the architect of the century". For a while, it seemed that we had really missed with our timing. When the piece finally appeared it felt like we were taking a Canute-like stand against the inexorable tide of Decon, and of its arch-champion Daniel Libeskind. [1]

Nevertheless, as subsequent history shows, our article correctly anticipated certain developments, and in a very timely manner indeed. Now, a little over a year later, Libeskind has become a mere spectator of the showcase New York project by which he would put the world to rights; and his one-time champions are steadily melting away (Pogrebin, 2004). In London in July, meanwhile, an application for grant aid for Libeskind's £70m "Spiral" extension to the Victoria & Albert Museum was rejected by the Heritage Lottery Fund, on the grounds that it "did not deliver well against our key requirements of conservation, education and enjoyment of the UK's heritage" (Byrne, 2004). [2]

Libeskind's original design for the WTC site was progressively revised, to the point where little of it is now left. While the impression was being spread around that the whole world wowed about Libeskind's vision, the real powers controlling reconstruction — the Star Architect's understudies, you might say — progressively adopted a more conventional style.

Is there clear evidence of cause-and-effect here? We're not so sure, and our feelings are ambivalent. Libeskind's fall from grace is clearly due more to the ever-shortening attention span of the fashionistas who set the cultural agenda, than to well-reasoned, scientific arguments. The fact that commentators can now dismiss Decon as acidly as once they rejected all things traditional is hardly reassuring: particularly when, as we see on the WTC project, it paves the way for commercial mediocrity.

Many people question how this could possibly have happened. After all, New York City was sold a vision more than a practical building, after a long and vicious media battle had been waged against supposedly traditional (and eminently practical) design proposals. Libeskind's vision won out, with a great deal of fanfare. Yet now we have a gradual return towards the faceless brand of corporate architecture.

The result is, strangely, a feeling of regret and loss. So much effort could have been saved by adopting a humane design in the first place. And it needn't have been modest: a soaring monument, yet adapted to the human scale and feeling in those regions where people have to walk, live, and work — a vision that does not abuse monumentality to discomfort human beings. What took place since awarding the project is indeed an evolution towards a design more adapted to the "geometry of life"; starting, however, from a fundamentally non-adapted basis.

As such, the end result will always be suboptimal, as any evolutionary biologist can explain. Moreover, we note with regret that what drove the evolution of the design were not so much forces adapting it to the human scale, but rather ones of profit maximization. [3]

The world needs an architectural vision; we just happen to disagree with Libeskind's particular vision. The answer is not, however, a return to the faceless and lifeless boxes of the 1960s. That would represent the worst brand of retrogression, but is unavoidable when people eventually discover that the vision has problems. Any vision, from the most wonderful to the patently absurd, comes up against harsh realities, at which time practical compromises have to be made. Deciding on which parts of an architectural vision to save depends on whether those will give something back — such as an enhancement of human life. Does the design offer spiritually nourishing qualities worth paying a premium for? (Yes, we are being incredibly idealistic here; we passionately wish to see a new architecture in the new millennium based on the "geometry of life"). Reality begins to dissect the vision to see what is behind it: a sound philosophy of form that supports life; realizable ideas for a better world; newly acquired scientific understandings; whatever of value.

We exposed all the ideological flaws of deconstruction at the very beginning of this debate. We identified the theory as being based on what has proved to be empty intellectual discussion, which invents a fanciful but meaningless language that fails to connect to the product. Once Libeskind entered the limelight, journalists such as Deroy Murdock (2003) had a closer read of his published writings (Libeskind, 1997), and came away with a very negative impression. Ultimately, the deciding factor was a more mundane one: what we labeled as the "geometry of death" is not very practical to build, and does not provide enough rentable office space.

Libeskind was never really the problem. The problem was and is, first of all, the role played by Star Architects. All too often, they help unwittingly in paving the way for mediocrity, and the consequent despoliation of our cities. The WTC project is not the first one in which a Star Architect has secured legitimacy for an approach that a sizable component of the public roundly rejected. Dazzled by the performance, and perhaps briefly entranced by the heart-wrenching appeals to our emotions, we are too satiated to notice when the Star leaves the stage and is replaced by some less glamorous assistants.

Second, Star Architects lead us to accept that a comprehensive, all-encompassing, "artistic" vision is the best way to solve a problem as large as that of the WTC. It was clearly too large for any single individual, and the gap between ambition and achievement will be even larger with the team that succeeds Libeskind. Significantly, the best proposal for the site so far has come not from an architect or planner, but from the New York Times's film critic, A. O. Scott, who argued for some low-tech interventions to stimulate "the ferment of the streets", and warned against "too much planning". Indeed, if there is a subtext to the piece we wrote about Libeskind, it is that "too much planning" is bad for you, but that there is a mathematical/scientific cure.

And so, in retrospect, Libeskind's star may grow dimmer, but there are plenty of other "Stars" ready to take his place. It might be worth saying that New York contains one of the most sophisticated audiences for the arts in the world. If this audience can be fooled by the Disappearing Star phenomenon, then any audience can.

NOTES:

1. Canute was an 11th Century King of England, who vainly ordered the tides to retreat, to demonstrate the limits of kingly powers.
2. This proposal was the second main focus of our original article. Because the project was dependent upon a hefty sum of public money, it looked increasingly unlikely that it would be built. It was officially abandoned after the First Edition of this book.
3. This is, in fact, a central question in genuine architectural theory, but not one that is addressed by today's crop of academic architects. Is it mathematically possible to transform a design representing the "geometry of death" into one embodying the "geometry of life" by minor or major adjustments? Christopher Alexander has invested several decades of effort in answering it. Translated into practical terms, this becomes: can we save existing Decon buildings through costly renovation after the present craze has fizzled out, or are we going to be stuck with fundamentally useless structures that have to be demolished?

12. POSTSCRIPT II: A LETTER FROM HILLEL SCHOCKEN.

I first became aware of the Israeli architect and urbanist Hillel Schocken through his interesting article "Intimate Anonymity" (Schocken, 2003). In it, he correctly diagnoses why many urban spaces fail despite having good architecture. We corresponded and became friends. Hillel is acutely aware of the human dimensions of architecture and urbanism, and is opposed to the disconcerting practices we see around us today. He has done some very sensitive restorations in Israel, including the home of Chaim Weizmann, designed by Erich Mendelsohn. Hillel is in fact directly linked to Mendelsohn via his grandfather, who commissioned Mendelsohn to build three Schocken department stores in Nuremberg, Stuttgart and Chemnitz. Though Hillel's built work is, to me, somewhat uncomfortably modernist, it is original, attractive, and as adaptive as modernism gets. The same can be said of Mendelsohn, who was rejected and marginalized by the other more famous modernists because he dared to be more imaginative than them (and a far better architect!). When Hillel visited Berlin recently, he wrote me his very strong personal impressions of the Berlin Jewish Museum. This letter is an important document, since it arises out of the direct experience of a perceptive user, and also confirms my own analysis of that building. I am very proud to be able to include it in my book.

Hi Nikos;

Sorry for not responding in detail to your questions on the "Holocaust Museum", or rather, as it is called, the "Jewish Historical Museum" in Berlin. I'm so frustrated with its apparent success that it seems the entire world is deaf to any criticism of it.

Architecture seems to be in a continuing crisis for a very long time, possibly since the 1930s. From a profession that solved the clients' programmatic problems and reflected accepted cultural values of society, it has become esoteric and egotistic, reflecting the whims of the architect as an individual artist. Buildings are no longer expected to be understood by their users through architectural means. One is more and more exposed to pseudo-philosophical architectural talk. Faced with this situation one cannot escape being reminded of the "Emperor's New Clothes".

In your essays on Libeskind (*Death, Life, and Libeskind*) and others you assume the role of the little boy from that story. Your analysis based on the idea of structures that embody "Life" and those that embody "Death" is both original and illuminating.

I would like to offer you some additional points of criticism to Libeskind's Jewish Museum in Berlin that I believe help clarify why his architecture and that of other Jet-Set Starchitects becomes "dead". After half an hour, my son begged me to get out of that building as soon as we could. And he was right. This is another instance that is worth investigating the public reaction more than what the architect actually says.

Firstly, the museum is part of the Historical Museum of the City of Berlin and was supposed to cover the long and important Jewish chapter in the history of Germany and the city. It is true that the dark period of the Holocaust is an important part of that history but it certainly isn't the only story. Jews lived in Germany for many generations and their contribution to German culture and to the European and Western culture in general was immense. Jews played a significant part in almost all walks of life such as science, literature, commerce, economics, the visual arts, music, theater, philosophy, etc. The museum was supposed to show all of that. True, the exhibits try to do that but Libeskind's building makes this effort utterly useless. People still call the museum "The Holocaust Museum". This is a direct result of Libeskind's over-prolific rhetoric, relating the plan to "the yellow star that was so frequently worn on this very site". One asks, why is it necessary to evoke the notorious yellow Star of David if no one can read it either in the resulting building or in its plan?

Secondly, I think architects should be barred by law from talking about their buildings! The architecture must talk to the public in a purely architectural language. In the case of Libeskind, this is an even greater problem. In various places in the museum there are little signs telling the visitor what the architect expects them to feel in this or that space. In the "Garden of Disorientation" (as I believe it is called) — an outdoor space with a grid of slanted concrete columns — there is a sign saying something like: "Mr. Libeskind expects you to feel disoriented ...". Sorry, I felt bored. I also felt uneasy to express my feelings as at every corner there was a guard making sure that I did not take my jacket off (as it felt quite stuffy). "You should put your jacket on or give it in at the cloak room ..."

Thirdly, the circulation in this building is purely absurd. Every now and then there are circular red stickers on the floor with white arrows telling you where you should go. This is, to me, a symbol of the architecture's failure to self-explain the building to the public. Libeskind has built three underground "roads" which are supposed to tell three different programmatic stories. He is certainly not original when he uses the term "road" with relation to long, narrow, boring and monotonous spaces that usually come under the term "corridors". He is following in the footsteps of the "illustrious" Le Corbusier, who called his endless dark and threatening corridors that run along every third floor of his monstrous *Unite d'Habitation* "streets". Both compensate for the poor performance of their architecture by using verbal terms that are supposed to convince the timid visitor that night is day.

Fourthly, the internal spaces of the museum are simplistic and rectangular. Libeskind "compensates" for his total lack of spatial understanding by perforating the elevation with diagonal slots for windows that relate to the outside composition of the elevation with no regard at all to their effect on the interior. This is the reason why many architects who experienced the building before, and after, the exhibition was installed say "it was better empty". The exhibits are a real nuisance for the architecture and vice versa.

Despite all this, the Jewish Museum in Berlin has met with almost unanimous acclaim from both architectural critics and the public at large, which reflects the sad state the architectural profession finds itself at the beginning of the 21st Century. Architects are no longer required to meet the client's needs. They are no longer responsible for the harmonious weaving of the building into an existing fabric. Success is assured by the mere shock effect a building creates. The stranger, the better. Cities across the world are looking for Jet-Set Starchitects to design for them a project that will "put them on the map", a project the like of which was never seen before.

Again, this is a modern version of the "Emperor's New Clothes". Libeskind's pseudo-philosophical thinking coupled with the right public relations effort can sell ice to the Eskimos. Architectural critics as well as the public at large are proved again to be fools. The world is in urgent need for a little boy ...

All the best
Hillel Schocken

PART 6

WARPED SPACE

A REVIEW OF: "WARPED SPACE. ART, ARCHITECTURE, AND ANXIETY IN MODERN CULTURE" BY
ANTHONY VIDLER. MIT PRESS, CAMBRIDGE, MASSACHUSETTS, 2000.

The book's title promises a treatment of the concept of space that is relevant to Architecture and Urbanism, which immediately appealed to the reviewer when he was asked to review this new work. One should not approach the title, *"Warped Space"* too literally: one is likely to be challenged to find much about Geometrical Space or any coherent statement referring to generalized geometries. The author's notion of warping is also intriguing since it clearly is not connected to a literal or scientific definition of the term. The author must therefore propose a philosophical approach to the concept of space. In this regard a reader may be puzzled as to why certain thinkers in this area are not mentioned (i. e., Herman Sörgel) while others are mentioned only in passing (Gaston Bachelard).

A cursory review of the table of contents suggests a critical historical review of the treatment of space from the time of early modernism to the present in support of the view — which many of us share — that little has changed in this regard except to make the spatial experience of the built environment even more unpleasant. However, should one be interested in an exegesis of the disconnect between architectural design and the interaction of human beings with space, such a reader may be puzzled by the author's approach.

A reader familiar with deconstructivist presentation may be better able to appreciate Professor Vidler's treatment of the topic. One who may not be as familiar with such an approach is likely to struggle, however, especially if on a quest for definitions or the suggestion of a thesis. This book presents a problem of comprehension, since reading it is a particularly demanding experience because the author's thoughts are difficult to follow. Having carefully read the Introduction twice, its message about the book's aims and scope is still unclear. The rest of the book poses a difficulty for both reader and reviewer. Whereas the text throughout the book reads as if it is making a definite point, no overall direction emerges when reading an extended selection, and one is left disoriented.

Professor Vidler is apparently working within the scholarly tradition, with references to other work and the inclusion of footnotes. Quotes by Sitte, Freud, and other well-known psychologists and urbanists bring a reader no closer to comprehending the book's central thesis, however. The foundation of any scholarly work should include an overview of the problem, placing the author's viewpoint and contributions within a rubric of other contributions.

Despite the complexity of architectural and urban space, and the rich and varied insights on the topic by other authors, this book presents only opinions of the deconstructivists, and selected material that might support those opinions. The work of Bill Hillier, Julienne Hanson, and the space syntax community is not mentioned, nor is the large body of results by environmental psychologists such as Oscar Newman and Jack Nasar. That omission seems curious in a treatise interested in anxiety in public spaces.

We don't know if the author agrees or disagrees with the opinion of Léon and Rob Krier that early modernism set a dangerous precedent of deliberately making psychologically uncomfortable spaces. Instead, there are statements by Le Corbusier — who arguably never understood urban space — on how he hated street life; and a not very illuminating discussion of some early modernist filmmakers' treatment of cinematic space. One reads of Le Corbusier's psychological anxiety experienced on the Acropolis, but finds no reference to the classic analyses of its spaces (Doxiades, 1972; Martienssen, 1964).

Finding something that would help draw the interest of the typical reader of the Journal of Urban Design is also difficult. For example, some criteria or a set of guidelines on how to analyze, judge, or construct a type of architectural or urban space that is perceived as more human than what we find during much of the twentieth century; anything that can be of use to a practicing architect, urbanist, and interested citizen. It was clearly not the author's intent to treat such material.

The second half of this book is a collection of essays promoting a certain group of contemporary artists and architects, including Mike Kelley, Greg Lynn, Toba Khedoori, Martha Rosler, Eric Owen Moss, Rachel Whiteread, and Daniel Libeskind. Many of these tend to be visual artists who wish to make a philosophical statement rather than design a practical structure. Indeed, one of the few built constructions discussed in the book is a solid block of concrete that was poured into an empty terrace house, and the house (which formed the shell or mold for the concrete) was demolished. Another is a giant sculpture of a Brassiere that fills a large room. We are therefore entirely within the whimsical world of the artistic avant-garde, but in that case, the connection to real buildings and experienced space is very tenuous indeed. As mentioned by Professor Vidler, Rachel Whiteread's solid concrete block was attacked virulently by the London Press, and by London County Council for impeding either planting or new construction, since it is more solid than a Bunker. What are urbanists to make of a solid block of concrete without an interior?

In the essay on the group of Viennese architects known as "Coop Himmelb(l)au", Professor Vidler correctly identifies them, along with Friedrich Hundertwasser, as being dedicated to an uncompromising attack on the architectural status quo. But then, Hundertwasser — who really understood how to create human space, both interior and exterior — is not mentioned further. Instead, the bizarre and totally impractical projects of Coop Himmelb(l)au are praised for reasons that are hard to comprehend.

There is moreover no hint that, at least in our top architecture schools today, Coop Himmelb(l)au is moving closer to becoming the status quo, against which followers of Hundertwasser have to battle for acceptance.

The author adopts the expository style of the deconstructivist philosophers, which connects thoughts and phrases in an alternative manner, and which ultimately make no sense to scientifically-trained individuals.

This topic has been treated at length by Alan Sokal and Jean Bricmont (1998), who argued their point via a celebrated hoax published in a Deconstructivist journal. In accepting deconstructivist philosophy, and in deciding to feature architects who claim a legitimacy on the basis of that philosophy, Professor Vidler is unavoidably forced to use their unique style of discourse. Many of us, however, find that terribly confusing.

The reviewer apologizes to the author in advance, for no personal slight is intended in this review. The reviewer is probably missing the true point of his book altogether, while some other readers might find it instructive. Nevertheless, the reviewer's view is that this is not a book for the average reader. People like the reviewer will find it difficult to extract much useful information from the book, whereas it could be recommended to architects who already accept the deconstructivist style of discussion.

ACKNOWLEDGMENT.

The reviewer would like to thank Professor Peter Vefeades of Trinity University for helping with this review.

PART 7

TWENTIETH-CENTURY ARCHITECTURE AS A CULT

1. INTRODUCTION.

I have found, to my surprise, that architects are not interested in laws of architecture. They prefer to design buildings on the basis of artistic fashion and ephemeral philosophical concerns. The same reaction greeted the efforts of my distinguished colleagues, Christopher Alexander and Léon Krier, to reform architecture as a discipline. Another recent attempt was initiated by Prince Charles. Despite having the vast majority of the British public in agreement with his humane vision of architecture, the Prince's attempt ultimately failed.

How does the architectural profession so successfully repel attempts at reform? I believe that the answer is to be found in a system phenomenon. Architecture is a cult, and the last thing a cult wants is to be transformed into a proper scientific discipline. The reason is that the two types of system have very different internal structures, which in turn generate a form for the controlling power structure. There is no smooth transition from a cult to a discipline based on logical precepts.

Architecture is not set up to be stable to received input in the same way that science is. In science, there exists large-scale and long-term systemic stability. By contrast, contemporary architecture, like any other belief system not founded on rationality and experiment, is susceptible to catastrophic system collapse because it cannot tolerate minor changes.

The moment when society decides to abandon architecture as a cult, and replace it with architecture as a field based on logical reflection, the present architectural power structure will cease to exist. A new power structure composed of new people will be supported by a new educational system. Establishment architects realize that their continued prosperity depends on prolonging the current system, and are doing a marvelous job of reinforcing its hold on society.

2. DEFINING A CULT.

A system may be identified as a dangerous cult if it has the following characteristics, combining aims with techniques:

1. It aims to destroy
2. It isolates its members from the world
3. It claims special knowledge and morality
4. It demands strict obedience
5. It applies brainwashing
6. It replaces one's worldview
7. It has an auto-referential philosophy
8. It creates its own language, incomprehensible to outsiders

I will show here that contemporary architecture satisfies these criteria.

3. ARCHITECTURE AND CULTS.

Few people today connect architecture with religion. And yet, up until about the last two centuries, architecture could not be distinguished from religion. Today, architecture has broken away from religion in forming its own cult. Architecture competes with religion because it promises transcendent pursuits to its practitioners. It offers mystical enchantment, with insights left to be discovered purely by the power of creativity, and thus an opportunity for any initiate. The architect sees a chance for transcendental expression beyond the utilitarian uses of a building. Despite the modernists' proclaimed insistence on functionalism, they too were enchanted by their own ideas of formal expression. From this, it is not surprising that architecture misused the workings of religion to further itself.

The Bauhaus and Taliesin — two "compounds" upon which contemporary architectural education is based — followed a cult structure. Walter Gropius established a strict, authoritarian cult regime for resident Bauhaus students. Johannes Itten, a follower of a cultish offshoot of the Mazdaist (Zoroastrian) religion, indoctrinated Bauhaus students into its mystical practices. Wassily Kandinsky, Piet Mondrian, and Theo van Doesburg (all Bauhaus teachers at some point) belonged to the Theosophist movement led by Helena Blavatsky. They subscribed to the mystical cosmology of fellow Theosophist Dr. M. Schoenmackers, whose astrological theories decried that only the primary colors yellow, blue and red could be used.

On the other side of the Atlantic, the cult practices at Taliesin were organized by Olgivanna Wright, Frank Lloyd Wright's third wife, who was a disciple of the Greek-Armenian mystic George Gurdjieff. Gropius put into place his anti-traditionalist principles as soon as he became head of the architecture department at Harvard University in 1938, providing the model for postwar architectural education. Schools around the world soon copied what he and Wright had done.

It is irrelevant whether the spiritual groups mentioned above represented beneficial, benign, or harmful cults. Cult methods were applied to make architecture into a new cult, and an extremely dangerous one because of its virulence and destructive aims. A key aspect of modernism was an absolute belief in the necessity of eliminating all pre-modernist architecture.

The point where architecture turned into a cult can be identified with the abandonment of traditional building culture. Like science, architecture has a vast store of practical knowledge and technical skills that one needs to master before making original contributions. By throwing all of that away, the modernists could offer instant gratification to those who joined the cult. They attracted followers using the myth of the creative genius. Young architects still had to train for several years, but their time was spent very differently. Instead of learning and absorbing a core body of knowledge, they trained for allegiance to the architectural cult.

4. BRAINWASHING.

Cult indoctrination begins by tearing down a person's confidence and self-esteem; i. e., one's emotional equilibrium as established via the childhood development of one's intuition and senses. Tactics for achieving this include mental and physical humiliation to discredit what are already automatic and natural responses. After one's major point of internal stability and referential attachment to a worldview is effaced, that candidate is open to any kind of indoctrination.

For several decades, architectural novices have been conditioned by the message that sensual gratification from ornament and architectural forms, surfaces, and colors is a criminal act. It is asserted that such sources of pleasure are fit only for primitive peoples and social degenerates. Indeed, a cultivated non-response to sensually emotive architectural elements is supposed to characterize the intellectually advanced individual. As a psychological and physiological reaction to those forbidden elements is normal, however, this message induces feelings of guilt and worthlessness, as required to break down a student's spirit. Self-esteem is then rebuilt using the modernist repertoire of alien, hostile forms and surfaces — and, from then on, only the cult's reality is considered valid. One of the slogans of the Bauhaus was "starting from zero". Its aim was a radical restructuring of human consciousness. Every incoming student was subjected to intense psychological conditioning designed to cleanse every preconception regarding architecture, so as to re-wire the student's neuronal circuits.

The studio method of architectural training lends itself perfectly as a technique for cult indoctrination. A student's project is judged — without having a basis of proven logical criteria — as to how far it resembles currently fashionable buildings. The student's grade is entirely up to the whim of the teacher. It is no wonder then that, despite the widely-pronounced aims of limitless creativity, all students' projects tend to look the same and to conform to stylistic dogma. Students who don't adopt the cult's beliefs are eliminated before they can get their degrees, so they never join the architectural profession.

5. THE CULT OF DECONSTRUCTIVISM.

In a devastating hoax, the two physicists Alan Sokal and Jean Bricmont (1998) have exposed some of the most prominent French deconstructivist philosophers as charlatans.

Charlatans are not protected in the scientific world. The society of their peers would expel them from positions where they could continue to do harm. Science needs to protect its foundation more than its individual members, something that will not occur in a power-driven discipline that lacks a scientific basis. In the architectural arena, deconstructivists are unassailable because the discipline is based largely on cult beliefs. Those who use deconstructivist philosophy to justify their bizarre constructions are now at the top of their profession.

There is something dangerously wrong with a society that ignores the exposure of intellectual impostors. If part of a system is pathological, this puts the entire system at risk. Systemic connections will eventually infect the rest of the system (in this case, society as a whole), and thus destroy it. Our civilization appears to be so complacent with its recent technological progress that it does not recognize threats to its very existence. We are distracted by technological toys and are not applying our scientific knowledge to keep our society in healthy working order. More traditional cultures are aware that something is dreadfully wrong, but they don't know how to react in a constructive manner.

Architecture schools are training graduates who are indoctrinated into deconstructivist philosophy, yet are unable to design a simple building fit for human sensibilities. Deconstructivist buildings, moreover, have been shown to remove life from the environment. Life here is defined in mathematical terms as a measurable degree of organized complexity that is characteristic of biological forms.

None of this is even remotely perceived by either practicing architects, or students who would become architects, because the discipline has become entirely self-referential. There is no contact with outside reality, which is arrogantly stated to be the deconstructivist's principal aim.

The deconstructivist agenda is to destroy the logical foundations of knowledge and reasoning, in a way that would make it impossible to reconstruct it afterwards (see Part 9). For deconstructivist architects, there is no more utopia, only nihilism.

6. ARCHITECTURAL CULT SYMBOLS.

As psychological conditioning is used to reformat the minds of architecture students with an "approved" set of images, this indoctrination develops negative associations for "disapproved" images of traditional buildings. A remarkably effective propaganda campaign has successfully linked traditional architecture with all the ills of history. To many, a Classical building now stands for something evil, and a building in local vernacular style as a serious impediment to progress. Just as experimental animals and human prisoners-of-war are conditioned to react automatically to a particular stimulus, architects have been conditioned to feel a physical revulsion for new buildings in traditional styles. They have been brainwashed by the cult to identify the cult's "enemy" without reflection.

Modernism's cult symbol is an empty rectangle, with the concept of emptiness expressed by its interior being just as important as the sharp rectangular edges.

Since modernist dogma strictly forbids ornament on the human range of scales 1cm — 2m, there exist no true modernist symbols on those scales to which human beings can connect. The imposition of modernism's alien aesthetic is achieved by creating a void. Its symbol is precisely the absence of symbols. The mental image of "pure" form erases living structure from our world.

Theo van Doesburg (of De Stijl and the Bauhaus) is credited with saying that: "The square is to us as the cross was to the early Christians". Here we encounter a philosophical shift of levels, from visual symbols to an abstract ideal. The modernists worshipped the unattainable abstraction of geometrical purity, and this displaced all visual and architectural symbols of the past (Mehaffy & Salingaros, 2002). This indicates the transference of values from traditional symbols and rules (which could EXPRESS religion) to an abstract ideal (which therefore COMPETES with religion).

Deconstructivism is an offspring of modernism that retained many of its parent's cult symbols; for example their sharp edges and high-tech surfaces. Seeking novelty from within a severely limiting style, deconstructivist architects abandoned early modernism's horizontally-aligned rectangular geometry to create broken straight lines, diagonals, and curves. Modernism's ideological aim of eliminating the copying of historical forms and symbols was achieved via severe geometrical abstraction. The only possible direction to move from empty abstraction — without returning to the ordered complexity of traditional architecture — is to destroy forms altogether. Because modernism as a thought system denies organized complexity, it could only evolve into disorganized complexity.

Architectural cult symbols act like viruses to infect the built environment (Salingaros & Mikiten, 2002; see Part 12). They have even parasitized established religions, with the consequence that postwar religious buildings are spreading the cult's ideology rather than their clients' spiritual values.

7. THE SOLUTION.

Now that the architectural cult has become the establishment, it controls architectural education and the media. Deconstructivism today permeates the arts, literature, philosophy, and the social sciences, so where are we to find sanity and support? There are two disciplines that are opposed to cults, and which will provide the natural allies for a humane architecture of the present and future.

These are SCIENCE, and RELIGION. A destructive cult's weakness is that it is cut off from both science and God.

Unfortunately, modernists misused science atrociously, and now the deconstructivists' considerable propaganda machine is taking over terms like "fractals", "nonlinearity", "chaos", and "emergence". We need to tell the world the truth: that the new sciences point unequivocally to traditional architecture as being rooted in the same generative processes that create the rest of the universe. A new, humane architecture can bridge the gap between science and religion, and this alliance will generate a better world.

8. POSTSCRIPT: THE AUTHORITY OF THE GOSPELS
(DECEMBER 2006).

I cannot resist adding some thoughts I have had since publishing this Part of the book as an article in 2002. Those experiences have deepened my conviction that we are dealing with a broad, deeply entrenched, and ultimately unsettling phenomenon. I am more than ever convinced that it is a manifestation of intellectual fundamentalism and cult-like artistic isolation. These are diverse observations, loosely woven within the cult theme.

Some time ago I dipped into the religious literature to read about those authors' understanding of the wonders of the universe. Being a scientist, this section of bookstores had never really attracted me. I wanted to find anyone who might think like me, however, who sees "value" in forms, and I was exploring every possible venue. Architecture is about constructing a built world to complement and replace the natural world, so I would expect architects to have some respect for what nature does. Remarkably, what I read in the architectural literature is profoundly depressing. Texts on "theory" show a disdain for natural forms and processes, while at the same time pretending to learn from biological structures. I don't believe such declarations one bit — looking at the results as a scientist, I can see no real understanding of biological form.

Anyway, imagine my surprise when I discovered a stack of genuinely positive writings by religious authors. Here indeed is what is missing from other parts of our literature: the wonder at the beauty of nature, ultimately interpreted as the beauty of God's work. A profoundly positive interpretation of biological structure leads to the value of human beings. The same sense of wonder is felt by some (though not all) of our greatest scientists. The notion of the word "sacred" arose in religion, and it is here applied to humanity. I read about a deep respect for the human animal as more than an animal.

Sure, we eventually come up to a divide on Darwinian processes (an unfortunate philosophical division between religion and science), but that's another matter. I wish to emphasize the positive and deep appreciation of natural structure I discovered. Aside from one point (which is important, and which I discuss below), it felt to me that I had found a significant community of writers who felt exactly as I do about the wonders of the universe. The universe, far from being mechanical and pointless, is alive and full of wonderful mystery. This is not an anti-scientific point of view; it is merely anti-reductionist.

The only aspect that caused me to step back was their referencing system. Throughout my religious reading program, I read what appeared to resemble scientific text (albeit without equations!), with footnotes and references to higher authority on every page. Used to reading scientific papers, I subconsciously treated those reference numbers as pointing back to some experiment, or to a theoretical model verified by separate teams of scientists so as to establish its validity. Eventually, I saw that all references were to the Christian Gospels. Now, there is nothing wrong with referring to what is deemed to be an ultimate authority (the Word of God, no less), but scientists cannot really take that as a substitute for physical experiments. This glitch did not in any way diminish my pleasure at the texts themselves, which I have already stated, provide a most inspiring appreciation of the beauty in our world.

So far, my discussion has been restricted to Western Judeo-Christian religious thought, with which I am most familiar. Nevertheless, there exists a vast body of literature on the world's diverse religions that confirms the same feelings of wonder at the profound aspects of the universe. Every distinct human group has evolved its own religious understanding of observed complexity, contributing some of the most beautiful pages of literature ever written. This is also the source of humankind's greatest architectures, inspired by different — though equally intense — religious sentiment.

Contemporary architecture is erasing those traditions ever more systematically, however. It appears to me that this is occurring most efficiently in places of the world where a totalitarian anti-religious regime in power for several generations has already erased that country's traditions. Switching cults is relatively easy; replacing religion with a cult takes more effort. It is a simple matter for a totalitarian government to embrace the cult symbols of contemporary architecture, passing them off as symbols of progress.

I wish to turn the religious referencing method around. I will use the example of a massive three-volume text on contemporary architectural theory that I recently received and carefully went through. It consists of essays by many different authors, who apparently employ the same kind of referencing system! But now, the references are to the cult leaders: Deleuze, Foucault, Heidegger, Lacan, Latour, etc. (I should say that I have nothing against Heidegger, only with his adoption by the architectural cult). The texts I read here are full of quotes by those "luminaries of thought" (indeed, the essays are by-and-large simply commentaries rather than the development of any original thesis), with a footnote to the references. The essays' authors do not propose their own observations, but limit their role to an interpretation — a "close reading" — of others' writings.

Readers are supposed to accept the authority of the above group of thinkers, unquestioningly. Meaning is attributed to the words themselves rather than to any coherent result or thought. This is a faith-based method of discourse. But the implied authority is neither to scientific experiment (the wisdom of nature), nor to Divine Wisdom. What if, like myself, a reader believes with considerable justification that this is all a shallow and futile exercise in relativist epistemology? And yet, this body of pseudo-philosophical texts is treated with exactly the same reverence as the Gospels.

I know that the biologist Richard Dawkins would like to lump both sets of authoritative texts (religious, on the one hand, and pseudo-philosophical, on the other) into one heap, but I disagree with Dawkins for the following reason. Traditional religions have provided humankind with aspirations and hopes for untold millennia, which is the reason why human beings (and the human capacity for thought) evolved alongside their religions. Human evolution is a symbiosis of biology and culture, which Dawkins seems to undervalue. Cults, on the other hand, have been destructive because they are intellectually fundamentalist. The cult of contemporary architecture is a particularly nasty phenomenon — as is beginning to be recognized in public reaction to the recent crop of Art Museums and Libraries erected around the world!

Although I have explained that I do not subscribe to the referencing system of the religious literature, I respect its use in that specific and very limited context. (Religious writers run into serious problems when they attempt to write scientific texts using the same system). Nevertheless, even as a layperson, I am terribly offended by the system's appropriation in presumed texts on architectural theory. There is in effect an implied comparison of Derrida with Saint Paul; Foucault with Saint John; Heidegger with Jesus. Sorry, but the very idea provokes an ugly physical revulsion. But that's what those authors (graduate students, highly respected architecture faculty, and Deans of Schools of Architecture) are currently doing. It's the accepted referencing system for contemporary architectural discourse.

While employing the faith-based method of discourse, contemporary architectural writers nevertheless lack any of the sense of wonder that religions are based upon. Instead, theirs is a bleak outlook, detached from the living world; seeing (and reveling in) the worst that humans have done. It is reductionist in the extreme, focusing entirely on the words of its cult leaders.

My interpretation of this as a cult phenomenon is supported by the extreme narrowness in the authors' choice of references. It's always the same names. That's astonishing to see in the work of so many authors supposedly covering a broad variety of topics relevant to architecture. The majority of researchers working in the field (both outside and within architectural academia), along with their evidence-based results, are stubbornly ignored. A vast body of published work simply "does not exist". This is not an innocent case of ignorance due to academic over-specialization, but rather the imposition of a narrowly-defined reality for the cult. It is a jarring experience to be reading along in a discussion of complex adaptive systems, expecting it to develop into an insight on evolving urban form — and to find instead that it leads to a quote by Deleuze. The logical development is broken abruptly. Why?

Architects are not used to reading: they are visually oriented. Moreover, having had to read architectural theory has forced architects to develop a strange and peculiar manner of reading, because for a long time, such texts have been of a strange and peculiar nature. Architectural texts have been very confused and impressionistic, so those who have grown up with them developed a superficial method of skimming them rapidly. That habit, however, makes it very easy for architects to read text that makes no logical sense, and not to notice that anything is amiss.

To highlight the difference I am talking about, consider the number of books used in typical physics versus architecture courses. The physics course has one textbook crammed with information. A student is not even expected to cover all of its chapters. The architecture course, by contrast, may have a required reading list of up to twenty books or more. These numbers tell you that the architecture books are simply meant to provide "an impression". An architecture student trained to skim architecture books therefore cannot easily read science, because that represents a vastly different psychological and cognitive experience. It might take quite a while to retrain architects to read text for content.

Another telling point is to notice the curiously similar final page of all those book chapters on contemporary architectural theory. Some articles may be interesting to read, whereas others are meaningless, and would be an embarrassment to any serious disciple. Nevertheless, all of them usually end with the same declaration of cult allegiance: they propose the small pool of currently fashionable architects as models to follow and adore. If they have illustrations, it is always of deconstructivist images (the cult's icons). Regardless of the actual discussion, whether it is about fractals, complexity, neural networks, emergent processes, self-organization (the very topics I write about in an architectural context, with altogether different conclusions!), we are inevitably led to the "anointed ones". All half-dozen Starchitects! No other architects are ever mentioned. The cult followers are obliged to support their common self-reinforcing faith.

As if further proof were needed, something else happened to drive this point home. I recently assigned my new architecture students to read two of my papers, and two papers by my friends. The students were supposed to make extensive notes and collectively write an in-depth review of all four papers. I hoped that after doing this, they would grasp the topic, and save me from having to lecture on everything from the beginning. Imagine my surprise when I read their reviews: they were full of quotes from the "approved" cult authors! None of those references appeared in any of the four assigned articles, however. My students (intelligent ones, by the way) did not seem to have read the assignment; rather they took this as an opportunity to promote the cult authors. Little of the papers' actual content seemed to have registered. They did not even realize that I criticize the authors whom they quoted in their review! Cult reality overrides information input, even in a homework assignment.

PART 8

AGGRESSION IN ARCHITECTURAL EDUCATION: THE 'COUP' IN VISEU

Now that this book is making significant inroads into the contemporary architectural arena, one question keeps coming up over and over again: "Why are students continuing to accept brainwashing by modernist and deconstructivist ideologies; why don't they go to another architecture school and learn genuine architecture?" This is an excellent question, but one that has been carefully anticipated by the academic establishment. The answer is that THERE ARE NO OTHER SCHOOLS ONE COULD GO TO. An incredible power struggle has kept any innovative, forward-looking teaching institution from teaching real architecture, usually by threat of de-accreditation. Those few institutions that could get around this blackmail were simply closed down or taken over. I originally wrote this essay when the Traditional School of Architecture in Viseu, Portugal was taken over by a group of modernists. It shows that not only the students, but also a whole institution can be forcefully converted.

Today we are seeing a substantive shift in architecture away from the stylized debate of the elite toward a growing concern for the human dimension. Architectural programs hoping to remain viable over the next century must begin to open up to ideas outside the current paradigm (and not by systematically dismantling everything they perceive as a threat!). New scientifically based theories not only underpin the sensibilities of both the New Urbanism and Traditional and Classical schools; they provide a real basis for the need to change, and also the way to change (Salingaros & Masden, 2006). If modernist schools fear the values of a more human architecture, then let them design the big-box stores, sewage-treatment plants, and warehouses. This would allow the design of buildings that are closely related to human beings (houses, apartments, schools, churches, offices, markets, shops, museums, theaters, factories, etc.) to be conceived from within a body of knowledge that is more human in nature. If the thought that something can be learned from preindustrial (i.e. traditional) models fundamentally violates some persons' beliefs, then they must reconsider those beliefs. If they are unwilling or unable to consider any body of knowledge outside their own, then ultimately they will fail. The cost of this failure is taking its toll on students, architects, and everyday human beings.

Architecture and Urbanism students beginning the 2004 academic year at the Catholic University of Portugal in Viseu were surprised to find a new director and 13 new professors. Commentators have interpreted this move as a takeover, changing the direction of the school from traditional to modernist. To me, replacing the traditional architecture school in Viseu by a modernist faculty is an event of momentous significance. Of course, I'm affected indirectly because my good friend Lucien Steil was on the faculty, and José Cornelio-da-Silva, whose work I know and respect, was its director. (Both went to teach for one year at the University of Notre Dame's Architecture program in Rome. Lucien created Katarxis Urban Workshops with Michael Mehaffy and myself and is now with the Prince's Foundation in London. José has his practice in Lisbon and has become my design partner).

I would like to try and ignore personal issues here and focus on the long-term meaning of the takeover. If we count the number of places that a student could learn traditional architecture in recent years, we come up with 4 and 1/2. We have Notre Dame, the University of Miami, and, until now, Viseu. Prior to that, the Prince of Wales's Institute, headed for a while by another good friend of mine, Brian Hanson, was operational for several years, and helped to train many young people who are now very much sought-after. It was forced to close down. With the recent change in Viseu, that leaves no other institution in the European Community in which one can train. There are many traditional architects in Europe with whom a student can arrange an apprenticeship, but that now becomes more of an individual effort. The 1/2 remainder is Yale University where, to his great credit, Dean Robert A. M. Stern has always sought to balance traditional architecture with the latest avant-garde. If only that attitude were adopted at other schools!

John Massengale added his own informative comments after my essay on the demise of Viseu appeared: "There are over 125 accredited architecture schools in North America, and only two of them do not teach Modernist architecture as the core of the curriculum: the University of Miami and the University of Notre Dame. There used to be a third — the Oregon School of Design — but Modernist architects forcefully took control and ran it into the ground. I don't know how many schools of architecture there are in Europe, but I do know that there have only been two that based their curricula on the principles of traditional architecture and urbanism: the Prince's Foundation for Architecture & the Building Arts, and the New School of Viseu. Both suffered the same fate as Oregon. There are fewer than 30 schools of architecture in Great Britain, but having one teach traditional design was too much for the British architectural establishment, which mercilessly mounted personal attacks on Prince Charles (Massengale, 2004a)… There is no more insular, esoteric world than the elite architecture school today. One result is that the graduates of Miami and Notre Dame get many job offers, while graduates of Columbia often find themselves unemployable as architects (Massengale, 2004b)."

This information is not widely known. It could very well destabilize the fortress of pretense and futility that modern schools of architecture defend so vehemently. The truth is that an entire academic industry is producing graduates ill prepared to design buildings and cities that are adaptive to human use. This consortium of teaching programs annually turns out hundreds of confused young people who have been misled into believing that they are now architects. The system is desperately trying to protect its sovereignty — not by improving its methods, but by ruthlessly eliminating any competing ideas. That was clearly demonstrated in its intolerance of the three aforementioned programs.

As an aside, I saw Robert Stern here in San Antonio at the dedication of his new building, Northrup Hall in Trinity University. Stern joked with me that our mutual friend, the great classical architect Léon Krier and I were not supposed to like it because it looks modernist — but, on the contrary, I can testify to its excellence. Precisely because Stern is one of America's foremost traditional architects, he knows how to build an adaptive modernist building that has successful spaces, circulation, and textures. He understands why it is important to train architecture students to be real architects.

Even if we write off Viseu as just another victim of university politics, its disappearance as a place of learning traditional architecture and urbanism leaves an enormous gap in architectural education worldwide. I'm ignorant of the true causes of the takeover: whether it was to find nice, comfortable jobs for a team of architects; to institute a new program that might possibly attract more students than the old program; to bring political prestige to the entire university by promoting a more "contemporary" curriculum; or to eradicate modernism's sacred enemy, traditional architecture and all it represents. Whatever the reasons behind it, the job is now done, and architectural education is far worse off as a result.

In fact, the school at Viseu had rapidly achieved an astonishing international recognition as a European center for traditional architecture and urbanism, even as it was being undermined by its own university. The school organized an extremely successful international conference (to which I was invited but could not attend) just before its demise (Parham, 2004). This was where the forward-looking and innovative "Declaration of Viseu" was written (CEU, 2004).

Carroll William Westfall wrote a strongly-worded letter to the Bishop of Viseu condemning the takeover as an outrage. He gives powerful reasons why the change, evidently supported at the highest levels of administration, goes against Catholic tradition. Here is an extract from his letter: "It is, then, not merely the means that have been used to institute the new program but the content of the new program that are to be condemned in the sharpest possible terms. This is an act that will be seen as filled with the most profound shame. It is not too late to undo this unfortunate act. It will be difficult to restore the *status quo ante*, but surely the cunning that went into its dismantlement can be turned to reinstituting it. With its restoration will come a restoration of the seamless unity we seek between the Church and the world as it can be rendered in traditional and classical architecture and urbanism, and only by traditional and classical architecture and urbanism."

I know Bill Westfall, who is a great teacher and architectural historian. Even though I agree with him, I am afraid he is entirely too optimistic in expecting anyone to undo the coup in Viseu. Once taken, territory is rarely given up without a desperate fight. And, in this case, the takeover was executed with the collusion and apparent urging of a higher authority.

The fact that this occurred at the Catholic University of Portugal adds some irony to the story. By an incredible coincidence, I published an article entitled "Anti-architecture and Religion" in Portuguese in November of 2002, which must have been just before or about the time the machinations to undermine the architecture school at Viseu began. My article appeared in "Brotéria", which is a Jesuit journal read by Portugal's Catholic elite. [That essay is Part 9 of this book]. In that article I dared to state an uncomfortable truth: "It is as if architects formed by 20th century ideals have read Hans Urs von Balthasar's treatise [The Glory of the Lord: Volume I] linking beauty with the love of God — in order to do exactly the opposite. Everything that is natural, beautiful, sacred, and holy is negated, ridiculed, and suppressed; and moreover with a fanatical insistence. Not even the Church itself has been spared. In a remarkable adoption of what is fundamentally unholy, the Church has embraced modernist architecture. The result is that many people do not feel like worshipping anymore in new Church buildings that make them ill. They also question the wisdom of a Church that can no longer equate the beautiful with the Holy."

Because of this article, I don't think the administration of the Catholic University of Portugal can claim to be unaware of the long-term dangers of associating with modernist architecture and thought. Those who read my article (and I have good reasons to believe many did, according to my brother-in-law who lives in Lisbon) may have disagreed with it, but an important institution such as the Catholic Church in Portugal cannot afford to ignore the possible consequences of its actions. So, the question now shifts from the petty politics of replacing a group of faculty at a provincial university, to a philosophical allegiance between the Catholic Church and Modernism as an anti-religious cult.

Not being a Catholic myself, I am not in a position to discuss the grave issues resulting from this association. I only wish to raise the question of culpability that James Kalb writes about in his preface to this book. This regrettable incident cannot fail but harken back to earlier deceptions that the Catholic Church has fallen victim to (with profound and terrible consequences), and which have now returned to haunt it. The issue of culpability cannot be ignored — those who conspire with a destructive cult will have to share its guilt.

Modernist architects and their deconstructivist offshoot have been used to acting without accountability. Erase tradition; impose totalitarian philosophies on the people (but promising all along that it is a "liberation"); turn architecture schools into modernist and deconstructivist training grounds where one learns to grab power (but not to build habitable buildings); disseminate the most blatant propaganda by taking control of the architectural media; etc. are planned and deliberate actions for which they have never been held accountable. The most dangerous — and successful — of all strategies is to deceive and manipulate a powerful institution so as to further their own selfish cause.

This behavior is consistent with the change in architecture from a discipline serving human needs and sensibilities to a power-driven, fanaticized cult. Starting from the 1920s, modernist architects successfully applied military strategy and tactics to slowly take over the discipline of architecture. The rest of the world misinterpreted this process as a natural evolution of styles towards forms better fitted to contemporary society. That was an egregious mistake. The gradual elimination of traditional and humanistic architectures (and the institutions that train those who wish to practice them) should not be interpreted as a Darwinian selection, but rather as an aggressive takeover and extermination of what has irreplaceable value to humanity. Only those architectural styles dominate whose proponents are aggressive and ruthless.

Among those who fully understand what is happening is the prominent architect and urbanist Andrés Duany (co-winner of the 2008 Driehaus Architecture Prize). Immediately after the Viseu coup, he posted some comments on the Traditional Architecture listserver in which he outlined his disappointment. Traditional architects have ignored Duany's periodic warnings about mastering the military aspect of their profession. The result is that, as in the irreversible replacement of an animal species or a human society, traditional architecture schools are now being exterminated. Duany's fear of misapplied priorities is being realized. Let me quote portions of his postings:

"The problem with countering the avant-gardists (they are not modernists, and we cannot grant them that position) with Reason is that they have set up a field of combat that explicitly devalues the light of reason and privileges the raw force of unreason. In other words, they are set to fight by rolling us into the gutter in the night. By proposing to counter them with reason we are proposing to counter them with 18th Century gentlemen's dueling rules. They will continue to trounce us. Reason is but one weapon to be used in the appropriate circumstances. Power is another — and the only one they play by. Check out the details of the coup! Classic! Perfect! Can anybody not now see what utter sons-of-b*tch*s we are up against? Have I not been saying that we need to learn to attack, like them? What are we prepared to do now? Well ... how about some more moral superiority discussions? Want to bet that we lose Notre Dame and Miami within ten years? No student wants to take losers or wimps as role models. I don't particularly like to associate with them myself. After these humiliations we are powerless — without either viable organization or plan. What stunning lack of vigilance on our part! What tactical ineptitude! What lack of aggressive spirit! If these events are not a call to unity and action, I don't know what is."

Not too long ago, Elizabeth Plater-Zyberk (the Dean of the University of Miami's School of Architecture, Duany's wife, and co-winner of the 2008 Driehaus Architecture Prize) told me exasperatedly that "people on our side just don't know how to fight". That is quite true — they spend their time learning how to design and build sensitive and adaptive buildings. By contrast, the "other side" spends all of its time in mastering the arts of war and propaganda. Their main (phony) argument is that they are being innovative; never mind that they are religiously following cult dogma. What's really important is which power alliances can best promote some ridiculous visual fashion. The question is: how can the most powerful institutions be sold the deception of innovation and progress by means of sleek, shiny images?

Clearly, a small group of Portuguese architects cannot by themselves get rid of someone as internationally visible as José Cornelio-da-Silva. After a powerful institution has been duped into collusion, however, it is relatively easy. Those architects who oppose traditional architecture and urbanism are doing the right thing in terms of gaining territory and eliminating their competition. They train in aggression, AND INCREASINGLY CREATE AN ARCHITECTURE OF AGGRESSION, which obviously works. They have figured out how to take over architecture schools and will thus control architectural education for yet another generation.

On the whole, academic administrators are seduced by modernism because it gives them power to redefine the nature of reality. It offers them one more advantage in the exercise of bureaucratic power. If modernist architects could convince the Catholic Church as a whole, or even a small group of Catholic university administrators in Portugal to support their cult's extension of power, then that's quite an achievement. They have indeed scored a "coup", which merits the notice and even grudging respect of military strategists within our own camp.

Perhaps the world will now realize it is in the interest of humanity to finally act. Responsible institutions should shake the fog of propaganda out of their heads and realize they are being used in an exterminatory campaign. The future will forget nebulous arguments about architecture and false promises that "modernity comes via shiny surfaces" — but history will judge today's institutions as not being morally fit.

PART 9

ANTI-ARCHITECTURE AND RELIGION

1. INTRODUCTION.

In wanting to explain a cultural mystery — why the world renounced emotionally-nourishing buildings, and instead embraced buildings that literally make us ill — one comes up against severe obstacles. It is not that methods for producing humane buildings are unknown, or that there is a lack of architects to build them; society has made a conscious decision to build what it does. Furthermore, enormous energy is spent in convincing people that our contemporary built surroundings are good, even though almost everyone feels otherwise. There is a basic disconnect between what we feel, and what we are told we ought to feel — or forced to accept. Answers to these questions lead us from architectural theory into social beliefs and systems.

I wish to elaborate an idea that has often been expressed by Neo-traditionalist architects: that all styles are not equivalent in terms of their architectural consequences; some styles have deleterious effects not only on the built environment, but on society as a whole. Contrary to a working assumption accepted eagerly by our contemporary culture, the avant-garde is not harmless. Stylistic pluralism hides a danger because it accepts cults into society, and those cults would like to destroy society.

Within an architectural style, ideas and concepts are tied together that may have no logical relation to one-another. Someone builds a novel-looking structure, then comes up with irrelevant explanations for why the structure looks that way. To ensure success, the architect can link the new style to themes that preoccupy society at that time, promising that its adoption will help to move society forward in the desired direction. Building styles that have evolved over millennia do not suffer from such a dishonesty or logical disconnectedness; it is only hastily put-together styles that are flawed in this manner. A particular style's philosophical underpinning could make some false assertion or statement, yet appear to fit together in a superficially satisfying manner. It is this *satisfaction of fit* that fools the mind into accepting a stylistic structure; the mind usually does not examine the logical coherence of the whole message. There exists an innate mechanism in the human mind that enables this phenomenon.

2. RELIGION PROVIDES A STRUCTURE FOR MEANING.

It is undeniable that the greatest architectural creations of mankind arose as a response to religious fervor; the desire to express in materials what human beings felt towards their Deity and Creator (Alexander, 2004). Cathedrals, Churches, Mosques, and Temples around the world attest to this fact. Enormous investments of human energy went into creating these structures. With few exceptions, they reveal an absolute honesty of expression.

Religion arises out of the necessity to understand a universe that escapes our comprehension because of its profound and ordered complexity. Religion has in the best periods of human civilization acted to complement our scientific understanding of natural phenomena. It can and does seek to provide answers to questions that are too difficult for science to answer. By presenting a set of guidelines and rituals as a balance against the destructive side of human nature, the world's religions have successfully held humanity more or less from collapsing into chaos and barbarism.

All religions are based on worshipping some higher form of order, which means that a key aspect of religion is trying to recreate this order as a geometrical expression using physical materials. This process begins with the House of God and religious artifacts, but certainly does not stop there. In the first religions the creative spirit manifested itself everywhere, and not merely in special locations or in a special type of sacred artifact. Utilitarian objects were made with the same philosophy of striving to represent the complexity and beauty of the universe — as best understood by human beings at that time — in the things we built. Every religious person accepts that God is indeed everywhere, so for millennia we tried to build everything around us according to a higher logic. While this created a tension with the opposing forces of economy, utilitarianism, fashion, etc., this tension prevented our buildings and artifacts from ever being without life.

Religious belief is usually driven (though not with all people) by a need to accommodate oneself to the mysteries of the universe. A religious mythology provides not only rules for everyday conduct; it also gives consolation and stability against the frightening prospect that there is no meaning to life: that life itself might be a random and inconsequential event. A belief system thus gives purpose to our lives. In the same way, architects need a meaning structure for their profession, and, having abandoned traditional values, they will seek it in cults of their own making. Architecture has not yet developed a scientific basis that would obviate the search for meaning within mysticism and irrationality.

3. FRENCH PHILOSOPHICAL DECONSTRUCTIVISM.

A group of French philosophers started an anti-scientific fashion in the late twentieth century. In a series of writings that make little sense, they claimed that scientific analysis was invalid, and that ways of thought akin to free disassociation are more ethical. Their actual point is impossible to summarize, precisely because it lacks any internal logic (see Part 11). Nevertheless, the end result of this movement is to create a cult of anti-scientific followers, who now question all the scientific achievements of mankind, and indeed any progress achieved through science (see Part 7).

The answer to the inevitable question of how such a bizarre and destructive cult could have arisen in academia lies perhaps in a linguistic phenomenon. Deconstructivism started as a discourse in French academic circles. Those of us who speak French, and who might have read French philosophy, surely know that a gifted intellectual can argue aloud in French, and say very little of substance while appearing to be making profound statements. The French have a long tradition of scholarly discourse, which could be shallow in content but linguistically rich in flowery expressions and gestures. If this hypothesis were in fact correct, it would explain why the original French academic audience was enraptured by the deconstructivist discourses, whereas the texts in English translation make no sense at all. Nevertheless, those texts are read worldwide today — they are part of an established cult whose irrationality forms part of its mysticism.

4. DECONSTRUCTIVIST ARCHITECTURE.

Deconstructivist architecture can be described as the product of a group of architects creating their own cult by defining a new style of building. The style is easily recognizable as having broken forms, using "high-tech" materials for visual excitement, and intentionally violating the most elementary elements of balance, rhythm and coherence. Their only design tactic is a simple and random morphological gesture that removes sense from form. It is doubtful whether such architects understand the French deconstructivist philosophers (for those writings are in principle not understandable). They do, however, find in them a convenient philosophical underpinning — and a catchy label — to justify their own architectural cult.

Science tries to understand the ordered complexity of the universe. It follows a process of putting together different pieces of insight, obtained by different researchers and by different techniques, into a coherent picture. Sometimes scientists take apart a structure to study its parts, but only so that they can better grasp how the whole works. Deconstruction is the antithesis of this: it is the tearing apart of form just for the fun of it. It destroys the ordered complexity that nature has marvelously synthesized, and from which we ourselves arose. This destruction is quite simply a turning against the evolutionary forces that have created us.

The success of the deconstructivist cult is undeniable, however. Nowadays, the most prestigious architecture schools in the world have opened their doors to deconstructivism, and have hired those architects who have made themselves the prime representatives of this cult. Major corporations, Governments, and even established religious institutions compete for their favors, spending money on alien-looking commissions; large sums of money that could otherwise be used to build structures adapted to human beings and the human spirit. In a most absurd — and ultimately destructive — infatuation with an architectural fashion, the media promote the cult of deconstructivist images, spreading them while lending them respectability.

Finally, evangelical techniques are misused to sell deconstructivist ideas to third-world countries, by falsely linking bizarre forms with technological progress. Countries that buy this idea then foolishly destroy their vernacular, historic, and sacred buildings in order to supposedly attain a higher level of architectural culture. Quite the opposite eventually takes place after the initial excitement has worn off, as scarce resources are squandered in paying for expensive imported materials such as glass and steel. The result of this is an impending ecological disaster the world over. The damage done to our inherited architectural and cultural heritage is immense.

5. INTOLERANCE FOR HISTORICAL AND VERNACULAR STRUCTURES.

In so many instances, a perfectly sound older building has been demolished in order to make place for a much inferior new building. Renovation and adaptation are simply not considered — the vestiges of the past must be erased entirely. And yet, both in terms of structural quality, as well as in their connectivity to human beings, many older buildings simply cannot be duplicated today; they would cost much more to build than clients are used to paying nowadays, and few contemporary architects would even know how to build them. Perhaps this envy, the certain inability to approach the superior architectural standards and achievements of those outside the cult, is what drives their destroyers.

Despite the highly-publicized reaction of the various postmodernist architectural styles against early modernism, they have all retained modernism's intolerance for historical and vernacular structures. As is well known, it is still forbidden to build traditionally, and, when traditional elements are included for whatever reason, they can only appear as "jokes", and not as integral tectonic components. Those few contemporary architects who do build in more or less traditional styles are viciously attacked by the architectural establishment. If anyone dares to break the twentieth-century taboo against traditional architecture, then that architect risks ending his or her career.

It is no wonder then, that new traditional buildings spark such violent opposition and outrage from within the architectural community. Interestingly, this revulsion is comparable to that felt by ordinary citizens when confronted with bizarre deconstructivist structures, which in that case is driven by our built-in ("hard-wired" or biologically evolved) instincts for order. As a result of their training, most architects today consider traditional architecture as "impure", and that part of their professional duty is to purify the world through its elimination. In this conception of things, Neotraditionalist architects are traitors and enemies of the cult.

6. EVEN THE CHURCH ...

It is as if architects formed by 20th century ideals have read Hans Urs von Balthasar's treatise *"The Glory of the Lord: Volume I"* (1982) linking beauty with the love of God — in order to do exactly the opposite. Everything that is natural, beautiful, sacred, and holy is negated, ridiculed, and suppressed; and moreover with a fanatical insistence. Not even the Church itself has been spared. In a remarkable adoption of what is fundamentally unholy, the Church has embraced modernist architecture (see Part 10). The result is that many people do not feel like worshipping anymore in new Church buildings that make them ill. They also question the wisdom of a Church that can no longer equate the beautiful with the Holy.

For many millennia, the highest architectural expression was reserved for the House of God. This is true with all peoples and all religions. It is immaterial whether iconography was allowed or not: where it was, mankind created glorious mosaics, frescoes and paintings; where it was not, we created fantastic polychrome tiles, wood carvings, and carpets for our places of worship. Religious spaces in themselves symbolize by their geometry the highest expression of the love of human beings for their creator. All of this ended abruptly in the twentieth century — not only the creation of enlightened spaces, but also our attachment through architecture to a higher form of order in the universe.

Modernist architects broke up interior space into ill-defined volumes, using broken wall planes and extreme ceiling shapes and angles. A lack of closure (often aggravated by glass walls) destroyed the wholeness of individual rooms. Living spaces were either made cramped by lowering ceilings too far, or uncomfortable by raising the ceiling to two stories. To complement this assault on the user's senses, hard materials, previously reserved for external surfaces, were introduced into internal walls. In a special irony, modernist architects were commissioned to build churches (some of which were deemed unusable by their intended occupants), and to disfigure older churches through so-called "renovation".

We find ourselves at a difficult time in architectural history. It appears (and not only to the author) that the leading academic architectural institutions have adopted a philosophy and practice that represents anti-architecture. Furthermore, universities are teaching this anti-architecture to more than one generation of future architects. Persons outside the field naively expect that architects know what architecture is about, and that the most famous ones are a reliable guide to follow. Yet, nothing could be further from the truth. The discipline has been taken over by a destructive cult. It is not within the power of this short essay to reverse this catastrophic trend, but at least it can raise a warning flag to the rest of the world about an architecture gone crazy.

PART 10

CONTEMPORARY CHURCH ARCHITECTURE AND SAINT AUGUSTINE'S *'THE CITY OF GOD'*

This essay was an invited contribution to a special number of the Italian journal Il Covile on Religious Architecture. In recent years, new Churches built around the world, even in Rome by the Vatican, have spurred heated controversy because of their unecclesiastical form. Many Roman Catholics feel that those buildings' design makes them inappropriate for houses of worship, which is a pretty severe condemnation. The debate goes far deeper than Roman Catholicism, however, for it concerns how human beings connect to their God, regardless of their particular religion. The sacred character of the built environment is of the utmost importance, and extends beyond the physical confines of a house of worship. We need to know how to create a sacred everyday environment in general. Conversely, we also need to identify the methods that destroy the sacred character in buildings so that we can avoid them. In jumping into this topic, I have been profoundly influenced by Christopher Alexander's Book Four of "The Nature of Order" (2004), in which he discusses the relationship between architecture and religion.

1. DEFINING THE *'CITY OF GOD'*.

We often read of the *Civitas Dei* (The City of God) in the ecclesiastical literature. From one perspective, the *Civitas Dei* is also the conception of an ideal architectural-urban environment. But more than a prescription for an optimal urban shape, it refers to the adaptation of materials, shapes, and spaces to physical — and above all spiritual — human needs. Human beings are imperfect; they need a rapport with God, without which they are no more than the lower animals. The *Civitas Dei* offers us an idea and a material foundation that facilitates the relationship with our God. Therefore, the material part (i.e., the physical city) is none other than an entry door to the union of humanity with its Creator.

It is not easy to say which of our cities even approximately represents an image of the ideal *Civitas Dei*, but I can suggest the ancient and medieval centers of Italian cities as examples. At least some idea of the *Civitas Dei* survives in those places that have not been ruined from intrusions of a more modern character. In this inquiry the question immediately arises: "How do we characterize intrusions that alter the *Civitas Dei*?". Obviously, they are part of the *Civitas Diaboli*, because they prevent the union of the living city with the universe, and with the universal soul. This is for us an effective and simple image: one that distinguishes the *Civitas Dei* by contrasting it with the *Civitas Diaboli*. Following its occasional application to clarify philosophically complicated concepts, the opposition between good and evil is simple to understand.

Defining the *Civitas Dei* depends on its links; connections between human beings and their Creator, connections between different people, friends and strangers alike, between human beings and the built environment, geometrical and visual connections between adjacent buildings, between buildings and open public space, etc. These ties eventually lead to a deeper connectivity, which may also become spiritual. In scientific terms, the manifestation of the *Civitas Dei* on earth becomes an interconnected complex, not unlike a large computer program.

Everything must work together in a connected manner, but the urban links (let alone the spiritual ones) are not obvious, because for the most part they are not easily perceivable with scientific experiments. The structure of the city is not written in lines of software code; indeed, if it were so, we would not have all the urban and social problems that damage our society. A computer program can be corrected because the errors are obvious once you find them (the difficulty resides in finding them among thousands of lines of code). The same technique cannot be applied to the city. Today we are building disconnected urban fabric without realizing that this is a gross error.

2. DEFINING THE *'CITY OF THE DEVIL'.*

The *Civitas Diaboli* is the conception of a disconnected universe. Just like in pseudo-religious cults, indoctrination tactics begin with the separation of individuals from their society, family, culture, and the faith they were born into, in order to include them in the cult. From that point on, the cult defines a false alternative reality for them. The cult exercises its power, an enormous power that comes from controlling lost souls, persons detached from the real world. Those people depend totally upon the cult's false promises and lies. This disconnection is practiced in architecture and urban planning to construct the *Civitas Diaboli*, a disconnected environment that catalyzes an insidious separation between human beings and the universe. I am not speaking in theological terms, but in strictly human ones. We have nihilistic architects (some of them unfortunately very famous) who are making money constructing a disconnected environment.

How do we characterize a construction that belongs to the *Civitas Diaboli*? The easiest method is to study the connections, or rather the lack thereof. We need to search for the inner connections of a building to itself, its connections with nearby buildings, with open urban spaces, the connections between walls and surfaces and human beings, etc. The fewer connections we find, the more we approach a representation of the *Civitas Diaboli*. Minimalist architecture obviously denies such connections, and thus forms part of the *Civitas Diaboli*. Perfectly smooth walls, crude and rough "Brutalist" concrete — in sum, the entire vocabulary of the minimalist style. These deliberate effects cut visual and sensory connections and their application on the smaller scales, those that correspond to the range of scales of the human body.

Some architectural critics circulate a false idea, declaring minimalism to be "simple" in a positive sense, but they fail to understand that simplicity in nature is expressed using a profound complexity. Anything "simple" in nature hides an incredibly complex and organized mechanism. The correct descriptor is "coherent" and not "simple". Simplistic voids do not exist in nature.

The *Civitas Diaboli*, defined by Le Corbusier and other "heroes" of twentieth-century architecture, has been realized in the post-war period in many parts of the world. It is a shame that those monstrous and anti-human ideas have been linked to utopian political hopes, which have then played a key role in their proliferation. An abstract geometry, empty and dead, has come to be identified with economic and social development. Liberation from a suffocating and unjust past is sought through an expression of this geometry. It is like believing that drinking *Sani-Cola* makes you more beautiful, intelligent, and popular (a deceit that is very profitable for both *Sani-Cola* and for dentists).

In the spiritual realm, co-existence between God and Satan is impossible; here on the earth, the *Civitas Diaboli* destroys the *Civitas Dei*. The former replaces ancient environments with rectangles of concrete, steel, and glass. Living urban fabric is cut, erased, in order then to build sterile industrial spaces. Older buildings are destroyed because they are no longer fashionable, not consistent with the images of "pure" geometry. Even the old churches are "renovated", forced to conform to the minimalist style, "cleaned up" from the visual information that represented centuries of meaning and significance.

3. DECONSTRUCTIVIST ARCHITECTURE.

Deconstructivist architecture is very fashionable today, praised by our most respected (that is, highest paid) architecture critics. Even though it is very different from minimalism and brutalist concrete, it follows the same steps, disconnecting the primary aspect of surfaces. It is another expression of nihilism, introduced in the 1980s, and promoted by Philip Johnson, a very influential architect who founded the American Nazi-Fascist political party in 1937 (see Part 11). It is curious that the same man, characterized as a "diabolist" by the philosopher Bertrand Russell (*"Your friend Philip is a diabolist"* (Schulze, 1994; page 155)), had already introduced and promoted international modernism in the 1930s. Architectural deconstructivism proposes a complex visual shape, but one lacking organization and connectivity; and therefore without life or God. God loves imperfections, and human beings are imperfect. Satan, on the other hand, is absolute and intolerant since he is interested only in power. Whatever Satan cannot control, he destroys. Architectural deconstruction represents nihilism in materials, just as the pseudo-philosophy of deconstruction represents nihilism in society. Today's academic intellectuals adore these French theories — another example of how the most intelligent persons are capable of the most disastrous stupidities.

Building a new church in either a minimalist or deconstructivist style is a contradiction. How can one relate with God in a building that already disconnects in the elements of its architecture? Persons who find themselves inside such a church read in its structure (or, more accurately, feel deeply within their body and soul) its architectural message of disconnection. In fact, it is hardly possible to relate with other people in such a space. The very notion of Church as *Ecclesia*, the union of persons of common faith, becomes impossible. To connect oneself with God is perhaps achievable, but it demands a great effort of abstraction, which first of all must reject the negative sensory signals.

Many authors speak of a "pure" spiritualism, and assert that a setting within an abstract geometry helps establish the relationship with God, as the old Fathers found in the desert. But I don't believe such efforts to be appropriate for the old lady who goes to pray in her neighborhood church. The Church knew all of this years ago, as one can verify in the visual (and musical) richness of churches constructed in the past. In every built portion, in every detail, one can read the connection with God. Every piece of ornament serves to connect, and all the pieces form a complex whole that we perceive as a material and spiritual union. It is true that cases of incoherence and overload exist, but that is no reason to condemn a basic principle.

4. MARKET FORCES.

Now that the Church seems to have become a multinational agency offering religious goods, it is interested above all in public relations. It does not wish to lose its diminishing influence in today's society. Without a doubt, the Church's publicity advisors think that it must become "modern" and contemporary, or at least make an effort to appear as such. It is perhaps too difficult to change its anachronistic bureaucracy founded in medieval times, but far easier to adopt modern and contemporary architecture. The images of modernity become a visible symbol of public relations. Perhaps if the Church does not show its contemporaneity with empty and nihilistic images, people might abandon it for the American religious sects promoted on television.

Market forces are much too powerful — every product, be it soft drink, soap, or religion, must compete with all the others in the marketplace. At least, the American televangelists have understood how to project a contemporary image. Developing a pseudo-culture of nihilistic images, the United States have lost what remains of their traditional culture. Power controls through the manipulation of images, as we know very well from history.

A recent case proves my point. In September of 2004, the Catholic University of Portugal in Viseu fired its entire Architecture Faculty, a group that included the best living religious architects. It replaced them with another group of modernist architects (Part 8). Obviously, the Catholic Church of Portugal (which takes all the important decisions for the Catholic University System) decided to become more fashionable, and not be identified with a Faculty that promoted traditional architecture. Even the class of lay Portuguese intellectuals thinks that its country is unfortunately glued to a traditional past. They feel that this attachment must be overcome before their country can be considered truly contemporary. The future without a doubt belongs not to the faithful, nor to the meek, but to those who are part of the industrial/commercial power structure — who show themselves more contemporary through the images that define them as such.

5. ICONS AS SYMBOLS.

The cult of contemporaneity adores iconic symbols: simplistic objects and geometries, such as cubes and cylinders, without details, ornament, or subdivisions. Even the new cult of deconstructivism, which has openly broken with the Platonic geometry of the modernist architects, continues to worship high-tech materials like glass, steel, and polished titanium. Those materials express the clear, pure cult images, without life or information content. The adoration of such images is not far removed from the adoration of Christian icons, but in both cases one can arrive at an absurdity. Instead of finding in icons an entry into the spiritual world, faith is sometimes transferred to the materials themselves. But this practice is forbidden by Moses in the three great religions.

It doesn't matter. Those who consider themselves truly "contemporary" have founded a cult on the images expressed in futuristic-looking buildings. Ironically, Orthodox religious icons have lately become a very fashionable art object among the non-Orthodox, thus losing their intrinsic spiritual value. In the case of architecture, spiritual value has been transferred to constructions in a pure geometry. Here is the reason for why the architecture of the new churches looks so uninspiring. Images of contemporaneity are promoted like symbols of a new faith, and not as symbols of Christianity (nobody dares to admit that those images express nihilism). Churches built in this architectural style serve as symbols of the cult of contemporaneity, but serve neither the religion nor the Church that has commissioned them.

PART 11

THE DERRIDA VIRUS

1. INTRODUCTION.

Since the 1960s, deconstruction has sought to undermine all well-ordered structures. "Deconstruction is a method of analyzing texts based on the idea that language is inherently unstable and shifting and that the reader rather than the author is central in determining meaning. It was introduced by the French philosopher Jacques Derrida in the late 1960s." (Encarta World English Dictionary, 1999). This means that texts have no ultimate meaning, and that their interpretation is up to readers. Thus, deconstruction pretends to be a call of liberation from the hegemony of certainty.

It needs something ordered (either actual or latent) on which to act and then destroy. Thus, it is entirely parasitic. With one notable exception, what its advocates say about deconstruction is clouded by confusion. Since it is an attack on logic, it does not produce logical statements. According to Derrida: "All sentences of the type 'deconstruction is X' or 'deconstruction is not X' a priori miss the point, which is to say that they are at least false. One of the principal things in deconstruction is the delimiting of ontology and above all of the third person present indicative: S is P." (Collins & Mayblin, 1996; p. 93).

Deconstruction can, however, be understood by what it actually does. It dismantles structure, logical statements, traditional beliefs, observations, etc. When criticized for dismantling these entities, deconstructionists insist they are merely analyzing and commenting on text. This approach resembles the way viruses survive and proliferate.

Derrida himself has called deconstruction a "virus": i. e. an inert code that replicates itself by using a host. Its strategy is to make an unsuspecting host ingest it; to force the host's internal machinery to make new copies of the virus; and to spread as many of these copies as possible, in order to maximize the possibility of infecting new hosts. The virus requires a more complex host to invade and destroy, but cannot live by itself. Originating in France, deconstruction has "infected" most disciplines in universities everywhere. In an uncharacteristically clear statement, Derrida states his objectives: "All I have done … is dominated by the thought of a virus, what could be called a parasitology, a virology, the virus being many things … The virus is in part a parasite that destroys, that introduces disorder into communication. Even from the biological standpoint, this is what happens with a virus; it derails a mechanism of the communicational type, its coding and decoding ... [it] is neither alive nor dead ... [this is] all that I have done since I began writing." (Brunette & Wills, 1994; p. 12). Fortunately, since most people cannot understand it, it has influenced society only indirectly (Part 7).

Deconstruction erases normal ways of thinking. It may appear incomprehensible, but it is very effective: it erases associations that form coherent thoughts. It acts like a computer virus that erases information in a hard disk. The Derrida virus seeks to undermine any original meaning via a complex and entirely self-referential play of words (Scruton, 2000). Otherwise astute critics have made the mistake of dismissing Derrida as another obfuscating French philosopher. Yet, what he has introduced is much more dangerous. He turns knowledge into randomness, just as a virus destroys living organisms by disintegrating individual cells. Its properties can be summarized as follows:

(1) The virus is a very small amount of information encoded either as a list of instructions to follow or as examples to copy.
(2) Within an appropriate host, the virus directs the partial disintegration of order and connectivity in the host structure.
(3) The virus then directs the reassembly of portions of the host structure, but in a way that denies connections necessary to achieve coherence or life.
(4) The end product must encode the virus in its structure.
(5) A deconstructed product is the vehicle for transmission of the viral code to the next host.

Deconstruction has been remarkably successful in dismantling traditional literature, art, and architecture. Like a biological virus, deconstruction is careful to balance host survival with infectivity. It only partially destroys its host, because total destruction would stop further transmission. It breaks up coherent sets of ideas by separating natural modules into submodules. Some of these submodules are then selectively destroyed in order to subsequently reattach their components randomly into an incoherent construct. A variant of the Derrida virus does not attack a specific text, but scavenges a discipline as a whole. It works on the collected work of many authors dealing with a particular topic. Its components are then reassembled in a nonsensical jumble that is only misleadingly and superficially coherent and appears viable to those unfamiliar with the host discipline and its vocabulary.

2. DECONSTRUCTIVE ARCHITECTURE.

Deconstruction's most visible manifestation is in architecture, in a building style characterized by broken, jagged, and lopsided forms, evoking physical destruction. According to David Watkin's *"A History of Western Architecture"*

(2000; p. 674): "The leading architects of the populist yet aggressive architecture of Deconstructivism are Peter Eisenman, Frank Gehry, Daniel Libeskind, Rem Koolhaas and the latter's pupil, the Iraqi-born Zaha Hadid." Architectural theory has embraced deconstruction in order to reverse architecture's main *raison d'être*: to provide viable shelter. Deconstructionists claim that deconstruction is just another design style, and, as such, has a right to be articulated.

But alienating architectural structures can do far more damage than confused academics churning out nonsense. In infecting contemporary architecture, the Derrida virus attacks a form's internal organization and coherence, leaving forms embodying disorganized complexity. It has migrated from high-profile buildings to infect more mundane commercial structures, such as office buildings, hospitals, and stores. Since deconstructivists avoid any self-definition, most deconstructive architects deny being deconstructivists (Jencks, 1988; pp. 49-61). This may be due to the fact that architects do not like being branded with a particular label, or admit that they have changed their minds.

In the 1980s, Derrida worked with Peter Eisenman on a project for the *Parc de La Villette*, in Paris. It was to be a small garden embodying de-ontologized non-space (whatever that means), but fortunately it was never built. What Derrida said about the design demonstrates the anti-architectural position of deconstruction: "[It's a critique of] everything that subordinated architecture to something else — the value of, let's say, usefulness or beauty or living ... not in order to build something else that would be useless or ugly or uninhabitable, but to free architecture from all those external finalities, extraneous goals ... to contaminate architecture ... I think that Deconstruction comes about ... when you have deconstructed some architectural philosophy, some architectural assumptions — for instance, the hegemony of the aesthetic, of beauty, the hegemony of usefulness, of functionality, of living, of dwelling. But then you have to reinscribe these motifs within the work." (Norris, 1989).

Architecture's goals happen to be precisely what Derrida rejects: aesthetics, beauty, usefulness, functionality, living, and dwelling. They are its very foundation, absolutely essential and hardly extraneous to its practice. Architecture was never really subordinated to anything else; it arises out of and is an expression of human needs.

Deconstruction applied to buildings removes their architectural qualities, while "reinscribing" a useless and superficial semblance of order that appears only as abstract motifs. Even Derrida concedes that what he has in mind for architecture is not architecture as such. What he proposes is an architecture of death for the new millennium.

In a talk published by Eisenman's wife, Derrida says: "Now, if I were forced to stop here and to say what the architecture of the next millennium should be, I would say: in its type, it should be neither an architecture of the subject nor an architecture of *Dasein* [being; existence; life]. But then, perhaps, it will have to give up its name of architecture, which has been linked to these different, but somehow continuous ways of thinking. Indeed, perhaps it is already losing its name, perhaps architecture is already becoming foreign to its name." (Derrida, 1991). (On "the architecture of life" and "the architecture of death", see Part 5).

An architecture that reverses structural algorithms so as to create disorder — the same algorithms that in an infinitely more detailed application generate living form — ceases to be architecture. Deconstructivist buildings are the most visible symbols of actual deconstruction. The randomness they embody is the antithesis of nature's organized complexity. This is despite effusive praise in the press for "exciting" new academic buildings, such as the Peter B. Lewis Management Building at Case Western Reserve University in Cleveland, the Vontz Center for Molecular Studies at the University of Cincinnati Medical Center, and the Stata Center for Computer, Information, and Intelligence Sciences at MIT, all by Frank Gehry. Housing a scientific department at a university inside the symbol of its nemesis must be the ultimate irony.

Otherwise knowledgeable clients — including academics — have been seduced to commission tortuous buildings in the deconstructivist style. There are fellow architects who proudly proclaim the virtues of a new university building by a famous deconstructivist architect, such as the Aronoff Center for Design and Art at the University of Cincinnati by Peter Eisenman. At the same time, ordinary people consider it ugly, odd-looking, and senseless (Radel, 1996).

An example of this vanguard deconstructivist architectural style is Frank Gehry's celebrated New Guggenheim Museum in Bilbao, Spain, which represents an unnatural imposition of free-flowing ribbon forms sheathed in a continuous, shiny metal skin. Besides the deliberate disorientation, which it produces visually through absence of a vertical, Gehry has eliminated or randomized components that would otherwise contribute to coherence. A repeating form in the vertical or horizontal directions (or possibly both) ties a large surface together visually. Thus, in Classical and Modernist buildings windows are lined up so as to provide translational symmetry. In other instances, rotational symmetry ties windows together on some of the gorgeous Medieval Cathedral fronts; otherwise it is used on the plan of a circular building.

Gehry's Bilbao Museum dispenses with components altogether. There is no translational or rotational symmetry. Similar is the case with an office building in Prague also designed by Gehry, where the windows are carefully *misaligned* in both vertical and horizontal directions, as well as in their depth and attachment to the façade (which itself is strangely distorted for no apparent reason), and their internal structure made inconsistent so as to avoid coherence. (This is known as the "Ginger & Fred" building). Gehry explains: "I worked very hard trying to devise a window that looked like it was attacking the form ... I thought of it like a swarm of bees coming at a wall." (Friedman, 1999; p. 210). Gehry also reversed the natural progression of small to large as elements approach the ground, so that the windows actually get larger as they get higher.

The sense of incoherence is reinforced by the lack of substructure at decreasing scales (Alexander, 2002; Salingaros, 1998). Gehry avoids any scaling similarity by using smooth metallic skin (Salingaros, 2000a). In his Prague office building, each window could be roughly similar to the entire façade when scaled up by a factor of 10, but this is far too large a factor for the two scales to connect visually and thus generate a certain coherence, so the two scales remain visually disconnected (Alexander, 2002; Salingaros, 1998; 2000a).

In the 1920s, modernist architects who were driven by an ideological fanaticism to dismantle the world's architectural traditions used industrial materials. Gehry uses them for the same disconnecting purpose. For example, his Prague office building has two towers — one solid and the other glass. Glass walls and polished metal surfaces generate anxiety, because the eye cannot focus on the surface — the former is transparent, whereas the latter is mirror reflective. In addition, such surfaces do not produce any sensory input from touching. Industrial surfaces are alien to nature and therefore hostile to the touch. This effect is by no means limited to a strictly sensual reaction, but is due to visual and tactile perception of the material surfaces' microstructure.

Some contemporary art long ago graduated from avant-garde silliness, to launch an aggressive attack on aesthetics. Invoking physical revulsion — in a clever ploy to emotionally validate its nonexistent content — was a way for artists to attract media attention. This is reflected in the architecture of the new museums, which explains their puzzling resemblance to memorials to mass murder. Thus, the same design approach is applied by Daniel Libeskind in his Jewish Museum in Berlin (which commemorates the Holocaust), and to his proposed extension for the Victoria and Albert Museum in London. The playful innovations by a small group of architects riding a wave of stylistic fashion for fame and profit are neither benign nor innocent. Alarmingly, other museums are planning new additions to house genuine art in such uncompromisingly hostile environments (Part 5). These architects erect huge deconstructivist symbols everywhere, thus becoming instrumental in propagating the virus.

When all is said and done, deconstruction in architecture is merely a continuation — after a lengthy pause — of the 1920s' Constructivist movement, exemplified by Konstantin Melnikov's Rusakov Club for the Transport Worker's Union in Moscow, and Vladimir Tatlin's unbuilt Monument to the Third International Communist Congress. The post-revolutionary Russian avant-garde married radical politics to a style of broken architecture. It is hard to find intentional dislocation in architecture before the Constructivist movement (and its contemporary, the Bauhaus movement in Germany). In *"A Dictionary of Architecture"* (1999; pp. 162-163), James Stevens Curl defines this movement as follows: "Constructivism: Anti-aesthetic, anti-art, supposedly pro-technology, Left-wing movement originating in the USSR ... Russian Constructivism's anti-environmentalist aspects, jagged overlapping diagonal forms, expression of mechanical elements, have proved to be potent precedents ... for the followers of Deconstructivism, notably Hadid, Koolhaas, and Libeskind."

Deconstructivist buildings resemble ruins whose structure has been somehow violated: Warsaw, Dresden and Hiroshima immediately after their bombing; buildings after a major earthquake; Manhattan after 9/11, etc.

These structures encode their physical violation in what remains of their destroyed form, and this quality is sought by some deconstructivist architects. Industrial materials tend to produce jagged, fragmented ruins that remain so because they weather very poorly or not at all. But the weathering of natural materials generates an altogether different type of ruin; one in which time and nature — often helped by human interventions at reinforcing and partially restoring what is left of the structure — try to minimize the form's violation.

Derrida's virus infected contemporary architecture even before the latest deconstructivist fashion. Its impact can be seen in "postmodernist" buildings (popular between 1965 and 1985, and thus contemporary with deconstruction's spread in philosophy and literature). These are marked by the reassembly of non-cooperating but identifiable architectural elements. That is exactly what the Derrida virus does when it acts on architecture as a whole, rather than dismantling a single concept for an individual building. It uses a haphazard repertory of pieces taken from various older buildings, historical styles, and materials, and carefully reassembles them in a manner that avoids combinatorial coherence.

Reactions to postmodernist buildings such as James Stirling's Neue Staatsgalerie in Stuttgart are not as alarming as those to deconstructivist buildings, because the Derrida virus operates on fewer scales. The whole is disturbing in the way it is put together (actually, *not* put together), but the pieces seem unobjectionable and even attractive. Since smaller elements are themselves copied from genuine architectural styles, they tend to be coherent on their smaller, internal scales. In the postmodernist case, disorder is manifested only on the larger scale, which is incoherent. In the deconstructivist case, the Derrida virus acts on many different scales, so that even smaller architectural elements are randomized. Again, randomization needs to stop somewhere, otherwise the building becomes unusable. Unlike modernist architects, who work with a very restricted — though often strongly coherent — stylistic vocabulary, postmodernist architects are open to using a variety of architectural elements torn out of context from all periods. By rejecting any context, rather than working within any coherent style, postmodernist architects always chose to apply classical and other historical quotations with "ironic" intentions, never as genuine tectonic elements, and thus never attaining (by design) the balance and connectivity of traditional architecture.

After their initial infatuation with deconstruction, some architects have turned to other, weirder influences for design inspiration, such as blobs and folding. Yet, the pervasiveness of deconstruction has not allowed any genuinely adaptive architecture to emerge. The Derrida virus is still at work.

Many architects desperately try to innovate, while studiously avoiding human needs, because these point in the direction of traditional, pre-modernist architecture. Comfortable, pleasing architecture that resembles older non-modernist buildings is taboo for ideological reasons. It is vilified by the architectural establishment. This is the dark secret of contemporary architecture: a cover of questionable innovation hides a doctrine of hatred of traditional forms. Unfortunately, most people are ignorant of what goes on inside the closed architectural establishment.

The most disturbing development is cutting-edge architects, who profess to embrace the "New Sciences" predicated on buzzwords, such as fractals, complexity, emergence, chaos, self-organization, Darwinian processes, etc. (Part 3).

3. TRUSTING THE ARCHITECTURAL EXPERTS.

A biological virus has to overcome a cell's defenses in order to enter it and manipulate it to produce copies of itself. The Derrida virus is one of many social viruses that act through human agents. People are predisposed to reject illogical belief systems that contradict common sense and intuition. They have built-in defenses against being taken over by destructive doctrines (although cults successfully override this mechanism). A telltale sign of cults trying to assume power is hearing that common sense is unreliable, and that "experts" should be trusted instead. Self-proclaimed experts present themselves as having superior knowledge, based on abstruse philosophical texts, written in an incomprehensible esoteric language. Any claims that experts possess intelligence and knowledge that contradict (rather than reinforce, extend, or, better, explain) our ordinary perception are classic setups for indoctrination.

A small group of promoters everywhere praise deconstructive buildings. Clients rely on them for advice in choosing fashionable architects. The media repeatedly turn to those same people for architectural criticism. They, again, sit on juries that award architectural prizes. They are all certified "experts," who perpetuate a wave of architectural fashion by undermining commonsense public understanding of what is real and what makes sense. Having attracted attention, self-proclaimed architectural experts lash out at whatever threatens their ideals, namely traditional architecture that embodies traditional values. They label what they personally dislike to be old-fashioned, unexciting, retrograde, reactionary, dangerous, fascist, etc.

This reverses commonsense values, while calling for the extinction of all that is intuitively perceived as right (McFadyen, 2000).

Because of the costs of major architectural projects, the power politics played out in this arena can make or break people. It has nothing to do with style, but has always been that way because of economics. Contemporary architecture reveals a frightening picture of raw power, in which global architectural fashion is driven by a small group of power brokers (Brodie, 1991; Schulze, 1994). They influence the architectural media, decide on many of the major architectural commissions, and control who is appointed in key academic positions in architectural schools.

Architecture favors the propagation of almost any style, once a few well-placed people have adopted it. Boundless ambitions, an immense power base, various architects tied together by obligations, loyalty, mutual loathing, and the exchange of favors, threats, deals, and payoffs, shameless self-promotion, lucrative commissions — all of these elements constitute an unholy alliance that promotes a global architectural fashion. Now, this political machine is working to propagate the Derrida virus.

Deconstructive architecture was put on the map by an exhibition at the Museum of Modern Art in New York City, organized by Philip Johnson and Mark Wigley in 1988. While some of the architects featured there had already established their reputation, Johnson first brought them together under the common "Deconstructive" label, and launched that style on a global scale. The show included projects by Bernard Tschumi and the team Coop Himmelb(l)au (comprised of Wolf Prix and Helmut Zwiczinsky). This event had a tremendous effect in validating — or manufacturing — the new style, for it was the same Johnson who back in 1932 had launched the "International Style", also by an exhibit of that name at the Museum of Modern Art. The modernist style went on to conquer the entire world, establishing Johnson as the power broker who defined the built environment for the better part of the 20th century. On that earlier occasion, Johnson's assistant was Henry-Russell Hitchcock (Schulze, 1994).

In a striking parallel with the case of Paul de Man in literary deconstruction, Johnson, the figure instrumental in launching deconstructive architecture, was compromised by pro-Nazi sympathies as a young man. Eisenman claims that what motivated the then 82-year old Johnson to try his hand a second time at creating a new architectural style is that: "... he wants to go out ... with a jump that puts him back in favor with the left, or what is thought to be left intellectually, in other words so he's not seen as someone of the right ... he has always been worried about the left and I think this is one time where he maybe is co-opting the left." (Jencks, 1988; Sorkin, 1991).

Johnson had attended two Nazi political rallies where Hitler spoke (Potsdam in 1932 and Nuremberg in 1938), and followed the Wehrmacht when it invaded Poland — by invitation of the German Propaganda Ministry — as a correspondent for a right-wing American publication. This did not affect his standing within the architectural community. What is interesting here is not what Johnson did in his past, but rather what attracted him to deconstructive architecture. In a 1994 interview, Johnson said: "My philosophical outlook dates from a time and a way of thinking that differs from the liberal, acceptable, politically correct line that we all subscribe to today ... There is no such thing as the good or the true or the beautiful. I'm a relativist. I'm a nihilist ... I learned the German language, when I was young, because I was interested in reading Nietzsche ... That's why I was initially attracted to Hitler, who totally misunderstood Nietzsche, really. But there was enough similarity between them so I got very excited about it ... The hierarchy of important things in the world starts with art, not with looking for truth, or science, or anything." (Lewis & O'Connor, 1994; p. 175).

The catalogue for the Deconstructivist Architecture show at the Museum of Modern Art explains that: "Deconstructivist architecture disturbs figures from within ... It is as if some kind of parasite has infected the form and distorted it from inside ... The alien is an outgrowth of the very form it violates." (Johnson & Wigley, 1988; pp. 16-17). This is the Derrida virus but, disingenuously, the catalogue denies any connection between the architectural style and Derrida's philosophy. As Roger Kimball points out about this catalogue (1990; p. 136): "The lurid overtones of violence and corruption are intentional; they are, in fact, central to the ethos of deconstructive architecture ... Disturb, torture, interrogate, contaminate, infect: these are the words [chosen] to explain and to praise deconstructivist architecture."

This dangerous intellectual game is rooted in a nihilistic philosophy, and supported by an immense power base. To be fair to some architectural critics, they initially labeled deconstructivist architecture as nihilistic. Later on, however, they had to "toe the line" or be out of a job, so they are now among its most fervent supporters. Respected architects — who have previously demonstrated their skill in putting materials together to create a coherent, habitable form — are now calling for destruction (Varnelis, 1995).

A 1939 letter recounts Johnson's impressions of the German invasion of Poland: "Everything was fine and dandy in Berlin when I left … I came again to the country that we had motored through, the towns north of Warsaw … The German green uniforms made the place look gay and happy. There were not many Jews to be seen. We saw Warsaw burn and Modlin being bombed. It was a stirring spectacle." (Schulze, 1994; p. 139). Now, "stirring" is surely an odd term to describe destruction and slaughter on a massive scale. More that half a century later, his wartime memories still triggered the same sentiment: "… the burned-out village was in the Second World War, and I was on the wrong side. So we don't talk about that anymore … But it was a horrifying sight … And it was so beautiful. That's a horrible thing to say, but ruins are beautiful. You can't help it. Fascination with ruins, it's endless." (Lewis & O'Connor, 1994; p. 33).

The Museum of Modern Art show was organized in 1988. By now, deconstructive architecture has gained its own momentum, and any questions raised about the circumstances of its birth are only of historical interest. Johnson may have given it a boost, but its current popularity is due to genuine client demand. Derrida responded to the charges that deconstructive architecture is a pure expression of nihilism. True to form, he employs the standard strategy of confusing the issue by dissolving the meaning of words: "And who knows what nihilism is or isn't? Even the people who object don't raise the question "What is nihilism?" … So when people say [Deconstruction] is negative, nihilistic and so forth, either they don't read or they are arguing in bad faith." (Norris, 1989; p. 10).

4. THE TRADITIONAL PATRIMONY.

Some traditions are anachronistic and misguided, but as reservoirs of traditional solutions against which to check new proposals they are of immense importance. A new solution may at some point replace a traditional solution, but it must succeed in reestablishing the connections to the rest of knowledge. In the context of social patterns, architecture, and urbanism, new solutions are useful if they connect to traditional social, architectural, and urban patterns (i. e., all those before the 1920s). If there is an obvious gap where nothing in a discipline refers to anything outside, then there could be a serious problem.

Recently, Edward Wilson has introduced the notion of "consilience" as "the interlocking of causal explanations across disciplines" (Wilson, 1998a). Consilience claims that all explanations in nature are connected; there are no totally isolated phenomena. Wilson focuses on incomplete pieces of knowledge: the wide region separating the sciences from the humanities. He is happy to see it being slowly filled in by evolutionary biologists, cognitive neuroscientists, and researchers in artificial intelligence. At the same time, he is alarmed by people in the humanities who are erasing parts of the existing body of knowledge. These include deconstructive philosophers. Wilson characterizes their efforts as based on ignorance. On Derrida's work, he writes: "It ... is the opposite of science, rendered in fragments with the incoherence of a dream, at once banal and fantastical. It is innocent of the science of mind and language developed elsewhere in the civilized world, rather like the pronouncements of a faith healer unaware of the location of the pancreas." (Wilson, 1998b; p. 41).

Unfortunately, most of the humanities today subscribe to belief systems that damage the web of consilient knowledge. Although never directly expressed, the goal of deconstruction is to erase institutions of knowledge. What Derrida has said is alarming enough: "Deconstruction goes through certain social and political structures, meeting with resistance and displacing institutions as it does so ... effectively, you have to displace, I would say "solid" structures, not only in the sense of material structures, but "solid" in the sense of cultural, pedagogical, political, economic structures." (Norris, 1989; p. 8).

Many people crave novelty without regard for possible consequences. This craving is often manipulated by unscrupulous individuals. Not everything that is novel is necessarily good. An example of this is a new, artificially-developed virus unleashed into the world. Because of the immense destructive power that humanity now possesses, it is imperative to understand possible consequences.

In a hilarious hoax, Alan Sokal developed a nonsensical deconstructive critique of well-known scientific claims in an article submitted for publication to a pretentious, deconstructive academic journal (Sokal, 1996). None of the referees for that journal challenged Sokal's account before accepting the article as worthy of publication. Sokal was so obvious in his deception that he assumed it would have been exposed; but it was not. Subsequently, Sokal and Jean Bricmont (1998) exposed deconstructivist criticism as nonsensical and showed that several respected deconstructive texts are based on nonsensical scientific references. This is only the most famous exposure of nonsensical deconstructive writings; there are many others (Huth, 1998). In a debunking of deconstructivist texts, Andrew Bulhak codified the deconstructivists' literary style into a computer program called *"Postmodernism Generator"* (1996). It is remarkably successful in generating nonsensical texts that are indistinguishable from those written by revered deconstructivist philosophers.

Putting aside the question of truthful content, a discipline is not valid unless it rests on a solid intellectual edifice. One characteristic of a coherent discipline is hierarchical complexity, in which correlated ideas and results define a unique internal structure. Like a valid bank note, this structure should be extremely difficult to counterfeit. That is not the case with deconstruction. Thus, a phony article in Statistical Mechanics, using all the appropriate words and mathematical symbols in a nice-sounding but scientifically-meaningless jumble, would be detected instantly.

Even a single mistake in such an article could not survive unnoticed. It is the function of referees to check each and every step in the argument of a scientific article submitted for publication in a professional journal. The very survival of the discipline depends on a system of checks that identifies and expels bogus contributions. By contrast, the survival of deconstruction — in which there is nothing to verify — depends upon generating more and more deconstructed texts and buildings.

A well-crafted deconstructive text does make sense, but not in any logical fashion. It is a piece of poetry that abuses the human capacity for pattern recognition to create associations, employing random technical jargon.

As Roger Scruton has pointed out: "Deconstruction ... should be understood on the model of magic incantation. Incantations are not arguments, and avoid completed thoughts and finished sentences. They depend on crucial terms, which derive their effect from repetition, and from their appearance in long lists of cryptic syllables. Their purpose is not to describe what is there, but to summon what is not there ... Incantations can do their work only if key words and phrases acquire a mystical penumbra." (Scruton, 2000; pp. 141-142).

The use of words for emotional effect is a common technique of cult indoctrination. This practice reinforces the cult's message. Whether in chants that make little sense yet can raise followers' emotions to fever pitch, or in the speeches of political demagogues that rouse a wild and passionate allegiance, the emotional manipulation *is* the message. Even after the exposure of the deconstructive philosophers' fraudulent character, their work continues to be taken seriously. Deconstructionist books are available in any university bookstore, while respectable academics offer lengthy critical commentary supporting these books' supposed authority. By affording them the trappings of scholarly inquiry, the impression is carefully maintained that they constitute a valid body of work.

Followers of deconstruction apply the classic techniques of cults to seize academic positions; infiltrate the literature; displace competitors; establish a power base by employing propaganda and manipulating the media, etc. They use indoctrination to recruit followers, usually from among disaffected students in the humanities. As David Lehman put it: "An antitheological theology, [deconstruction] ... shrouds itself in cabalistic mysteries and rituals as elaborate as those of a religious ceremony … it is determined to show that the ideals and values by which we live are not natural and inevitable but are artificial constructions, arbitrary choices that ought to have no power to command us. Yet, like a religion-substitute, deconstruction employs an arcane vocabulary seemingly designed to keep the laity in a state of permanent mystification. Putatively antidogmatic, it has become a dogma. Founded on extreme skepticism and disbelief, it attracts true believers and demands their total immersion." (Lehman, 1991; p. 55).

5. THE DE MAN HERITAGE AND ITS CONSEQUENCES.

In 1941, the late Paul de Man, the most accomplished literary deconstructivist, wrote some very direct, undeconstructed prose: "… despite the Semitic meddling into all aspects of European life … a solution to the Jewish question which envisions the creation of a Jewish colony isolated from Europe would not involve deplorable consequences for the literary life of the West. It would lose, all told, a few personalities of mediocre value … the war will only bring about a more intimate union of two things that have always been close, the Hitlerian soul and the German soul, until they have been made one single and unique power … the future of Europe can be envisioned only within the framework of the possibilities and needs of the German spirit … a people which finds itself called upon to exercise, in its turn, a hegemony in Europe." (Kimball, 1990; pp. 96-97). These statements no longer shock, as they did when they were rediscovered after de Man's death. Neither does the cover-up that followed his exposure.

Derrida (who is Jewish) tried to deconstruct de Man's anti-Semitic and pro-Nazi writings so that their original meaning was obscured by a fog of "interpretation". Like a cult, deconstructivists closed ranks and vilified journalists who reported on the de Man case.

For Lehman, the danger of deconstructivism was demonstrated not merely by de Man's youthful writings, but much more so by the denial brought into play by his surviving peers:

"How benign a method could [deconstruction] be if its proponents could so blatantly use it to explain away inconvenient facts and turn an unfortunate truth on its head? … Over this fallen idol the self-styled iconoclasts revealed themselves to be, after all, a thoroughly idolatrous crew." (Lehman, 1990; pp. 242-243). Consider the following parallels. As with deconstruction, the Nazi concept of science was relative: Jewish scientists were excluded, whereas racial pseudo-scientists were legitimated. This attitude is overshadowed by the chillingly effective use the Nazis made of technology, and exemplifies nihilism, since it is predicated on an underlying duality of dominance/destruction. Thus, when he realized he was losing the war, Hitler ordered the leveling of Paris (which, fortunately, never happened).

In viral terms, infection occurs because the virus possesses an attractive shell, which it offers to its host. No host would knowingly allow a virus to enter it, but is invariably tricked into doing so. Biological viruses possess an exterior protein that the cell finds metabolically attractive, and so ingests them; some computer viruses are encapsulated in a message purportedly coming from a friend; the Derrida virus promises "liberation from oppressive hegemony", itself a relic of the 1968 slogans in France.

This alternation of a destructive doctrine with a false promise of liberation is a recurring theme of revolutionary movements that have periodically scourged humanity. To the extent that it threatens to destroy everything else, deconstruction is not simply a worldview among others. Deconstruction takes advantage of a bad misunderstanding, which confuses multiculturalism with nihilism. A method to erase knowledge, masquerading as a new philosophical movement, cannot be quarantined within academia. Indoctrinated students eventually enter the real world threatening to create havoc.

Deconstruction involves a will to destroy. Much of it comes from absolutizing subjectivity. Shut off from the outside world, the individual is locked in an internal version of reality prone to corruption. Deconstruction seeks to achieve precisely this end: isolation, then corruption. Deconstruction isolates itself in order to protect its secret of a nonexistent content. It spins a cocoon of incomprehensibility as a defense mechanism. Unfortunately, modern physics set a dangerous precedent when it stopped making sense and no longer related to everyday experience. It made sense in a different dimension, a different scale in space and time, even though its observable consequences constitute the physical universe.

As a result, its legacy is that of formal systems that contradict common sense. Taking this as its point of departure, deconstruction devalues common sense and rejects customary wisdom. It declares everything that falls short of formal proof to be irrational, but then provides an irrational formal structure to replace what it has destroyed. As a virus, it has invaded civilization, erasing collective common sense while spreading with astonishing rapidity.

Once formed, worldviews are unlikely to change and are trusted more than any direct sensory evidence. These internal worldviews become so much a part of oneself that they are unlikely to undergo any modification, unless one is forced to do so. For this reason, those who have adopted a cult philosophy deny all evidence that threatens the cult's vision of reality. Rational arguments make no difference. Jared Diamond (2003) asked: "Why do some societies make disastrous decisions?". He was surprised to find that the most common answers assume that human beings have an innate reality check that prevents disastrous decisions. Yet, historically this has not been the case. Human beings seem inclined to fall into a kind of uncritical groupthink. The failure of the resulting group decisions has often led to the collapse of entire civilizations.

According to Diamond:

(1) Short-term gains often ignore possible long-term losses. A decision-making elite may advance its own interests to the detriment of society at large;

(2) People tend to be fanatically attached to irrational and self-serving beliefs, linking them to values they hold sacred; they tolerate no challenges and ignore their negative consequences;

(3) There is often denial of mounting evidence of a disaster because the truth, or coming events, are too horrible to contemplate;

(4) Signals pointing to a problem are not taken seriously. Previous disasters that arose under similar conditions are conveniently forgotten; society concentrates on the present and ignores its past;

(5) A novel threat is dismissed by assuming the continuity of a comfortable familiar situation (i. e., an unfounded belief in the inertia of the system), even knowing that change is often unexpected and discontinuous.

These indicators help to understand why deconstruction has been embraced so broadly.

Consider the case of architecture. The buildings of some deconstructivist architects have been called unusable, even by critics who usually support this group. Yet, those architects continue to win coveted commissions and international competitions. They are eagerly sought out by private clients, foundations, corporations, churches, and foreign governments, and are routinely invited to submit entries by the sponsors of major global architectural projects. Having built one dud, they are immediately begged to construct another. Their work is validated because they are awarded the most prestigious architectural prizes. They hold the most lucrative academic appointments and train tomorrow's generation of architects. They are invited to lecture at other institutions, even though their talks invariably make little sense. They present a confusing jumble of disjoint ideas and irrelevant imagery expressed in the approved jargon — usually nothing more than a self-serving attempt to justify their own buildings after the fact. These lectures are then published and studied as if something meaningful was being communicated.

Clients have bought into this deception, associating deconstruction with excitement and progress rather than with viruses and nihilism. Eventually they pass on: individual sponsors die (which is why they wish to be memorialized by architectural statements); decision-makers at foundations and corporations move elsewhere; university deans become vice-presidents at other institutions; mayors are not reelected; cabinet ministers are replaced; governments change.

But architectural forms infected with the Derrida virus remain. Those who made the initial decision to build them (often against the outcry of citizens and architects with uncorrupted common sense), though responsible, cannot be held to account or even traced.

As deconstruction is fast becoming institutionalized, its containment is a political problem. Regardless of who made the decision to build a deconstructive building or hire a deconstructive architect, the highest power itself (companies; universities; foundations; cities; churches; countries) is ultimately identified with the final result. Converting an architecture school to a training ground for deconstructivists implicates the whole university. Building a National Museum as a showcase to the world implicates the entire nation. Building a church in this style anoints nihilism with the blessing of organized religion. To admit that it had all been a bad mistake makes the entity look foolish.

Institutions are understandably unwilling to lose face, because their existence relies on their ability to make wise decisions. Therefore, they might not be ready to question their original choice, and continue praising the style in order to cover themselves. By so doing, those high-level institutions promote the Derrida virus by giving it a visual form, and by condoning it, reinforce its propagation.

6. APPROPRIATE DEFENSES.

An effective strategy for defending institutions against the Derrida virus could be formulated once its weak points are understood. A virus reduces structural order. It is the simplest form of organized matter that manages to reproduce. Below a certain complexity threshold, structures cannot really be alive. A virus lies close below this threshold and is parasitic on more complex structures. The only way to stop the Derrida virus is to fight it on its own terms, and not on the level of intellectual debate.

That is a mistake several authors have made. They have dealt what ought to have been devastating blows to deconstruction, yet it survives unscathed.

The virus is unaffected, because it is neither alive nor dead. It is not complex enough to destroy by trying to take apart.

Derrida said as much, but no one paid sufficient attention: "[The virus] is something that is neither living nor non-living; the virus is not a microbe. And if you follow these two threads, that of a parasite which disrupts destination from the communicative point of view — disrupting writing, inscription, and the coding and decoding of inscription — and which on the other hand is neither alive nor dead, you have the matrix ... I allude to the possible intersection between AIDS and the computer virus ..." (Brunette & Wills, 1994; p. 12).

Since the virus is not alive, it cannot be killed, so it makes no sense to attack it with either ridicule or with logical criteria such as truth and consistency. Those techniques are suited to falsifying and dismantling infinitely more complex systems, which have a corresponding vulnerability. The Derrida virus is simply a piece of information encoded in human neuronal circuits and in the external physical environment. It resides in the minds of indoctrinated individuals programmed to spread it, and in buildings and texts that infect us through visual systems. The only way to stop it, therefore, is to stop its modes of informational transmission.

Deconstruction in architecture follows the methods of disintegration and incoherent reassembly of its philosophical/literary parent. Its founder, Derrida, admits that he intentionally introduced a virus into the collective subconscious. Applications of this method have generated a vast amount of deconstructed text and a number of deconstructed buildings. The deconstructivists' exclusionary practices in architecture have almost succeeded in eliminating all traditional architecture from consideration. The technique is to brand traditional architecture "bad," retrograde, non-innovative, fascist, an impediment to progress, etc. This proscription includes new and innovative architecture that somehow resembles traditional architecture. It is unlikely that those converted to deconstruction can be persuaded to abandon their irrational path. Sanity and rationality, however, is likely to be restored among future generations of architects.

ACKNOWLEDGMENT.

I am indebted to James Kalb and John Wenger for helpful suggestions.

PART 12

BACKGROUND MATERIAL FOR "THE DERRIDA VIRUS".

INCLUDES SECTIONS CO-AUTHORED WITH TERRY M. MIKITEN

This part collects extracts from some of my previous papers on architecture and urbanism that develop the viral theme. It discusses the scientific ideas for understanding deconstruction in architecture as a viral phenomenon, thus providing background for "The Derrida Virus" (Part 11). This material also helps to link the related though distinct notions of antipatterns, architectural viruses, cults, and memes.

1. INTRODUCTION.

I consider contemporary architecture as a collection of informational viruses infecting global society. A virus imposes a particular informational structure — consisting of its own genetic material — on the environment. It encodes its template by using pieces from disassembled complex structures. It replicates and proliferates by producing numerous copies from its template. The viral analogy has considerable explanatory power, and helps to validate our own basic intuitions, which have been at odds with many aspects of design movements since the early 1920s. Most important, it allows us to see those architectural styles — often presented as the antithesis of each other — as belonging to a single genus of structural typologies.

My previous papers dealt mostly with architectural viruses from the modernist period, which preceded the deconstructivist period of today; yet the discussion applies equally to the most recent viral mutations realized as images published in the current architectural magazines. Before we can define a virus, we need to understand very clearly what it is that the virus attacks. My understanding in this context considers evolved solutions to be healthy, since unhealthy or damaging solutions would have been eliminated by natural selection over a period of many generations. Societies promoting unhealthy architectural and urban typologies become extinct because of the stresses inflicted by the geometry upon the people (or other destructive practices such as pollution and land mismanagement), thus stopping further transmission.

What is healthy for human civilization, and what is not is the same distinction as that between organisms and viruses; the latter parasitize the former. In the ambiguous world of architecture (and human society), there are indeed criteria that distinguish between analogues to these two classes. Particular arrangements of matter are closer to our evolved biological make-up — in the sense of supporting our health and wellbeing — than others. These insights lead to a framework for understanding contemporary architecture (Part 11).

One component of the explanatory framework comes from *"A Pattern Language"* of Christopher Alexander *et. al.* (1977). Pattern languages codify and organize evolved architectural solutions, such as the need for windows on two sides of every room, the necessity for ornament, or the advantages of small parking lots. These represent an accumulated store of verified knowledge about our interaction with the modern world; what geometry or practice works best in any given situation and in a given culture.

The criterion for choice is the pattern that makes us feel more human when we inhabit a space or perform a function. Each inherited solution is a "pattern", and all patterns together combine into a language just as words combine to form our spoken and written language (Salingaros, 2000b). Traditional societies used pattern languages to build virtually everything, and the products work very well.

Although pattern languages arise in every human endeavor, they conflict with the reigning architectural doctrine of our time. In any study of pattern languages, "antipatterns" (doing the opposite of what traditional experience and our feelings tell us to do) keep coming up. Architects deliberately do the wrong thing over and over again, in the face of tested inherited solutions, because of the mad pursuit of innovation, or because they are following the totalitarian dictates of an established power elite. An antipattern thus acquires a false validity simply because of familiarity engendered by repeated use. It sticks in the mind, and eventually contaminates our stored knowledge about a discipline. Once that happens, it is extremely difficult to get rid of an antipattern and so prevent it from interfering with valid patterns.

What is the function of an antipattern? Its only purpose is to materialize an image conceived in some individual's mind, and to spread itself around the world. In doing so, it typically destroys existing or latent complexity and order. This mode of operating is characteristic of an artificial virus. In an earlier paper on pattern languages, I identified antipatterns as viruses that propagate via transmission among the minds of human beings. In the extracts that follow, I use the terms "architectural virus", "antipattern", "stylistic rule", and "meme" (Dawkins, 1989) to mean essentially the same thing examined from different perspectives. A "meme" is a simple piece of information (an idea, image, or tune) that propagates among human minds, as defined in Section 4, below.

2. STYLISTIC RULES AND THE REPLICATION OF VIRUSES.
(Salingaros, 2000b)

During a time of crisis, or in the desire to be totally innovative, established disciplines sometimes willingly replace their pattern languages by stylistic rules. Those are entirely arbitrary, however, coming either from fashion or dogma (someone in authority pronounces a rule that is never questioned), or they refer to a very specific situation that does not apply broadly. Stylistic rules are incompatible with complex patterns. The mechanism by which stylistic rules propagate bears essential similarities to the replication of viruses. A stylistic rule is usually given as a template, and proponents are required to replicate it in the environment. Its success is measured not by how well it serves any human activity, but rather by how many copies are produced. Stylistic rules frequently have no connection to human needs: they are just images with a superficial symbolic content. While some are benign, many are pathological.

Many stylistic rules are anti-patterns: they are neither accidental, nor the simple preferences of an individual. They intentionally do the opposite of some traditional pattern for the sake of novelty. By masquerading as "new" patterns, they misuse a pattern language's natural process of repair to destroy it. Patterns work via cooperation to build up complex wholes that coexist and compete in some dynamic balance. By contrast, stylistic rules tend to be rigid and unaccommodating. Their replication in many cases fixes the geometry of built form so as to exclude human patterns. Any single stylistic rule is capable of suppressing an entire chain of linked patterns on many different scales. A destructive stylistic rule, like a virus, is an informational code that dissolves the complexity of living systems.

Today's architects are trained to use a limited vocabulary of simple forms, materials, and surfaces. Their possible combinations are insufficient to even approach the structure of a language. This replaces an accumulated literature of patterns corresponding to words, sentences, paragraphs, chapters, and books that encapsulates meaning from human experience and life. Few people realize the enormous consequences on society of adopting a particular design vocabulary. Decisions concerning architectural style affect the surrounding culture; contrary to what is widely proclaimed, one person's visions are not restricted to a building as a single artwork. A single visual template can eventually destroy a culture just as effectively as a deadly virus.

3. HOW PATTERNS ARE DISPLACED BY ANTI-PATTERNS.
(Salingaros, 2003a)

Human language — both spoken words, and the pictorial language of images — quite possibly drove the brain to expand fourfold in order to accommodate the increase in information input. The problem is that destructive memes also use the replicating process intrinsic in the human mind to propagate themselves throughout a population. We apparently have no defenses against virulent memes, and cannot distinguish between them and benign memes. A frightening picture emerges of human beings being manipulated by inanimate pieces of information that, like viruses, care only for increasing their number at the expense of their human hosts. Major human catastrophes can be attributed to, or are certainly helped by, a destructive meme that spreads to the population and drives it to do what it does unquestioningly.

A meme is more like a simple visual image rather than a reasoned description of how something is made. Successful memes are very easy to remember. A collection of simple memes could pretend to form a language, which could itself be perfectly consistent internally; nevertheless, they cannot coexist with a pattern language that respects complexity. The best example comes from government. Fascism and totalitarianism clean up the messiness of human society by displacing our most deeply held patterns of human values. They have an undeniable appeal, however, otherwise they would not take over the collective mind of nations every few decades. Each time that happens, people again fool themselves into believing the demagogues who tell them that life's complexities can be drastically simplified.

4. MEMES AND ARCHITECTURE.
(SALINGAROS & MIKITEN, 2002)

While our topic is architecture, it is instructive to discuss for a moment a parallel situation in biology where these ideas are routinely useful. In considering how microbes attack tissue, as for example those in the oral cavity that cause tooth decay, the scientist studies the tendency of a microbe to adhere to the tooth surface. Microbes that have the greatest stickiness are also likely to have the greatest virulence; i. e., cause the most serious disease. The logic is straightforward: the stickier the microbe, the greater the number that will adhere to the tooth at any one time. Research shows that the surface of tooth enamel has a certain chemical structure, and the virulent microbes have a corresponding chemical structure that binds to it; rather like the two mating surfaces of Velcro.

Individual memes, or images, are the equivalent of agents that "infect" memory. Each image has a set of attributes that makes it more or less likely to stick in memory and to be transmitted to others. In the universe of Art and Design this mechanism is readily apparent. The volatility of design themes drives the world of fashion, where the business and sales force creates a strong pressure for selection that is Darwinian at its core. New mutations arise with regularity, and these are tested against the environmental forces in which they appear. The life and death cycle can be swift for unsuccessful fashion styles.

The same is true in architecture, where there is an undeniable and changing "fashion". Nevertheless, a fashion arrests the adaptive design process, in which selection evolves specific solutions to individual problems that are exquisitely suited for their job and surroundings.

Architectural memes are more nearly analogous to physical replicating entities such as viruses, than to more general memes representing only ideas. The reason is that the former are encoded as actual structures (other than neuronal circuits). It is only their replication that occurs through memetic transmission; the artifact in this instance has a physical existence outside the human mind.

An architectural style thus exists in two very different forms:

(1) as an ideology codified in books and taught as a tradition in architecture schools, which perpetuates a group of memes in people's brains; and
(2) as images represented in the built environment.

Each aspect reinforces the other. The built environment serves as a source of continuous re-infection by visual architectural memes. The image/building/image cycle has positive feedback, and can lead to an exponential rate of infection.

5. ENCAPSULATION OF IMAGES IN THE MIND.
(SALINGAROS & MIKITEN, 2002)

A meme boosts its virulence by linking itself to other attractive memes, which then shield the original meme. The advertising industry is founded upon techniques of encapsulation: either physical packaging, or the packaging of products within ideas. A commercial product sells just as much because of an attractive package as for any other factor. An effective marketing strategy links a product via emotional appeals to self-esteem, sex, status, power, individuality, etc. It is not a coincidence that modern advertising techniques developed alongside modernist design, and early modernist architects showed a keen interest in psychological manipulation as it was then being incorporated into the advertising industry. Le Corbusier actually made a living from mass media and commercial promotion independently of his work as an architect.

A biological virus remains infectious against the continuous development of antibodies by host organisms. The way it does this is to change its encapsulation so that it is no longer recognized by the host. This is said to be one of the mechanisms for the resistance of the HIV virus to therapy. In exactly this fashion, modernism successfully changes the shell in which its memes are packaged. Modernist ideologues accomplish this switch with great dexterity: almost a sleight-of-hand. As soon as one of the encapsulations is identified, and it is realized that it does not lead to the promised benefit, the shell is changed to a new one. The central core — containing images that erase information and complexity from the environment — remains the same.

6. THE TRANSMISSION OF A STYLE AS A VIRUS.
(SALINGAROS, 2003B)

If we oversimplify a form language and call it an architectural "style", then we can discuss and explain some events in architectural history. We are now faced with a serious contradiction. Why do some design styles proliferate even though they are poorly adapted to human use and sensibilities? Even worse, it appears that the most damaging, least adaptive styles actually proliferate with the greatest ease.

The answer is frightening in its implications for our civilization. In analogy with the replication of viruses, the crudest minimalist form languages spread the fastest in society. That is simply because they encode a minimum of information. The "style" as an informational unit to transmit among human minds in a population carries over better when it is simplest. A few catchy images, such as flat sheer surfaces, transparent glass walls, pilotis, shiny "industrial" materials such as polished steel, etc. define a simplistic style. Never mind that the components of this protolanguage do not define a true form language; the public accepts them because of propaganda from respected authorities.

We know how the spread of a virus can be accelerated, as part of the arsenal of biological terrorists. First, disguise the pathogen in seemingly attractive substances, so as to have the victims consume it voluntarily. This corresponds to the promise that modernist architecture and planning solve social problems and liberate oppressed classes. The people buy that.

Second, artificially spread samples of the virus in as many places as possible so that the maximum number of persons will become infected. Here the media plays a key role, showing and praising modernist structures and urban projects.

Why did this occur only at the beginning of the twentieth century and not before? I believe that it had to do with radical social changes spurred by population pressure so that for the first time, some people were willing to sacrifice adaptive design in exchange for the false promise of a better future. Prior to that, people on all socioeconomic levels shaped their environment as far as they could to provide physical and emotional comfort.

Another contributing factor was the creation of a new communications network formed by the convergence of telephone, telegraph, newspapers, magazines, and film. The new media tied the world together as never before, yet also made possible the rapid proliferation of advertising and political propaganda. The spread of modernism could never have occurred were it not for the new media. Just as in the case of internet computer viruses, which could not exist before the internet, crude architectural form languages could spread only through architectural picture magazines.

7. EXPLAINING THE UNLIKELY SUCCESS OF MODERNISM.
(SALINGAROS & MIKITEN, 2002)

The rate of transmission of a visual style among human minds depends on several factors. Considered simply as information, the success of an architectural style is governed by the speed at which the associated memes can propagate. The situation is akin to percolation or diffusion: copies of an object (a piece of information encoding the style) have to pass from one human mind to another. This resembles the mechanism by which infectious agents spread in a population. Individuals in the population have little control over the process. Propagating agents are obviously not selected by the host, since they parasitize their more complex hosts. The process is infection rather than competition. An epidemic occurs when a virus has evolved an unbeatable advantage over its hosts.

8. A COMPLEXITY THRESHOLD.
(SALINGAROS & MIKITEN, 2002)

By sacrificing the structural complexity needed for metabolism, viruses gain an unbeatable advantage over more complex, metabolizing life forms that they infect. There is a parallel here with modernist design as it competed with more complex architectural styles such as Art Nouveau and the Classical style. Any style that attempts to adapt itself to human physical and emotional satisfaction, as well as to local materials and climate, will necessarily exceed a certain complexity threshold.

In neglecting those needs — indeed, in making it its explicit aim to ignore them — modernist architecture crossed the complexity threshold going downwards. This brought it an unprecedented advantage, but removed an essential quality that we associate with "life".

Although "life" has not been rigorously defined as a concept, biological life consists of two components: metabolism, and replication. The apparatus for metabolism represents much of what we observe as biological structure in every organism. The machinery for replication, on the other hand, occupies only a limited portion of an organism's structure. A virus replicates its encoded genetic information without being able to metabolize. It is the simplest possible life form, and by this definition, it is not "alive" in the sense that a more complex metabolizing organism is. In an analogous manner, modernist structures, though immensely successful at replicating in the built environment, do not possess the same degree of "life" (measured in terms of organized complexity) as do more traditional architectural styles that adapt to human use and emotional needs.

There is a debate going on in evolutionary biology as to whether viruses developed before, concurrently, or after metabolizing life forms. The third option argues that parasitic replicators have to have a population of more complex organisms to parasitize before evolving.

A probable scenario for this third option is that some incomplete pieces from the replicating apparatus of an organism found it possible to lead an independent existence outside the metabolizing structure. Whatever the actual case, this third option is intriguing for its parallel to modernist architecture. With the above analogy, modernism could not have taken root before society became complex enough to support it. The intuitive perception of modernist buildings as "alien" forms invading our cities (and minds) makes more sense in a society that is so morally and ideologically confused as to be in no position to stop the invader.

Evolution relies strongly on the organization of complexity. The metabolizing structure of all life forms exceeds a certain complexity threshold. Natural selection pushes many organisms to become more complex.

It is true that some species reach a plateau when their structural complexity provides a reasonably good chance for survival and reproduction. Those that do this have no need to change as long as their environment or ecological niche remain stable. Nevertheless, the direction of evolution as defined by the progress from elementary life forms to humans is one of increasing complexity. A sudden decrease in organized complexity thus appears as a catastrophic reversal akin to species extinction. Just as when viruses kill off a population of mammals, or when computer viruses erase a host of hard disks full of organized data, so the organized complexity of the built environment is decreased when Nineteenth-century buildings are replaced by modernist ones.

9. ANTI-PATTERNS THAT DESTROY URBAN INTERFACES.
(SALINGAROS, 2003A)

Most of the known architectural and urban anti-patterns were created by Charles-Edouard Jeanneret-Gris (Le Corbusier). Characteristic of all viruses, there is no completeness in the sense that we have an organism that metabolizes and interacts with others in an ecosystem. What we have is a nonliving informational code, or meme, whose sole purpose is to reproduce itself. For this reason, a mind-virus is given as a simple image, and not as a formula or solution to a problem. I have noted below some of the most destructive urban anti-patterns.

These have infected the minds of people alive today, and work to displace patterns from the collective subconscious. This is the reason why it is extremely difficult to reintroduce Alexandrine patterns back into today's society.

1. ABSOLUTE RECTANGULAR GRID
2. SEGREGATION OF FUNCTIONS
3. SHEER CONTINUOUS WALLS AT STREET LEVEL
4. BUILDING SETBACKS
5. EMPHASIS ON THE LARGE SCALE
6. SEPARATED BUILDINGS
7. VERTICAL STACKING
8. GEOMETRY OF STRAIGHT LINES
9. NON-INTERACTING UNITS
10. UNNATURAL MATERIALS
11. SUPPRESSION OF GEOMETRICAL PATTERNS
12. ELIMINATION OF THE HUMAN SCALE

This list underlines my point. There is no scientific support for any of these twelve anti-patterns, despite the false claims made by Le Corbusier, and repeated later by his apologists. Scientific investigation of human interactions proves that these twelve anti-patterns prevent the normal activity in a city that drives people to inhabit urban regions in the first place. Anti-patterns become so deeply embedded into a culture, however, that any questioning of them threatens many people's essential being.

Those persons are certainly unwilling to admit that they have allowed themselves to be infected with mind-viruses. Their mind is their self, and so they will defend their prejudices as forcefully as they will defend their life.

Taken as a set of working rules, the above dozen anti-patterns have been used in a method of urban design to build cities throughout the world. They combine well together, and support each other. They have a consistency, which is mistaken for adaptivity. Because of this consistency, they give a result that is standard and easily identifiable: it is the modernist anti-city that treats human beings as emotionless machines. In a recent essay entitled *"Geometrical Fundamentalism"*, Michael Mehaffy and I argue that the application of modernist urban anti-patterns around the world, by erasing the traditional urban fabric, is in part responsible for the rage the non-industrialized world feels against the industrialized nations (Mehaffy & Salingaros, 2002).

10. CONCLUSION.

I have put these extracts from my previous papers here, along with some introductory material for the following reason. I am convinced that anyone reading them together (which would otherwise be difficult to do, as the ideas are scattered among my papers on architecture and urbanism) will see the viral analogy as reasonable, and perhaps even inevitable. Furthermore, the thesis touches on so many different topics that I hope to inspire other writers to use this as a unifying theme for treating many disparate phenomena in contemporary society.

How did the idea of deconstruction as a virus occur to me in the first place? The father of Deconstruction, Jacques Derrida, actually admitted in 1994 that he developed his method on the basis of viral infection (Part 11). It thus resembles a genuinely artificial virus, analogous to the computer viruses that plague the electronic world today. I had labeled certain architectural styles as viruses in my previous papers long before I read Derrida's account of it (having avoided him in part because Derrida is deliberately convoluted and incomprehensible). His admission serves as a confirmation: a sort of prior "signed confession" discovered after the viral structure had been deduced from the evidence of its observed effects.

PART 13

THE NEW ARA PACIS MUSEUM

The Roman Emperor Augustus built the "Altar of Peace" (Ara Pacis) in Rome in the year 13 BCE, as a monument to the stability of the Roman Empire. It is a small building surrounded by wonderful relief sculptures, and fortunately remains in an excellent state of preservation. Many of its pieces were recovered in the 1930s, and the architect Vittorio Morpurgo constructed a simple modernist building to house the Ara Pacis in 1938. Because of its association with the Fascist regime (Morpurgo worked for Benito Mussolini) and the fact that the building itself was rather depressing, Roman citizens have long wanted to replace it. In 1996 The American architect Richard Meier was designated to construct a new cover. The frankly non-adaptive character of Meier's design unleashed strong protests and sparked off an architectural debate. The new museum building finally opened in 2006, to clouds of controversy.

Unlike many of our friends, I am really happy that the new cover for the *Ara Pacis* in Rome is finally finished. This building is the new symbol of cultural and philosophical development for a particular class of Italians. That group of people is part of a very select international community, with which it shares values and ideals, and also interests, so that this phenomenon is not simply Roman, Italian, or even European.

Some of my Classical architect friends waged a long and intense battle against the design of Richard Meier (Younés, 2002). Unfortunately, I must admit, without having any result, in spite of the time lost in futile debates, the hard work spent preparing counter-projects much better adapted to the Augustean altar (which no one in any important position ever looked at), and the anguish of seeing logical arguments blocked by empty words. Even I had been invited to participate in the opposition, but I declined. Not because I liked Meier's building, but because I was convinced that it was a lost cause. The battle was political and ideological, not architectural, and therefore a Classical design was excluded from the very beginning.

Many times in history a process begins, which cannot be stopped before it reaches its natural conclusion. Humanity has never been able to arrest history's great evils before they provoke a horrible destruction. Nobody wants to listen to the prophets who predict the coming evil: people are too busy, or they are seduced by the fashions of the times, or they do not believe that the evil could be so devastating. "Perhaps it is only a passing phenomenon", "It will disappear in a few years", "Surely they are exaggerating",

"Nothing can be judged without waiting a little", "These are emotional and alarmist reactions", etc. Fighting too strongly from the beginning only sets up a negative polarization, and gives birth to irreconcilable oppositions that foment a left/right dichotomy in what is a non-political space. Instead, one has to let time and events flow slowly, and at the end see what has really happened. In the end, you stare evil directly in the face.

For many years now, a contemporary architectural fashion is developing all over the world. Its purpose is purely nihilistic: to destroy every trace of architectural life in the built environment. Beyond destroying shapes directly, it also ingeniously incorporates death in the forms themselves. It constructs death. It replaces all our cities, all of the earth, with structures that incorporate death.

When you see a new building of this kind in Los Angeles, few people are alarmed, because that great city is already an absurd confusion of architectonic trash, skyscrapers, open parking lots, freeways, etc. The beautiful Los Angeles of the 1930s is all nearly destroyed in this sense. Moreover, to be truthful, it's not such a great achievement to remove architectural life from where it does not even exist. It is much more rewarding to eliminate life from where it is concentrated. For nihilist architects, the challenge is to achieve the maximum damage — which means to operate in a place full of life. You can build all the architectural absurdities you want in the desert, or in the outlying suburbs, but that gives only minimal satisfaction. It is like shooting at a cardboard target: it does not give the same thrill as shooting at the flesh of a living being. You don't hear the cry of the wounded animal; you don't see the blood spurting out … really, true pleasure comes from killing, and obviously, one has to kill something that's living.

One does not need a doctorate to be able to identify those places which this nihilistic architecture has set as its the maximum targets. They are our old cities, sources of both Western and Eastern civilizations, and also the source of architectonic life for all times. Athens, in front of the Acropolis; Rome, right in the historical center; Beijing, inside the old city; London, next to the Victoria and Albert Museum, and numerous other design projects now being promoted using seductive images …

This fashion cannot be stopped just because we don't like it — it is a socio-political phenomenon with enormous inertia. The architects are not responsible; it is the politicians who give them the jobs, as one gives the dog a biscuit. This is the means of self-promotion for a class of politicians who wish to be remembered as progressives, leaving behind them grand architectural works as their testament. Exactly the way Mussolini did. An eternal memory to themselves established with monstrous constructions ("progressive" in the eyes of some). We who dare to criticize them are de-

131

fined as retrograde; religious traditionalists lost in the 19th century; fanatics of the left/right; revolutionaries; anarchists; Fascists; stuck to ancient ideas; against social and philosophical development; against technology; against the immense American dominance in the world of the arts; and other inelegant epithets.

Let's come back to architectural fashion and its future. Although Richard Meier is not a deconstructivist architect, and is therefore not nihilistic, he does not design living forms. Meier designs pure shapes in an abstract geometry, and surfaces that are sometimes attractive but always sterile. The issue of architectural life never seems to enter into his concept of design; one sees only a smooth purity. In his design objectives, and in his formal approach, Meier is not all that far away from the lack of life seen in the works of deconstructivist architects, even though his expression is distinct.

Now that the *Ara Pacis* project is finished and opened to the public I have a small, though minimal hope that the Italian public will be a little more awake than other people in other parts of the world. Once people actually see the *Ara Pacis*, there is the possibility that a direct physical experience with one's body and one's own senses will lead to a realization of what this is all about. One needs to see and experience the paradox. Augustus's altar, constructed by the emperor to celebrate the life of the Roman Empire, is a structure that is quintessentially alive. It contains in its geometry and in every detail the fecundity of human and natural life. It is structured according to a complex geometry that nourishes our living being. That is, the original *Ara Pacis*! It offers an incredible contrast to the largely dead structure recently constructed to protect the ancient altar.

If we can clear our brain from the confused propaganda with which some commentators declare Meier's *Ara Pacis* an architectural masterpiece; if we succeed in clarifying our thoughts, perhaps will be able to hear our soul whispering: "it does not harmonize with the altar", "it is rather strange and disconnected", "the light gives us a headache", "it is a sterile place that has nothing to do either with the Rome of Augustus, or with our contemporary Rome brimming with life".

Be careful not to be tricked by the skillful architect. In some places he uses a beautiful stone with natural microscopic details. But the feeling of life disappears when one walks away from those surfaces. Life does not exist on the large scale, nor is there any geometrical harmony. Who can criticize the windows? They are beautiful, nicely ordered, and clear. Nevertheless, they contribute to create a psychological atmosphere with the spirituality of an automobile showroom containing the latest models. This is a mechanical geometry, not unattractive, but surely without life. Even though the ability of the Italian public to think clearly about architectural issues is reduced after indoctrination by the mass media, it is not entirely impossible that a direct architectural experience will awaken them.

The new building-cover is considered to be very original, because twenty years ago its architect won the Pritzker architectural prize, offered by the American avant-garde. Nevertheless, its rectangular shapes make us think of Giuseppe Terragni; the glass walls of Walter Gropius; the horizontal windows of Le Corbusier; the useless swimming pool of Ludwig Mies van der Rohe, the white wall of Adalberto Libera, the wall of brutalist unfinished concrete of Le Corbusier; the wall of travertine limestone of Ludwig Mies van der Rohe; etc. In spite of this presumed "originality" dating back to the 1920s and 1930s, all the different pieces do not coordinate: the shapes are isolated, every tectonic component being detached from a non-existent unity. The purity of the separated forms hides a stubborn geometric idea, which applies to create a disconnected building — a building that is incoherent, and in the final analysis, dead.

Another paradox: the "hard" plaza, the fountain, the steps, the isolated external column (a symbol of power): all this harkens back to a Roman memory in the not-so-distant past. So many efforts, so many passionate debates, so many political maneuvers, in order to end up with a building that seems perfectly adapted to Mussolini's Forum from the 1930s. Can we be proud of this coincidence? Granted, the old cover by Vittorio Morpurgo was ugly, but at least it had a symmetry that is now lacking. It was replaced for political reasons (because it was constructed in 1938) rather than aesthetic ones. Aside from the symmetry, in what ways is the new cover so very different from the old one?

Even worse, since one cannot find life in many architectural element of the new cover, the structure consequently absorbs the life of every living thing around it. Instead of giving us energy, it takes our energy and weakens our soul. For example, notice how the smooth internal column sucks the life from the sculptures on the *Ara Pacis*. It is an interesting phenomenon — nobody could imagine that a simple column could do so much damage. You have to pay the entry to the museum in order to verify this effect! Already the American newspapers proclaim: "one reason to visit Rome is to see the new museum, the world-wide architectural masterpiece by Meier". Well then, all the rest of Rome would be just trash if American tourists came mainly to see this building.

If the Italian public ever begins to understand the foundations behind this style of contemporary architecture, it will not be long before it begins to ask uncomfortable questions: "Which critics and architectural reviews proclaim this project to be a great work of art?", "And with what criteria?", "Why in our architecture schools today are all styles expressing life uniformly condemned?", "How come nihilists control the architectural media?", "Why, despite the negative criticisms from so many architects, politicians, journalists, and interested citizens, did the *Ara Pacis* project proceed ahead all the same?", "Why did the Vatican bring Richard Meier to Rome in the first place in order to build the *Tor Tre Teste* Church, thereby promoting him as a fashionable architect?".

Hopefully, the public will pose these questions. Perhaps it will, but nobody will answer. The established power base has ultimate control, and is not obliged to explain anything; rather, it will probably issue a cloud of propaganda in self-defense. Power is too deeply entrenched — there are too many persons who risk losing face. More than a few isolated individuals (who can always hide themselves after retirement), major institutions risk losing their reputation (and therefore their control). Those cannot allow the possibility that a small mistake, like the promotion of a strange building, can ruin everything. Here we are talking about an immense power base, driven by corporative greed and reinforced by academic fanaticism. This power comes from the deep conviction that a "progressive" architectural style is tied to the future, to economic and industrial progress, development, and with new building contracts (representing billions of Euros for projects of this type).

I'm talking about power that is monolithic and thus dangerous, because when it perceives a threat, it reacts in a totalitarian manner. The stylistic debate is only a smoke screen whose purpose is to distract architecture students from the true financial objectives. We find ourselves faced with an unexpected wedding of convenience between the European Left and American cultural imperialism.

The *Ara Pacis Augustae* is now finished, and it would be a waste of time to try and change anything after the fact. The true danger is lurking in the immediate future. There is a long line of avant-garde projects that are preparing to destroy Italian cities with their monstrosities. The architects are very few — the same names that work in the international "jet set", supported by ambitious and unscrupulous politicians. Compared to the others, Meier is rather benign and therefore preferable. Without any hesitation, I would propose Meier instead of the deconstructivists!

The problem is that the *Ara Pacis* project was only the preliminary foreign intrusion into the living body of historical Rome. We are dealing with a global phenomenon: a movement dedicated to incorporating death in the form of buildings, promoting the new fashion. The task has already begun, to the accompaniment of a chorus of academic architects. If we really are interested in protecting architectural life, we have very little time to chase such projects away. We need to stop these visions of death before it is too late.

At the end we will not be able to make excuses, because the damage will be far too great: "That building looked much more interesting as a design than it is in reality", "Nobody could imagine that an architectural style could inflict so much damage", "In the world of Art everything is allowed even if it is harmful", "It was not our fault", "We were manipulated by the media and by political interests", "Nobody ever told us the truth", "The academics said that architecture has nothing to do with life, that architecture never touches our body and our health", "The experts have always assured us that those who criticize these new buildings are all crazy", "We have seen these buildings promoted on television", "Even the Church has supported this as architectural progress …"

PART 14

THE NEW ACROPOLIS MUSEUM

To emphasize that Greece has finally reached the cultural level of the other European countries, its present government [1] chose the Swiss (now American) architect Bernard Tschumi to design The New Acropolis Museum. Surely, with this Museum, the Greeks demonstrate that they are up-to-date! Another goal behind this choice was to convince the British Government that it is time to return the Elgin Marbles (sculptures taken from the Parthenon in 1802) to their country of origin. In a bold gesture of optimism, the upper floor of the museum will remain empty awaiting the imminent return of the Elgin Marbles. As Tschumi optimistically declares: "I truly believe that the day the museum is finished, the marbles will return".

Nevertheless, the rest of the world does not share this self-confidence. On the contrary, Tschumi's name provokes laughter among certain architectural circles. The American journalist Robert Locke, in an article entitled *"America's Worst Architect is a Marxist"* presents Tschumi as a poseur: "an architect of gags that fall flat". His architecture's theoretical bases are characterized as absurd: "Tschumi's theoretical writings, the basis of his reputation, are a tangled mess that alternately induces dizziness and puzzlement as to whether the author actually knows what philosophy is, or merely heard it described by someone in a bar once ... The worst of this stuff is so self-evidently empty as to defy attack" (Locke, 2001).

The truth is that Tschumi became famous for his theories without having built anything at all. His buildings in *Le Parc de la Villette* at the edge of Paris are rightly called "follies" since they are meaningless. They startle and puzzle anyone who sees them. According to Tschumi, they represent "programmatic instability ... the Park is architecture against itself". As for his first building in the United States, Columbia University's Lerner Center (where he was Dean of the Architecture School), it is widely considered to be a total failure. Its chief feature is a stubborn refusal to harmonize with its surroundings. Critics call it "an agitated, irrational mix — an architectural fiasco — a dud" (Nobel, 2000).

Who selected this man to erect a museum on Athens's most sacred ground? Are there no serious architects such as Christopher Alexander and Léon Krier so that we are forced to turn to marginal characters? And why did we forget Greek architects of international stature such as Demetri Porphyrios? [2] Sure, France's Socialist Government under Mitterrand first validated Tschumi; but this happened mainly for political reasons. Tschumi bears a scar from the 1968 street fighting during the leftist Paris riots. Exactly the same ideological and formational roots are shared with the leader of the Greek terrorist organization *"17 November"*.

We don't judge Tschumi unsuitable because he might belong to some political ideology, however. The problem is that the building he is proposing for the foothills of the Acropolis doesn't harmonize with anything [3].

Millennia of Greek architectural tradition form a root from which many fertile branches have grown over the ages — from before Classical antiquity, to the Neoclassical style of the early twentieth century, up to the adaptive modernism of the architect Dimitris Pikionis. Now, however, Greece is calling on someone to reveal the latest, but always sterile, ultra-contemporary style. Obviously the Greek nation judges its own buildings to be worthless — since they are irrelevant to what the great international architect from the United States wants to teach. This represents a national shame.

Like a first-year student who has not yet become aware of the life embodied in traditional architecture, and who is impressed only by shiny objects and whatever looks strange and precarious, Tschumi does not appear to distinguish between living and dead architecture. Of the museum, he says: "The argument of the building is that you can address the past while being totally contemporary, totally unsentimental. The way to address a complex problem is with total clarity". If there were no sentiment involved, why should the Greeks insist on the return of the Elgin Marbles from London? These words show that Tschumi has understood neither the Greek soul, nor what constitutes a complex system.

Contrary to what he states, his design for the museum is anything but contemporary. It simply reproduces the discredited typologies of the early Modernists from the 1920s, confused together with the works of the Bolshevik architects Konstantin Melnikov and Vladimir Tatlin.

It further embraces the disintegrating influence of French pseudo-philosophers such as Jacques Derrida. Tschumi's architecture, instead of uniting and organizing complexity, intensifies it. It avoids any relation to its historic environment, remaining an introverted expression of selfishness — a glass greenhouse in Athens's harsh summer heat [4].

I am not accusing Tschumi — someone else chose him [5]. The committee responsible for this project initially invited Daniel Libeskind and Arata Isozaki (who are even worse architects than Tschumi) to participate in the competition. Somebody in Greece who is impressed by things foreign must have become very excited by the crazy, twisted forms presented as the latest fashion in architectural journals. Now that the Acropolis Museum has become a matter of honor for a powerful group of politicians, architects, and journalists, however, how can this mistake not proceed any further? The Greek Government does not dare to admit that it made a blunder in such an important decision.

For this reason, it is pushing this project towards completion. The present government can fall tomorrow (perhaps as a result of this fiasco) [6]. Unfortunately, if this project is not stopped soon, we will have a structure in front of the Acropolis that deconstructs — and desecrates — the sacred site for many years, until it is torn down and replaced by a more suitable, adapted building [7].

The Acropolis Museum makes Greece into a laughingstock among those who know the dark reality of architectural politics. The world is starting to awake from the nightmare of a perverse architecture supported by a small but very powerful and fanatical clique. Contemporary Greece shows with its immature behavior — chasing after all the most tasteless and superficial fashions — that it needs some intellectual development. The country that defined Western Civilization needs to establish confidence in its own identity, and appreciate what it gave to the rest of the world all these centuries. Greece is suffering from such an intense feeling of inferiority that it denies its rich heritage, calling upon so-called experts to show it how to build alien structures.

This sad story reminds me of a time when the more developed countries would send bad goods to Greece — rotten meat, contaminated grains, etc. — sometimes with the collusion of the government then in power. Now this stuff is sent to the poorer African countries. But it seems that as far as architecture is concerned, Greece is still part of the Third World. Greek citizens have not yet learned to distinguish the phony from the genuine in architecture (maybe ordinary Greeks can; but apparently not those in a position of power and responsibility). Like fools, we continue to swallow whatever clever confidence tricksters sell us. And this in a country with a theatrical and cinematic tradition of clever comedies — plays and black-and-white films from the 1950s in which imposture, pretense, and deceit play the dominant role!

The British will certainly tell Greece that the Elgin Marbles had better stay where they are now, until it becomes a serious nation.

Since certain "contemporary" Greeks turn with such hatred against their architectural heritage, who can believe them when they declare a deep appreciation for their sculptural heritage? The upper floor of the Tschumi museum is condemned to gather dust — empty.

Let this be a lesson to other countries eager to cash in on the alleged "Bilbao Effect", where an alien structure introduced into a neglected city is supposed to attract hordes of tourists. First of all, the long-term consequences of such a manoeuvre are not yet clear, not even for Bilbao.

Second, Athens has always been a central tourist destination, and was never undeservedly forgotten — it doesn't need another architectural attraction to bring in tourists.

Third, what proof is there that those tourists who get excited by a deconstructivist building will also appreciate the Parthenon? Do tourists who go to Bilbao also appreciate its unique nineteenth century urban fabric? Cities and governments out to grab headlines had better understand these inconsistencies before they ruin their genuine attractions in a greedy pursuit of the tourist dollar.

NOTES:

1. Reference is to the Socialist PASOK government, which fell on 7 March 2004, one week after the publication of this article.
2. I asked Demetri Porphyrios on the occasion of his being awarded the Driehaus Architecture Prize, why he did not get to design the Acropolis Museum. He smiled and answered graciously: "Very simple — the Greek Government did not ask me".
3. This essay should not be read in strictly political terms. It suffices to point out that opposition to the project came both from the center-right New Democracy party (which won the subsequent elections), as well as from the KKE (the Communist Party of Greece) and the Synaspismos (an independent party on the left). I felt I had to refer to Tschumi's politics only because the media make so much out of his supposed political leanings. Good architecture is totally independent of any political affiliation or dogma — a lesson we have learned from both Léon Krier and Christopher Alexander.
4. I did not try to analyze the architectonic faults of the proposed building, for two reasons. The first is that my theoretical writings demonstrate that this kind of architecture is not architecture at all. The second is that, as in all similar fashionable projects, the published images prevent an effective representation of what the building is going to feel like. They provide only an innocent, impressionistic, and ethereal image for public consumption.
5. Criticisms of Tschumi's architecture have been around for years — I am merely quoting published material. In spite of this, he was selected unanimously for this prominent project. The Greek Government chose to believe what certain so-called experts told it, and to ignore others' opinion on the matter. Incredibly, it chose to ignore sensory information, instead going along with an abstract ideological line.

6. See Note 1.
7. Some readers misunderstood this article as being all about Bernard Tschumi. It is not. Tschumi is probably doing the best he can. What I am criticizing is the process of selection. The Greek Government chose from among the worst living architects, and got (in many people's opinion) a bad design as a result. The deeper problem is that Governments the world over have been advised — no doubt by prominent international and local architects — that the best architecture has a certain "look". For swallowing this deception (i. e., of the essential deconstructivist "look"), someone has to be held accountable. Maybe the watershed is finally being crossed — when the selection of an alien architecture comes back to haunt those who commissioned it.

POSTSCRIPT: ARCHITECTURAL CANNIBALISM IN ATHENS
(November 2007).

It gives me scant pleasure to see what is happening in Athens, my own city. After writing my article on the museum-monster back in 2004, I have been waiting patiently for the time when I could announce "I told you so!" Nevertheless, now that the time has finally come, I am deeply sad and so angry at the turn of events that I can hardly say anything. In the latest development (summer of 2007), the new museum's extremely powerful backers belatedly realize that two historic buildings (part of Greece's architectural patrimony) partially block the view from the museum's cafeteria. Therefore, they must be destroyed! The Greek State appears to be acting in a deep trance and going along with this, deaf to protests by international bodies, oblivious to thousands of signatures, newspaper articles by eminent architects and cultural figures, etc. It does not realize that it is being misled by smooth-talking propagandists for the avant-garde. My fellow Athenians are only slowly waking up to the reality of a fanatical and destructive ideological movement. The international concern about a contemporary starchitect building threatening (and actually destroying) local culture has become a rallying call for similar events elsewhere in the world.

I grew up in Athens. My family lived in the old part of the city, near the center. As a young boy, I walked and played in the historic regions and archaeological sites. Those places formed my character and being. My ancestor Angelos Salingaros fought on the Acropolis, defending it during the siege of 1826. It thus pains me deeply now when I see Athenians keen to destroy Athens's architectural and urban character, in a frenzy of supposed modernization. Most of old Athens has already fallen victim to a post-war building boom that replaced the old courtyard houses with ugly five-storey apartment blocks. It would be hard today to find in Athens even a single example of the courtyard house, whose typology goes back to ancient Greece (and was transmitted via Rome to the Islamic world and Spain, then to the New World, and to California of the 1920s). A few neoclassical buildings remain, built in the period between the end of the nineteenth century and the beginning of the Second World War, but not many (Salingaros, 2005).

Like so many other countries around the world, Greece is facing architectural cannibalism driven by the onslaught of a new worldview. This worldview is intolerant, substituting and replacing a nation's tradition, culture, and even its religion. But it is not imposed by an invasion of a foreign military force (unless you identify globalization and the international media, as many do, as insidious forces of occupation); architectural cannibalism is a civil war. A few Greeks have been brainwashed to destroy their own heritage. They desperately wish to conform to the cult of contemporariness.

Fanaticized ideologues whose minds are infected with alien images and anti-humanist principles are desecrating the city of Athens and its history. Willing, eager collaborators have betrayed their heritage and embraced the fashionable cult of architectural nihilism imported from Europe and the US. Even as the rest of the world begins to reject that nightmarish period of inhuman architecture and urbanism (Salingaros & Masden, 2007), some individuals within Greece are proud to promote it. Always a little behind the times, this group nevertheless makes up for its lag by showing a proper fanaticism in its willingness to pay homage to the cult.

The New Acropolis Museum is finally finished, a prime example of cult architecture. It is now threatening two protected neoclassical buildings, however, demanding that they be demolished in order to give it a better view of the Acropolis. Their removal will seriously damage Athens's historic urban fabric. There is general outrage in Athens, while at the same time, the present government is calmly proceeding with steps towards an eventual demolition of the previously listed buildings. I would like to focus away from my personal emotions (entirely legitimate), and formulate a sharp attack on the perpetrators, which is sorely needed.

The two buildings in question are numbers 17 and 19 Dionysiou Areopagitou Street, two architectural gems. One is Neoclassical (from around 1890), and the other more Art Deco (from around 1930). Architect Nikos Karydis admires number 17 especially: "The fantastic four storey Classical – Art Nouveau residence by Kouremenos, with its magnificent sculptures flanking the entrance, and its fine proportions and clever use of marble in the façade is one of the best buildings in Athens". This past July of 2007, while wildfires were devastating all of Greece and threatening to burn Ancient Olympia (that is, at a moment when national attention was focused elsewhere), the legal protection of these two historic buildings was lifted. [1] This procedure parallels the unexpected declassification of the new museum's site that lifted its archeological protection so as to allow excavation of the foundation columns. Many ordinary citizens are disgusted by the political maneuvers that have followed the project. Numerous lawsuits dogged this museum because of a string of such seemingly "irregular" procedures. But everything has been pushed through regardless, and by both successive governments.

I wish to compare the New Acropolis Museum directly with the two historic buildings that it now threatens with demolition. Despite unrestrained declarations of praise by its supporters, the museum building is of negligible architectural value. It has no coherence, no logic, and near zero degree of architectural life (Salingaros, 2006). It is a typical product of the deconstructivist fashion, albeit not twisted and contorted as the most extreme examples of that style. The two threatened and modestly scaled older buildings, by contrast, embody a highly elevated degree of architectural life. That life is what viewers intuitively perceive, and that is why this particular pedestrian walk, passing in front of the two buildings while facing the Acropolis, is among the most gratifying anywhere in the world.

The New York Times architecture critic felt he had to justify this abomination (the New Acropolis Museum) by calling it: "An impressive accomplishment: a building that is both an enlightening meditation on the Parthenon and a mesmerizing work in its own right (Ouroussoff, 2007)". How, I wonder, could the reviewer believe what he has written? He must certainly be dissociated from his feeling and experience. Such effusive praise has to be interpreted within its proper context, as New York architect John Massengale writes: "Like his predecessor at the [New York] Times, who handpicked him, Ouroussoff is an activist advocate for a small group of Starchitects. For Ouroussoff, ideology trumps experience (Massengale, 2005)... Mr. Ouroussoff knows his is not to reason why, his is to praise Starchitects to the sky (2007a)... And so it goes, while the architecture critic of the New York Times continues working as a press agent for Starchitects and their egocentric ideology (2007b)". The cult is self-reinforcing.

Far more perceptive and honest is John Massengale's own critique: "Bernard Tschumi's New Acropolis Museum [is] a behemoth completely out of scale with the buildings that shape the street... Tschumi's building is an alien invader that smashes the space, looms over it with no human scale and makes a terrific regional place look like any crass development anywhere. If the two buildings are destroyed, the continued assault on the character of the place would cause even more damage to Athens than the loss of a fine individual building." (Massengale, 2007c).

Those few Greek architects who support the demolition of the previously listed buildings wish to implement the modernist ideal of a building disconnected from its surroundings. Thus, the heated debate is also driven by ideology: the arrogance of the contemporary showcase building that needs to stand apart from its "inferior" older siblings. One Greek architectural academic supporting demolition of the older buildings urged that: "Athens has to invest in the highest level of contemporary architecture without reservations, and this demands ruptures". This is a cult statement by someone who dismisses humanistic, adaptive architecture as merely "nostalgia for the past". Failing to appreciate the historic urban fabric's enormous life-enhancing value, anyone holding those convictions can only damage it.

Prominent figures both in Greece and in the rest of the world are apparently shocked by the New Museum's design, which refuses to harmonize with anything in its environment. The design of the new building has an ultra-contemporary high-tech look, so that it relates to absolutely nothing in the long history of Greek architecture. People are also surprised at this manifestation of architectural "cannibalism", which has now exposed the two previously listed buildings to destruction. Puzzled observers interpret these events to be an inexplicable oversight or mistake by the architect, Bernard Tschumi.

I am neither puzzled nor surprised by all of this. It doesn't occur to critics of the design that intolerance and destruction are the defining characteristics of Deconstructivist architecture. Deconstruction is an architecture of aggression carried out by viral means. It is fundamentally nihilistic [Part 11 in this book]. Unfortunately, its cult followers and the architectural media have deliberately misled the public. Not to belabor the point, but the proposed demolition of the two listed buildings would also cut down a row of magnificent four-storey tall shade trees as well. Nothing should stand in front of the Museum! Whoever chose Mr. Tschumi should have known what they were getting. It is meaningless to complain now. Some people understood what the term "cutting edge" really means (literally!), but others only woke up suddenly after this building has devoured everything within reach.

Writer Vassilis Vassilikos (author of the book "Z") was appalled. "Mr. Tschumi attacks and is provocative. This triangular platform, the balcony of the Cafeteria… this open terrace is a concrete arrow aimed at the back of the two protected buildings, as if wanting to tear them down by its sheer vehemence. It is savage; it is from the third world. Naturally, it matches the monstrous conception of the whole museum. But such an aggression, which is unworthy of an important architect like Mr. Tschumi, I never expected. If the protected buildings are demolished, this arrow will then target the Acropolis itself, as if wanting to destroy it as well. Mr. Tschumi, is this the much-desired dialogue with the ancient monument? Oh, Melina [Mercouri], who started this project, you would now be on a hunger strike until they pulled down this arrow of revenge that is the terrace of Tschumi's Cafeteria (Vassilikos, 2007)".

A total of 25 houses were demolished to make space for the new museum. The two neoclassical buildings were legally protected. The original brief preserved these two buildings on the plan, and the design had to respect their position. Now that the museum is complete, however, someone seems to have changed his mind, or was planning to do this from the very beginning. The details of the controversy, according to many observers, can be reduced to a very mundane reason: having a better view from the Museum's cafeteria terrace. At present, the clients of the Museum's cafeteria will have to face the back of the two listed buildings, which were never designed to be particularly attractive. The Greek press is saying that the expected income from tourists lunching at the Museum Cafeteria overrides any concerns for historic preservation.

The irony in all of this is that the Greek Government (actually two successive governments, which, while disagreeing on almost everything else, have exerted their considerable power to build the New Acropolis Museum) could be seriously risking its reputation. Far from promoting architectural and cultural enlightenment through an ultra-contemporary new museum, it could conceivably be accused of embracing a preposterous (and ephemeral) architectural fashion while destroying its priceless heritage. How has history judged those governments who, in the past, demolished their historic buildings so as to impose an idiosyncratic idea of architectural modernity?

It is worthwhile analyzing the conditions under which so many reasonably good people were led to commit senseless acts of destruction. After all, these are government officials, not professional vandals. Furthermore, the project evolved during a peacetime democracy, so there was ample time and opportunity for citizens to complain if they did not agree with what was going on at the time. Sadly to say, a majority of the Greek public was duped into enthusiastically supporting the idea of the New Acropolis Museum. It became a national cause, acquiring a certain degree of mass hysteria that usually goes along with such causes. Successive governments presented the following propositions to the public (in my own words):

1. Greece desperately needed a new museum to house the antiquities related to the Acropolis, since the old museum is too small.
2. Bernard Tschumi is an important and accomplished architect, validated by international fame and demonstrated competence.
3. Famous architects are learned professionals, who are supposed to respect a nation's history and architectural heritage.
4. England will return that portion of the Parthenon frieze now displayed in the British Museum (known as the Elgin marbles) as soon as a new museum is built in Athens to house it.
5. This is a prestige project for "the greater national good", which should therefore be supported BY ALL POSSIBLE MEANS.

Point 1 is probably correct, whereas I would argue with point 2. Glowing projections of huge numbers of visitors to the new museum (totally hypothetical) are treated as ticket receipts already cashed in. I'm not so sure. What if visitors feel psychologically ill in the building, as they do in so many other deconstructivist buildings? What if they cannot focus on the sculptures because of the nasty glare (a basic design defect also present in Richard Meier's Ara Pacis Museum in Rome)? This quasi-religious conviction of superior architectural achievement makes a rational critique next to impossible.

Point 3 represents an honest mistake that anyone unfamiliar with current trends in architecture and what is misleadingly labeled "architectural theory" can make. I have tried to explain in my books and articles why assumption 3 is false; in fact, it is deadly wrong. So much damage has been done by deliberately confusing what is famous, good, and contemporary. In reality, it is more accurate to label the most famous contemporary architects as anti-architects. They are not interested in architecture that adapts to human sensibilities, or to the local culture, but only in imposing their monstrous ego on a hapless public. They disdain everything built at any time and at any location that has an intense degree of architectural life; since older buildings have this characteristic, those are their most frequent targets. This should not be misunderstood simply as an attack on the old, however, but as an attack on architectural life.

Point 4 is crucial here. The British Museum stated categorically that it is not ready to return the Parthenon sculptures to Greece. Despite this clear pronouncement, the Greek government decided to play a "clever" game of embarrassing the British government into giving back the sculptures. It would accomplish this by building a museum with specially designed spaces for their eventual exhibition. While that was admittedly an astute (if chancy) propaganda move, it has absolutely no basis in reality. It was a game of bluff played on the international political arena: a ploy based on the psychology of humiliation. When you don't have any real bargaining power, you can try to shame your opponent into capitulation. The propaganda campaign within Greece was so intense that it misled everyone, including those who initiated it. After a while, even the propagandists believe their own lies.

The Elgin marbles were used as the "hook" to manipulate public opinion into supporting the new museum. From the very beginning, those concerned made sure to link reality with fantasy so as to keep the project moving along, and this game continues today.

Now I come to the most disturbing aspect of the story. Point 5 encapsulates the New Acropolis Museum as an "important" project, for which no sacrifice was too great to make. A shared national dream backed by authority — from the State, a famous architect, and the international sycophantic press — permitted and even urged crimes against architecture, history, and civilization. As already mentioned, critics have accused the Greek government of the destruction of archeological antiquities on the site itself. Preparing the foundations of this massive building was bitterly referred to as "archeology by bulldozer". People who protested against this were labeled as spoilers; as being against progress and the national vision.

One Greek reprimanded the critics who revealed the destruction of the archeological site with these words: "You are writing in English, so as to slander our fatherland and the Greeks... You are doing terrible harm... Already [some people] are utilizing your disclosures as an argument so that the pieces seized from the Parthenon will never be returned to our homeland... I am saddened." After a certain point, promoters of the new museum wished that everyone should submit to a conspiracy of silence about what's happening here in Athens. We don't want the outside to learn of the atrocities committed against our archaeological and architectural heritage, because that would jeopardize our game of international bluff.

There was a church on the site, the Church of St. George. It can be seen on the original plans within the region to be preserved, and outside the Museum's foundations. One day it was demolished. Fait accompli! Critics of the project managed to film the destruction — carried out by a giant excavator. There is no mention of this act of barbarism in the press. I don't know if that was due to a lack of interest or to self-imposed news censorship. [2] Demolishing a church for no apparent reason (other than that it doesn't fit into a megalomaniacal conception for a new museum) is an egregious sacrilege. Did the Greek Orthodox Church not object? I have been unable to find out. When the residents of the two protected buildings were asked why they never complained before about the neighboring buildings falling victims to the bulldozer, they confessed that they kept quiet, reluctant to speak up: "We were faithfully supporting the higher public interest."

Seeing destruction around you and being intimidated into silence... until your own turn comes... seeing the nation's laws violated or manipulated by those who are sworn to uphold them... feeling helpless because protest makes absolutely no difference to the obsessive pursuit of a goal set by others... crying out for help but having your pleads silenced by both local and international authorities (in this case from New York)... this situation reminds me of past times when humanity slid into darkness. Surely, even then, the perpetrators' goal was "noble", working according to a frighteningly narrow interpretation of "the greater national good". After the destruction, what happens?

We usually associate the deliberate demolition of churches in our times with the regimes of Joseph Stalin and Nicolae Ceauçescu. Stalin dynamited the superb 19C Cathedral of Christ the Savior to make room for erecting the monstrous Palace of the Soviets. Le Corbusier (another Swiss/French architect, like Tschumi) eagerly took part in the architectural competition without any problems of conscience, but failed to win the commission. Maybe God objected to this project, since the foundations kept flooding, and the proposed modernist (actually, totalitarian style with typical misuse of stripped classical elements) building could not be erected. The only thing that could be built on the site was a giant circular open-air swimming pool (not very practical for swimming laps). After the fall of Soviet Communism, the Cathedral of Christ the Savior was rebuilt as closely as possible according to the original plans.

I propose that, whatever the future holds in store for the New Acropolis Museum (remodeling to make it more modest? pulling down the problematic cafeteria terrace?), succeeding generations of Athenians have a moral obligation to rebuild the tiny Church of St. George. This martyred building will, like its much more important brother in Moscow, stand for the memory of a dark past, in which people foolishly embraced a warped idea of architecture and urbanism, founded upon intolerance and destruction.

Digging deeper into the motivations for what happened — and what may still take place — uncovers a frightening reality. The archaeological antiquities, the church, the two historic buildings, and the gorgeous trees in front of them were annoying to the project for a new museum. Someone whose reality has been infected by images of a futuristic modernity tells us that they cannot coexist; they have to be demolished. But we don't normally destroy whatever annoys us... we need, in addition, the authorization to do so. Not only from the State as a legal document (and that was provided here without any hesitation), but we also require MORAL authorization. Deconstructivist ideology (and the clique that supports it) has identified whatever annoys the new building as being beneath human consideration; as expendable; as without cultural value; as an obstacle to progress; as having no reason for existence; as being a detriment to our own wellbeing!

Reality is thus forced to conform to an extraordinarily impoverished vision of the world. That imposes a clear value distinction: what is new, shiny, and fashionable is good, whereas whatever differs from this (arbitrarily-defined) ideal is undesirable — and will continue to trouble us until it is annihilated.

So many things are being lost in this bargain; therefore most people can see that it is a wretched deal. Athens is trading away centuries of its heritage for a few shiny trinkets. We are witnessing a few individuals seduced by "architecture as giant sculpture" infecting Athenians with their intolerant visions of a machine-age future. This mind infection then drives people into a culture of hatred for their own past. They cannot appreciate the timeless patterns of the Acropolis, nor the human experience of walking around the sacred hill and ascending up the path, nor the experience of living in the architectural palimpsest that is historic Athens.

NOTES:

1. The government official who cast the deciding double vote later tried to commit suicide by throwing himself from the fourth storey. His lawyer followed suit by throwing himself under a coming truck.
2. My friend the architect Anthony C. Antoniades lives in Greece and has followed the New Acropolis Museum project closely since its inception. He was surprised to learn about the Church of St. George (from me), whose destruction has never been mentioned in the public discussion.

PART 15

ARCHITECTURAL THEORY AND THE WORK OF BERNARD TSCHUMI

This essay tries to make sense of contemporary architectural theory. I discuss some aspects of deconstructivism, with emphasis on the theoretical contributions of Bernard Tschumi. In particular, psychological conditioning through images and subconscious associations is used to create an alternative reality. I identify this technique as programming that emulates a pathology, and relate it to an analogous technique in computer software.

1. ARCHITECTURAL THEORY.

In order to discuss any supposed contributions to architectural theory, it is necessary to define what architectural theory is. A theory in any discipline is a general framework that

(1) explains observed phenomena;
(2) predicts effects that appear under specific circumstances; and
(3) enables one to create new situations that perform in a way predicted by the theory.

In architecture, a theoretical framework ought to explain why buildings affect human beings in certain ways, and why some buildings are more successful than others, both in practical as well as in psychological and aesthetic terms. One important requirement of an architectural theory is to coordinate and make sense of scattered and apparently unrelated observations of how human beings interact with built form. Another is to formalize those observations into an easy-to-apply framework that can be used for design.

Sadly, architecture is only now embarking on a long-overdue formulation of its theoretical basis. It is not an exaggeration to say that up until now, the field has been driven by personal whim and fashion rather than being supported by any theoretical foundation. As a result of a serious misunderstanding (due to scientific ignorance by three generations of architects), a voluminous body of writings has been mistaken for "architectural theory", even though it is nothing of the sort. This material is taught to architecture students, and is studied by practicing architects; nevertheless, it merely serves to promote certain stylistic fashions and dogmas rather than an understanding of architectural form. Enough genuine architectural theory now exists to form a nucleus from which the topic can be built. This nucleus consists of the writings of Christopher Alexander (Alexander, 2002-2005; Alexander *et. al.*, 1977), Léon Krier (1998), the present author (Salingaros, 2006), and a few others.

Genuine architectural theory has developed into two parallel strands. The first is the approach based on solutions that work historically. Not surprisingly, this strand turns to traditional architecture, using its typologies in an innovative manner. Architects ignorant of this strand of architectural theory misjudge it, falsely thinking that it merely copies older models, whereas in fact, it is using a well-developed vocabulary to generate novel solutions. The second strand of genuine architectural theory is based on science.

Here, models from biology, physics, and computer science are used to explain how architectonic form emerges, and why human beings react in certain predictable ways to different structures. The scientific approach is in many ways complementary to the traditional approach to design. The main difference in practice is that, since the scientific approach is not tied to any specific typology, it leads to a much broader design vocabulary than does the traditional approach.

Architects have difficulties in appreciating the scientific strand of genuine architectural theory, because of certain misstatements in the body of existing architectural texts. Authors claiming to explain architectural form using scientific theories and their vocabulary are invariably confused, and so confuse the reader. Much of this architectural literature is plainly incorrect, but architects have insufficient scientific knowledge to realize this. Well-respected architectural commentators write misleading statements that are taken as meaningful explanations by architects and students, who then become so bewildered that they cannot appreciate genuine scientific explanations. They confuse spurious explanations for the real thing.

This regrettably happens because in architecture, there is as yet no basis for judging between a true and a false theory. Other fields were able to develop their theoretical basis only after they instituted such a criterion, putting in place a mechanism for distinguishing sense from nonsense. Architects erroneously believe that such a set of criteria can exist only in an experimental subject such as physics, without realizing that architecture is itself an experimental field. The problem is that the observational, experimental side of architecture has been willfully neglected for several decades, to the point where its practitioners have forgotten this fundamental quality of their discipline.

2. BERNARD TSCHUMI'S WRITINGS.

I recommend to everyone Tschumi's two books: *"The Manhattan Transcripts"* (1994a), and *"Architecture and Disjunction"* (1994b). The first is worth studying in great detail, since it helped Tschumi to become the Dean of Columbia University's School of Architecture in 1988. It contains a 6-page Introduction and barely 10 pages of text. The body of the book consists of indistinct black-and-white photographs (whose subject often cannot be made out), and line drawings by the author. Those represent cartoons of distorted and broken buildings. Their message is unclear, as is their relationship to the text. The same black-and-white drawings are reproduced, this time filled in with dull purple and red, in a separate section entitled *"Colored Plates"*.

The photos in *"The Manhattan Transcripts"* include the infamous one of a man being thrown out of a window, with the caption "To really appreciate architecture, you may even need to commit a murder" (1994a; page XX). What is contained in this book was judged at the time of its initial publication in 1981 to represent a novel architectural theory — and considered worthy of reprinting in a new edition in 1994. I cannot see any theory here that explains or predicts the effects of architectonic form.

If this is not architectural theory, then we need to discover exactly what the text conveys. There is an explanation in the Introduction and in the prefaces to each set of drawings, which sets out the underlying idea. For example, on page 8: "The first episode . . . is composed of twenty-four sheets illustrating the drawn and photographed notation of a murder". On page 14 we read: "And that's when the second accident occurred — the accident of murder . . . They had to get out of the Park — quick". And on page 8: "He gets out of jail; they make love; she kills him; she is free", and again on page 32: "But what could she do . . . now that the elevator ride had turned into a chilling contest with violent death?" This has nothing to do with architecture, of course, but it does help to establish a macabre psychological ambiance that is crucial to the project.

If I were pressed to come up with the message of this book (and this is necessarily a subjective opinion) I would say that it communicates violence; and projects violence onto buildings. This is in fact the visual message encoded in the cartoon drawings shown in the Color Plates. Forms that are instantly identifiable as buildings are broken, twisted, and dismantled; their component elements left precariously unstable.

Images that someone leafing through this book might at first glance dismiss as silly actually carry the clear message of undoing coherent structure. These images have a special quality that sticks to the reader's mind. By doing so, they act on one's subconscious long after the book is put away.

"The Manhattan Transcripts" are therefore not so much a presentation of architectural theory, as a collection of images meant to work subliminally, precisely the same way as in advertising.

Tschumi's later book *"Architecture and Disjunction"* (1994b) contains 250 pages of text. The book touts itself as "a lucid and provocative analysis of many of the key issues that have engaged architectural discourse over the past two decades". Nevertheless, I find neither lucidity, nor an analysis of design.

A phony theory can be easily dismantled by finding flaws in its arguments. As I can recognize no theory in this text, however, there is nothing to criticize. Tschumi instead presents disordered observations on a variety of topics.

For example, he remarks on violence and architecture (pages 132-134): "The integration of the concept of violence into the architectural mechanism — the purpose of my argument — is ultimately aimed at a new pleasure of architecture. Like any form of violence, the violence of architecture also contains the possibility of change, of renewal . . . two types of partial violence should be distinguished, types which are not specifically architectural . . . Programmatic violence encompasses those uses, actions, events, and programs that, by accident or by design, are specifically evil and destructive. Among them are killing, internment, and torture, which become slaughterhouses, concentration camps, or torture chambers."

Earlier, on page 88, Tschumi suggests a parallel between sexual bondage and architecture: "Similarly, the game of architecture is an intricate play with rules that one may accept or reject . . . These rules, like so many knots that cannot be untied, are generally a paralyzing constraint. When manipulated, however, they have the erotic significance of bondage . . . What matters here is that there is no simple bondage technique: the more numerous and sophisticated the restraints, the greater the pleasure." Tschumi's book is made more piquant by inserting quotations from the Marquis de Sade on unusual sexual practices. For example, he reproduces de Sade's ingenious solution to simultaneously committing incest, adultery, sodomy, and sacrilege with one sexual act (page 182). Read as architectural theory, this makes no sense; but within the context of psychological association, it contributes to reinforce a message.

3. PSYCHOLOGICAL ASSOCIATION IN TSCHUMI'S TEXTS.

Trying to pin down anything in Tschumi's writings is very frustrating; but there is something I wish to note. In *"Architecture and Disjunction"* (1994b; page 187), we are offered a supposedly scientific explanation of the design for *Le Parc de la Villette*. "The stated concern of the project was to apply theoretical concerns on a practical level, to move from the "pure mathematics" of *The Manhattan Transcripts* to applied mathematics . . . The other strategy involved ignoring built precedents so as to begin from a neutral mathematical configuration or ideal topological configurations (grids, linear or concentric systems, etc.) that could become the points of departure for future transformations." And again (page 197): "La Villette was the built extension of a comparable method; it was impelled by the desire to move from pure mathematics to applied mathematics".

Now, in addition to being an architectural theorist, I also happen to be Professor of Mathematics, and I can find no obvious mathematical content (either pure, or applied) in Tschumi's writings and buildings.

One could (although he himself does not do this) describe Tschumi's buildings as intentional but selective randomness introduced into ordered form. His designs destroy the order achieved by having a multiplicity of subsymmetries; he undoes those symmetries in order to define structures that are partially, though not totally, incoherent. Breaking vital connections and symmetries between component parts amounts to violence in terms of undoing the mathematical richness of coherent form. Such a drastic severing of internal connections kills biological organisms. In *"Architecture and Disjunction"*, Tschumi had already (sort of) summarized his basic idea: "The concept of violence also suggests different readings of spatial function — that the definition of architecture may lie at the intersection of logic and pain, rationality and anguish, concept and pleasure" (1994a; page XXVIII). This may be the key to understanding what is really going on. A psychological state of excitement, anxiety, and sensual urges (especially those triggered by the forbidden pleasures of combining violence with sex) is subtly created by the text and photographic images.

I am not presenting the above quotes in order to criticize them, since I don't know exactly what Tschumi wishes to communicate. Nevertheless, the theme of violence is evident throughout his work. He reproduces the defenestration photograph from *"The Manhattan Transcripts"* again on page 100 of *"Architecture and Disjunction"*, enlarged just in case someone missed it in its earlier, smaller, incarnation. Back in *"The Manhattan Transcripts"*, I recognized two shocking, revolting frames from the 1928 Luis Buñuel and Salvador Dali film *"Un Chien Andalou"*, in which a young woman's eye is slit open with a straight razor (page XXIV). Just in case we missed them then, these images are presented again in *"Architecture and Disjunction"* (page 158), therefore Tschumi must consider them important to his overall message. Is this a way of saying that nowadays, "cutting-edge" in architecture literally means the same thing as in Luis Buñuel's film?

To introduce a new architectural style, one needs to implant — using whatever means possible — images of a particular typology into architect's minds. All of this graphic and implicit, suggested violence in Tschumi's writings does makes sense if interpreted in a certain way. Tschumi unfortunately does not explain, but if true, then this would amount to a brilliant psychological trick.

Could it be (and here I am conjecturing) that the violent/erotic undercurrent in Tschumi's texts serves to fix his images of dismantled forms in our subconscious so that we somehow accept them and remember them?

Is their message one of shock followed by subliminal reinforcement, associating visual dismemberment of buildings with the forbidden thrills of dangerous sex and violence so as to make it more attractive? This would be very subtle, but nevertheless effective, psychological conditioning. I am not exactly sure of this, but the possibilities of subconscious association are there to be explored.

Tschumi makes the following confession in *"Architecture and Disjunction"* (page 210): ". . . my own pleasure has never surfaced in looking at buildings, at the great works of the history or the present of architecture, but, rather, in dismantling them". Have his clients bothered to read this statement? Does it convey an appropriate sentiment from the chosen architect of a museum facing the Parthenon? Furthermore, is this a master architect's statement to which young and impressionable students ought to be exposed? Tschumi is being honest here, so one cannot fault him: any possible criticism must be directed at those institutions that have commissioned his works and helped to propagate his message. Or, perhaps, our civilization has reached the point where it is thrilled to accept an architecture that does violence to form instead of putting it together coherently.

Suppose, for the sake of argument, that the association of architecture with violence is successful; how does such a conditioned mind view buildings from that point on? Every adaptive structure, which necessarily connects its component parts to each other and to adjoining forms, must appear dull and unexciting. The thrill of violence can only be triggered by breaking or destroying some ordered structure, yet this quality is entirely lacking in traditional architecture. In a mind-set that has been conditioned to get a physical thrill from violence, the opposite paradigm — consisting of adaptive, living forms — is unattractive. Not only that, but when a choice has to be made, then complex adaptive forms will be replaced by those that give the thrill of violence. We have here a selection criterion that, acting over time, will change the psychological character of the built environment.

4. INSTITUTIONAL VALIDATION OF TSCHUMI'S WORK.

I recently joined a debate over Bernard Tschumi's New Acropolis Museum being built in Athens. It was supposed to be ready for the Olympic Games, and to possibly house the Elgin Marbles if ever they are returned. In Part 14, I gave my opinion of the project (not a positive one, I am afraid), and used criticisms by other authors of Tschumi's writings and his previous work to support my point of view. Some commentators noted that The New Acropolis Museum could have played a role (albeit a minor one) in the downfall of the Greek Government. Tschumi's design for that building — consisting of a glass box on stilts — is only one of several problems facing this project. There are serious objections to erecting something on an unexcavated archaeological site, and critics allege that artifacts were destroyed while digging the building's foundations (which led to a lawsuit to block the project).

I believe there exists a philosophical relation between these two points. Deconstructivist design violates ordered structure in some way — more obvious in some deconstructivist buildings than in others. It represents a lack of respect (to put it mildly) for the ordered coherence embodied in traditional architecture and in the vast majority of human artifacts. Deconstructivist buildings make no effort to connect to and blend with their surroundings, for the simple reason that they wish to stand apart from them. Indifference to what exists on and around the site (in this case the Classical style of the Parthenon; the Neoclassical style of the New Greek State; local residents; unexcavated antiquities) can be understood as being consistent with the general disconnecting method handed down by the French deconstructivists.

Tschumi forged an alliance between architecture and French Deconstruction, applying Jacques Derrida's precepts to the pavilions at *Le Parc de La Villette* built on the outskirts of Paris. The architectural establishment subsequently propelled Tschumi into a brilliant career as architect, lecturer, teacher, and university administrator.

In the 1980s, architecture was desperately seeking a philosophical underpinning; something to give it both justification and renewal; anything unusual and exciting upon which to base a new movement in design. The profession seemed stuck in the modernist rut (the postmodernist stylistic fruit salad notwithstanding). To those who had bought into French deconstruction, Tschumi was seen as an ideal candidate to lead a progressive school of architecture. In the same year 1988 that Tschumi was appointed Dean of Columbia University's Architecture School, the Deconstructivist Show at the Museum of Modern Art validated all its main practitioners (Part 11).

Even those of my acquaintances who applaud Tschumi's earlier role happen not to like his latest work very much, however. They consider him *pas-*

sé. No one could explain to me why after years of criticism ranging from lukewarm to negative, and a general lack of commissions, Tschumi is suddenly being asked to build projects around the world. There is a noticeable boost in his practice. His current lecture circuit reveals him to be on his way up. The program for the 92nd ACSA (Association of Collegiate Schools of Architecture) Annual Meeting in Miami, Florida lists Tschumi as the Opening Keynote Speaker.

Being chosen to open an important national meeting indicates a considerable degree of prestige among one's peers. Tschumi spoke on March 18, 2004 in Florida International University's new Paul L. Cejas School of Architecture, a building he recently designed.

Tschumi's books have been validated by the architectural profession. Architects continue to buy them and read them, and teachers recommend them as texts in university courses on architectural theory. Anyone has the right to write what he or she likes, but when the professional architectural societies, the architectural journals, our major universities, respected publishers of architectural monographs, and governmental institutions praise someone for being a cutting-edge architect on the basis of such writings, then the entire system is responsible. The burden of liability in case something goes wrong falls squarely on those institutions.

It is not only our universities that have taken part in validating Tschumi as a serious architect and architectural thinker. Foreign governments have commissioned him to build important showcase buildings. François Mitterrand, the President of France, was pushing the pavilions called "folies" at *Le Parc de la Villette* while he was still in power.

As mentioned above, Tschumi designed The New Acropolis Museum at the request of the Greek Government, which defended it against a protracted series of criticisms. Do such institutions care about French deconstructivist philosophy? Probably not. What we are likely seeing is a self-feeding cycle of validation, where no one questions the true value (or potential for damage) of what is being supported.

In the field of architecture, which has lacked an objective basis for the duration of the twentieth century, impression counts for everything. This raises a question with our present system of architectural education. How can a student not be intellectually intimidated when they see their university build one of Tschumi's buildings? How about if their government builds a prestigious national museum designed by him?

Can anyone critically judge Tschumi's writings when their author is presented as an unquestioned authority backed by institutional support at the highest level? What if students perceive him as totally lacking in substance; if they are repelled by his message of violence to form? Do they dare to question the wisdom and competence of their teachers, administrators, and elected leaders for supporting his idiosyncratic vision of architecture, or do they instead suffer cognitive dissonance?

5. THE COLLAPSE OF FRENCH DECONSTRUCTION, AND ITS IMPLICATIONS FOR ARCHITECTURE.

Let us turn to Greek Mythology for a critical analogy. Two monsters that wreaked havoc but could not easily be defeated were Antaeos, the mythical giant who gathered superhuman strength from touching the earth — and the many-headed Hydra, whose heads kept growing back after being cut off. The hero Herakles (Hercules) was able to vanquish Antaeos by lifting him off the ground, thus cutting his contact and source of strength. Herakles got the better of the Hydra by cauterizing the wound with a flaming torch after cutting off each of its heads. Just like in the cases of both Antaeos and the Hydra, deconstructivist architecture draws its strength from somewhere, regenerating itself after each devastating attack. It has seemed impervious to criticism, always reaching back to its philosophical power base for new strength.

Realizing where the source of this strength lies, I present a new interpretation of the French deconstructivists in Part 11. Instead of accepting their writings as philosophy, as has been customary, I suggest that they are a kind of mental virus, whose purpose is to destroy ordered thinking and stored knowledge about the world. I draw detailed analogies between this type of mental virus (also referred to as a "meme") and the ways that biological viruses act. In honor of deconstruction's founder, I named this ingenious mechanism for meme propagation after Jacques Derrida. I should mention that in expressing this innovative and controversial thesis, I am by no means acting alone, and in fact draw support from distinguished allies in philosophy, science, and architecture.

This discussion opens up a Pandora's box of questions that eventually need to be answered. It has nothing really to do with any individual architect, but is a phenomenon tied to the current architectural establishment. If the French deconstructivists are not only exposed as being without intellectual merit, but their method as actually dangerous to our society and institutions, where does that leave deconstructivist architecture? Will it be able to survive as a style cut off from its traditional intellectual power base? It could indeed; for the following reason. In addition to its intellectual power base, deconstructivist architecture possesses a considerable political power base in those persons and institutions that have profited from it, and therefore have the most to lose if it ever collapses (Part 11).

What is immediately obvious is that, following the collapse of French deconstruction, deconstructivist architecture will henceforth likely be judged as a fashion — a sensational stylistic play for fun and profit. Finding itself without the crucial support of French intellectuals, deconstruction in architecture appears simply as a visual provocation, a radical form of posturing that helps architects make a career by getting noticed. In this game, users (i. e. human beings and their needs) no longer matter, since the goal is simply to be noticed enough to get the top commissions. Being provocative is what it is all about. No more an expression of our age — unless it is an expression of alienation and mass psychosis — deconstruction becomes a marketing phenomenon, alongside with perfume, fashion, junk food, and bizarre cultish behavior.

There are two possible interpretations of the impact deconstructivist architecture has on our civilization. The first considers it as just another style, which in a pluralistic society has a right to be expressed along with every other conceivable style. As such, while people may not like deconstructivist buildings, they cannot object to others who promote them. The second, alternative interpretation is much more categorical, however.

It considers deconstruction as genuinely harmful to our way of thinking, since deconstruction promotes a warped and skewed model of the physical universe. If this interpretation is taken in earnest, then the architects, clients, and sponsors of deconstructivist buildings are inflicting harm on our society.

These are very serious concerns, and it remains to be verified which of the two preceding interpretations is more accurate. If it turns out that it is indeed the second one, then the issue of culpability needs to be raised. Were clients and architects blissfully unaware of possibly negative consequences of their actions? Did none of them listen to pleadings from more sensitive people that such buildings are, in a fundamental way, "inhuman"? What happens to those institutions, including our universities, learned academies, professional organizations, and governments, which have supported and sponsored deconstructivist architecture all along? Are they also to be judged guilty by association?

6. PROGRAMMING THAT EMULATES A PATHOLOGY.

Architects and architectural critics have become expertly adept at fancy wordplay, sounding impressive while promoting the deconstructivist style's unnatural qualities. This linguistic dance is used to justify a meaningless architecture of fashion. The problem is that criticizing an empty but flowery discourse is like shadow boxing with phantoms — one can never win a debate against an opponent who creates an impressionistic cloud empty of tangible facts. My solution is not to debunk the style of contemporary architectural writing (even though that is sorely needed), but to try and explain what it models.

I would like to draw some interesting analogies between architecture and biology, psychology, and computer science. These analogies help to explain the peculiar language used to validate architecture as a fashion. In Part 11, I achieved some insights into how deconstruction acts by considering it to be analogous to a virus (or "meme", as an informational virus is otherwise known; Part 12). I now wish to stretch the analogy further and to suggest possible parallels with a pathology of the human brain, which would make the action of the Derrida virus more directly biological.

Studying deconstructivist writings gives me the impression that except for Derrida, who is very cleverly and deliberately obfuscating, their authors are suffering from some sort of brain damage.

The normal, evolved mechanisms that enable human analytical thought have apparently been scrambled, so that those authors seem mentally incapable of expressing a direct, logical statement. Their writings almost make sense; but not quite. The deconstructive method avoids closure. Altogether, this mimics the effects of a lesion that has destroyed part (but not all) of the brain, preserving linguistic facility and memory while damaging the ability to synthesize thoughts. Since synthesis depends on connectivity, which deconstruction erases, this suggests some new type of mental pathology with observable effects.

Louis Sass (1992) has drawn an interesting parallel between deconstructivist discourse and the speech patterns of schizophrenics. He finds the following common features:

1. Disorienting changes of direction.
2. Meandering sentences that never come to a point.
3. BLOCKING, or halting in the middle of a train of thought.
4. The use of meaningless words or phrases.
5. Cryptic references, along with the impression that they are essential to make sense of the present message.
6. GLOSSOMANIA, where speech is channeled by acoustic qualities rather than by meaning.
7. Flow that is governed by normally irrelevant features of the linguistic system.
8. DEICTIC AMBIGUITY, i. e. insufficient contextual cues to establish thematic coherence.

9. A focus on multiple but normally irrelevant alternative meanings of words.
10. LINGUISTIC ALIENATION, where a word is divorced from its object.
11. Banal and pompous phrases spoken with an exaggerated emphasis (as in the deconstructivists' willful use of quotation marks).
12. An irony that tries to disown the normal meaning of words at the same time as they are being used.

We are fortunate enough to have a direct statement by a prominent deconstructivist architect linking his creations with schizophrenia. Bernard Tschumi describes the series of strange structures he built at *Le Parc de la Villette* on the outskirts of Paris in the 1980s in *"Architecture and Disjunction"* (1994b; pages 177-178): "In this analogy, the contemporary city and its many parts — here *La Villette* — are made to correspond with the dissociated elements of schizophrenia . . . The transference in architecture resembles the psychoanalytic situation . . . This fragmentary transference in madness is nothing but the production of an ephemeral regrouping of exploded or dissociated structures".

In a paper entitled *"The Sensory Value of Ornament"*, I discuss some analogies between twentieth-century architecture and specific pathologies of the eye-brain system (Salingaros, 2003c).

So far, there is no indication that those who promote deconstructivist architecture actually suffer physical brain damage — it is more an EMULATION of schizophrenia rather than an onset of the actual pathology. The reason is that the emulation can be switched on and off. As long as they are not talking about architecture, architects and critics appear to have no problems using mental explanations to make sense of the real world.

We can understand this odd behavior by turning to Computer Science. It is often advantageous to use an operating system that emulates another operating system. The original computer mimics another, very different computer. The reason for this is to execute a program that is incompatible with the computer's basic operating system. I propose that deconstruction — both the literary and architectural varieties — emulates aspects of pathology on a biologically healthy brain. When the emulation ceases, the person reverts to acting perfectly normally. That has been my own personal experience in talking to some architects. They act as normal and pleasant characters while discussing general issues; but their language and behavior becomes bizarre and unreasonable as soon as the topic turns to architecture.

This model makes sense if we consider deconstructive discourse and design to be fundamentally opposed to our inborn sense of language and order. It would normally be impossible to talk or design in such a disconnected manner — analogous to the impossibility of running an incompatible program on a computer. The only way to run the program is to emulate a different operating system. Nowadays, this is standard practice, as most programs run on the basic operating system, with the emulation kicking in only when a specific piece of incompatible software wants to run. The basic incompatibilities are thus never noticed. Such a model compartmentalizes our brain so that it can execute mutually contradictory instructions at different times.

7. CAN THIS EVER BE CALLED ARCHITECTURE?

To those outside the architectural arena, much of its contemporary writing and thinking seems incomprehensible. What stands for theory appears to be engaged with issues and ideas divorced from human beings, being concerned with topics that are irrelevant to people's activities and sensibilities. The field is instead driven by images. Without a theoretical basis, such images can lead to full-size buildings that feel monstrous and alien to their inhabitants and neighbors.

What looks novel, cute, and exciting on a computer screen or magazine page may turn into a nightmare by distorting the lives of people who have to use it after it is built. Genuine architectural theory tells us which buildings are successful or not, and gives the reasons why. Unfortunately, that body of knowledge is felt to be outside architecture as it is currently defined by its leading exponents. Theoretical concerns such as the basis for hierarchical complexity in architectural form, and algorithms for generating adaptive structure are simply not part of fashionable architectural thinking. This material is not taught in the schools.

Within the current architectural paradigm, there is little interest in rules for creating an architecture suited to human beings, and for designing urban regions that are manifestly alive with human activity. Apparently, no one reads the few articles and books discussing those rules, and if they ever do, they certainly do not apply them. That is a consequence of a fundamental replacement of worldviews. Going back to the computer analogy, an operating system can replace functions normally performed by hardware — such as all interactions with the outside world — with software. Most important, a computer that is hard-wired to have one type of interface can be made to mimic an entirely different interface via the imposition of a new operating system. The human mind, which is hard-wired (on the basis of neuronal circuits) for a specific set of input/output responses with the world, is known to be subject to programming (through ideas) that changes how it interacts with the outside. This programming downloads a new operating system that emulates an entirely different (alien) machine.

Some puzzling architectural practices are now beginning to make sense. Contemporary architectural training substitutes a universe of alien images for the real world in the minds of impressionable students. Designs for proposed buildings have all acquired the characteristics of eerie computer screen images. Those ghostlike, translucent visions represent disassembled structures — they intentionally make it difficult to visualize a form concretely, so that not only the form's image, but also its informational encoding communicates disassembly. The real world of physical forms has thus been replaced by a virtual one conforming to a peculiar aesthetic. The distinction between building and image has dissolved, as an alien visual conception replaces the practical reality of a world built for living beings.

Deconstructivist buildings really took off when deconstructivist images could cross from the electronic media directly to the built environment. Images resident in virtual space can now achieve physical representation in a way that circumvents the human interface altogether. Recently, architects started using computer programs that control industrial robots, which can mill full-size prefabricated parts and molds in three dimensions. Prior to that, it was extremely difficult to construct buildings that violated the natural tectonic forces of gravity, hierarchy, and connectivity, because human perceptual hardware (our neuronal system) registers that violation by making us feel uneasy. Harnessing the latest technology has made it possible for images to jump from a computer screen to a final built form.

There is another point worth mentioning. A universe of alien forms is inhospitable to all types of genuinely adaptive structures, animate as well as inanimate. That is a world in which matter must strictly conform to specific images. Those images serve as material to be re-used. Eventually, as alien images have begun to replace more complex, coherent forms, alien images steal parts and information from each other. We are witnessing this phenomenon in contemporary architecture, where plagiarism within a severely limited vocabulary of "approved" alien forms, surfaces, and materials has become rampant. That is inevitable. All the "cutting-edge" buildings now tend to look very similar, since they are beginning to cannibalize each other's designs. So much for the myth of architectural innovation!

The architectural establishment (consisting of academic departments of architecture; practicing architects; architectural firms; associations of professional architects that meet for their periodic conferences; specialized publications devoted to architecture; and juries that award architectural prizes) encompasses a considerable body of people. Although it is impossible to generalize among such a heterogeneous group of individuals, the architectural establishment believes that what it DOES defines what architecture IS. It sets the current architectural paradigm. Nevertheless, after vigorously promoting deconstructivism, the profession has divorced itself from its own discipline. This is not merely a matter of changing fashions or inclusiveness — deconstruction cannot define life in buildings or urban regions, but only its opposite.

In computer science and complexity theory, the term "architecture" denotes the linkages among different system components. A system's architecture is the specific way in which its components are integrated into a coherent whole. This knowledge is embedded in the system's connective structure. There already exists a fundamental cross-disciplinary exchange between genuine architectural theory describing buildings and cities, and computer science (Salingaros, 2000b). Contemporary architecture, however, which intentionally disconnects building and city components from each other, cannot be called "architecture" in this widely accepted sense.

I need to explain the consequences of what is being claimed here. It seems that the profession has lost its discipline's central objective. Many architects are working within a paradigm that excludes what architecture ought to be — that is, buildings and urban fabric that facilitate human life and interactions. They apply a method that denies any system architecture. The necessary geometrical qualities are now avoided by those who wish to appear "contemporary". Instead, we are given convoluted excuses about novelty and relevance.

This is not a "different" architecture as usually claimed; but technically not architecture at all. Deciding to throw architecture's inherited knowledge into the historical trash pile, and to ignore scientific results that establish genuine architectural theory betrays a worldview inconsistent with the real world. It also reveals a dangerous combination of arrogance and ignorance.

Why are the professional associations, composed largely of architects who build functional but often nondescript and lifeless office boxes, apartment houses, and commercial strips, such enthusiastic supporters of deconstructivism? They themselves have nothing to gain from it, and do not apply it in their everyday practice — yet as an institution they are helping to promote its key practitioners. Many decent, practical architects support their deconstructivist brethren; perhaps longing for the latter's "star" status. There is little open criticism from within the professional organizations, so one must assume that everyday architects acquiesce to and even admire what the "stars" are doing. Are the anonymous commercial architects so completely mesmerized by the glitz and spectacle of the star architects that they cannot see what a monumental backlash this will bring to the entire profession?

8. CONCLUSION: THE NECESSITY FOR THEORY.

In this essay I pointed out which contemporary authors have in my opinion actually contributed to creating a theoretical foundation for architecture. I also argued that what is currently accepted by many architects as architectural theory is not theory at all, but rather a clever means to propagate a particular design style. Outsiders (which includes most people) naively assume that contemporary architecture possesses a theoretical basis, like for example chemistry and neuroscience, which explains why buildings ought to look the way they do. However, a mass of writings mislabeled as architectural theory only helps to generate and support certain images; those images are then copied, and used as templates for buildings in an alien style. That is not a theoretical foundation. Those writings fail to satisfy any of the accepted criteria for a theory in any field.

Every discipline has a store of knowledge accumulated over time, which explains a huge range of phenomena. (Architecture has been collecting information for millennia). Some of this knowledge is codified into a compact theoretical framework; other parts are strictly phenomenological but tested by observation and experiment. Facts and ideas combine in a particular manner, common to all proper disciplines.

The crucial characteristic of a valid theoretical framework is a transparent internal complexity coupled with external connectivity. This arises from the way explanatory networks develop in time:

1. More recent knowledge about a topic builds upon existing knowledge.
2. Older knowledge is replaced only by a better explanation of the same phenomenon, never because a fashion has changed — this process creates multiple, connected layers of knowledge.
3. A theory in one discipline must transition sensibly to other disciplines.

This means that there ought to be some interface, a border where one discipline merges into another, all the way around its periphery. Any theory that isolates itself because it is incomprehensible to others is automatically suspect. A tightly-knit internal connectivity, along with a looser external connectivity, provides the foundations for a mechanism of self-correction and maintenance. This holds true for any complex system.

Architecture as a profession has repeatedly disconnected itself both from its knowledge base, and from other disciplines in an effort to remain eternally "contemporary" (the much-publicized recent connections to philosophy, linguistics, and science notwithstanding, since they are now exposed as deceptions). This is, of course, the defining characteristic of a fashion;

the opposite of a proper discipline. Again and again, architecture has ignored derived knowledge about buildings and cities, and has embraced nonsensical slogans and influences.

Those who profit from the instability and superficiality of the fashion industry are deathly afraid of facing genuine knowledge about the world. It would put them out of business. Architects and critics periodically change the reigning fashion so as to keep the market stimulated. They have to devote an enormous amount of resources to promoting whatever ephemeral style is in vogue. In order to sell their fashion, they are obliged to suppress any application of accumulated architectural knowledge. This prevents a theoretical basis from ever developing. Ever-changing fashion is parasitic on timeless processes.

Critics dismiss neo-traditional buildings as facile copies of classical prototypes, even though those need not resemble anything built in the previous two millennia. The architectural media declare that "a classical column represents tyranny", and that by confessing to an attraction to classical architecture, we somehow support totalitarianism. At the same time, a liking for non-classical vernacular architecture of any kind is ridiculed. In this instance, we are branded as being ignorant and "sentimental" (which, in contemporary architectural values, is an unforgivable offense). Novel buildings with human qualities, which nevertheless have nothing to do with the classical typology, are also forbidden.

People are now misled to believe that the "architecture of the future" is necessarily broken and twisted, and made out of glass and polished metal. Any doubt is dispelled by awarding their architects the most prestigious prizes. Some of those who participate in disseminating this style act from an almost religious conviction. They fervently believe that they are doing civilization a favor, promoting the future and protecting us from backwardness and retrogression. Architectural schools are steeped in righteousness. Ever since the Bauhaus of the 1920s, many schools' aim has been to restructure society for the betterment of all people; whether those welcome this or not. If ordinary people are sentimental about past methods of design, and crave buildings that appeal to the human scale, that is only an indication of human weakness.

We stand of the threshold of a historic architectural reckoning. A new architecture mixes exuberant curved forms and fractal scaling with the broken forms of deconstruction. Let me suggest that architects who wish to be contemporary ought to drop their deconstructive baggage. They should instead extend a hand to those whom they have formerly disdained and slandered — I mean the traditionalists, and those innovative architects who respect human scale and sensibilities. By mixing novel forms with typologies that have undergone a competitive selection during historical time, we can define a new architecture that is fit for human beings instead of remaining forever alien. Younger practitioners have been duped into identifying novelty with the essential "alien look" of deconstruction. Nevertheless, a new generation of architects is intelligent enough to realize what is going on, and to snap out of an unfortunate deception.

9. APPENDIX: REACTIONS TO THIS PAPER.

Following the publication of my paper online, readers wrote in comments; others published a response on their own website. I was very curious to see how people would react to my arguments, as it would indicate whether the original points registered or not. Non-architectural readers were intrigued if not totally convinced. At the very least, my article opened up a healthy debate on the topic of contemporary architecture OUTSIDE the normally closed architectural circles. I was pleased that those architects who did not dismiss my arguments outright tried very hard to come to grips with what I had said. I never expected to convince them at once, and was delighted that they took the trouble to engage.

On the whole, however, my paper provoked the type of response I anticipated. Nearly every critique bore out my thesis on the existence of an architectural cult (Part 7). The reaction consisted of standard cult responses to an external threat. One may even consider this as a sophisticated scientific experiment, although that was not my original intent. Perturb the deconstructivists and their followers by criticizing their beliefs, and see how they respond. Interpreting their response then gives invaluable information on what type of system we are actually dealing with. This is especially important when the inner workings of an institution are shielded from the outside world, or when it pretends to be something it is not.

Architecture, as with all proper disciplines, requires an explanatory framework. Since its scientific basis is only now beginning to be developed (by Christopher Alexander, myself, and a few others) it continues to rely on unprovable assumptions. This means that its working basis is judged more akin to an implicit religion rather than a scientific discipline, which is understandable. Nevertheless, we do possess a set of criteria that distinguish between a true religion and a dangerous cult.

Religion helps to form and maintain a healthy society through evolved patterns and traditional knowledge tried over time. Its beliefs accommodate and facilitate human actions, and are consistent with human perceptual systems and emotional health. They start from a physiological basis of instinctive common sense. A religion or philosophy of life is a way of organizing experience and dealing with the world's complexity. The distinguishing feature of a dangerous cult is that it ignores experience, and tends to be characterized by narrowness, arbitrariness, and an emphasis on hatred. A cult ignores natural complexity, and inserts its own complexity into the environment. Consistent with this view of architectural deconstruction, I would like to analyze the responses to my paper on the basis of several classic cult stratagems:

A. CONVERT EVERYONE TO THE CULT
B. DISGUISE THE CULT'S TRUE AIM
C. CLAIM A SEPARATE REALITY
D. DENY THAT THE CULT COULD BE WRONG
E. USE A RAW POWER PLAY
F. OFFER A POISONED DEAL
G. ATTACK THE MANUFACTURED ENEMY

I will illustrate these points in what follows, using parts of readers' responses to my paper. It is remarkable that, despite the number of different responses, not a SINGLE one of the numerous devastating criticisms I raised was answered or even addressed. Instead, all responses fit more or less into the above classification. This helps to confirm a most damning characterization of contemporary architecture, though one that it vehemently denies.

If we consider deconstruction as a linguistic and iconic posture, then this explains why its supporters cannot come up with tangible principles that are worth defending. There is nothing there other than being conditioned to speak, write, and view reality in a certain peculiar manner.

A. CONVERT EVERYONE TO THE CULT.

It is no coincidence that those who criticized my paper invariably urged everyone to study the writings of Bernard Tschumi and Peter Eisenman in great detail. Naturally, they could not summarize what their purported message is; but were honest enough to admit that the message is "complex, challenging, not superficially apparent, hard to truly understand, an abstract means of representation, etc." They emphasized that one had to spend a great deal of time with those texts before expecting the message to come across — which is precisely the method of indoctrination. After becoming indoctrinated, one's mind is so disoriented as to be no longer capable of examining those writings using logical criteria. I view such incomprehensible texts as a set of mental exercises that psychologically condition initiates into the cult. Note that we are not dealing here with theoretical physics, which requires a language not known to everyone; architectural theory should be written in a common language understandable to every person. After all, they have to live with its applications. One respondent's excuse that contemporary architectural texts are "advanced works intended for those who are already conversant in twentieth-century theory and metaphysics" just doesn't hold.

B. DISGUISE THE CULT'S TRUE AIM.

Some non-architects were puzzled by the contradictory claims of myself and those architects whom I criticize: that we both value human, contextual buildings built to satisfy people's physical and psychological needs. Or, so both of us claim. Readers were sharp enough to realize that one of us is being disingenuous, since those conditions cannot be satisfied with two totally opposed styles of architecture. Admittedly, it is not easy to decide who is right, for the simple reason that the other side represents the architectural establishment. Well, my friends and I rely on the latest research of environmental and evolutionary psychology, whereas our opponents are supported by their vast political power — so which group is not being entirely honest?

C. CLAIM A SEPARATE REALITY.

If one lives in a different world run by different rules, then one is immune to being judged by the rules of this world. Cults create this impression in order to protect themselves. Here, respondents implied that architecture resides in the world of art, in which the criteria for a theory do not apply. In the real world, we need logical prescriptions for designing a building; whereas in the world of contemporary architecture we can supposedly "look for contradictions between architectural forms and the movements and events that take place in them . . . artistically explore the visual continuities and discontinuities between different ways of looking . . . compare visual relationships between our different methods of representing events in space-time." While all of this sounds good in a vaguely poetic manner, most people will not understand what it means. It is not specific enough to convey meaning in the world of our experience. (I don't understand the reference to space-time, even though I have published papers on relativity).

Even so, as it alludes to human beings interacting with structures, those interactions are amenable to a genuine theoretical description. I continue to insist on my original premise that we live in one universe, which is run on universally applicable laws. Only those unfortunate individuals who are suffering from some sort of brain pathology are forced to live inside their own separate reality.

D. DENY THAT THE CULT COULD BE WRONG.

This is not only a ruse to continue the cult's hegemony. More importantly, it is an essential mechanism for maintaining sanity among its members. Even indoctrinated persons cannot change their physiology, so while inside deconstructivist buildings they must feel the same anxiety experienced by the non-indoctrinated. This is the sacrifice that cult members are obliged to make: they have to support the cult's ideology despite the contrary evidence of their own sensory apparatus and physiological response.

For this reason, an intellectual "explanation" that appeals to novelty, excitement, and meaningless intellectual acrobatics is always offered, in the attempt to override an observer's natural anxiety. We are told that part of this type of architecture's attraction is its unusual excitement. Many people buy into this deception. Paradoxically, a disconnect between one's own senses and the cult dogma drives the convert even closer to the cult. Experiencing such a contradiction is disturbing, and so disorienting that an already emotionally insecure person clings even tighter to the safety offered by the cult doctrine. They have renounced the real world, so there is nowhere else to turn. Afterwards, he or she feels a worthier cult member by having avoided the temptation of incontrovertible evidence.

One respondent, who works in Peter Eisenman's Aronoff Center, obviously has to keep supporting the value of deconstructivist architecture or quit his job and move elsewhere. I'm not at all surprised that he considers deconstructivism to be "a powerful, revolutionary kind of theory".

E. USE A RAW POWER PLAY.

Those who commented on my article reminded me that what I criticize is tremendously successful commercially. Deconstructivist architects are being hired by important organizations across the world to build these buildings. Here is the power play: if all those clients, plus the professional groups and media accept this not only as valid, but as GREAT architecture, how can I argue against it? What has by now obviously become an institution could not possibly be duped so easily. The sheer number of people counts against it. Right is what the majority defines it to be. So, I was admonished (or bluntly warned) to give up.

F. OFFER A POISONED DEAL.

This ploy is a favorite of ruthless politicians and conquerors. They pretend to accommodate their opponents, who represent the opposite ideals, in a generous-sounding deal. The true aim is to get close enough — or buy time — so as to annihilate them when the opportunity is ripe: "Let's work together for the common good; we are comfortable with contradiction; we are interested in both X and Y types of architecture, etc." What the other side is offering in way of concession is unclear, however. I cannot resist referring to historical deals of this type; for example, Adolf Hitler's deal with Neville Chamberlain: "You allow us to take over Czechoslovakia, and I promise not to start a European War". And then we have Hitler's deal with Joseph Stalin: "I'll meet you half-way . . . somewhere in the middle of Poland . . . and we can remain friends".

I find ludicrous the repeated calls to accommodate both Alexander's work and deconstructivist philosophy. They are mutually contradictory. Despite confessions by some architects that they welcome contradiction, these two philosophies about the nature of the universe cannot coexist. As the present power base of architecture is set to promoting deconstruction, our part of the deal (like the other half of Poland during WWII) will be short-lived. Already, for several decades, Alexander's work has been neglected at best, or actively condemned at most architecture schools. In the classic Alexander/Eisenman debate of 1982, this contradiction was clearly spelled out for everyone to see (Alexander & Eisenman, 1983). The roots of today's architectural madness were already painfully obvious back then. This newly-found "tolerance" smells to me like the obvious ploy that it is. My own papers on the scientific basis of architecture make the distinction between the two camps clear. I show in great detail why, of the two opposing world-views only one (ours) is connected to the real universe (Salingaros, 2006).

G. ATTACK THE MANUFACTURED ENEMY.

When all else fails, the cult has to rally the faithful around an abstract idea of the enemy. This is the predictable response, but one that is usually misunderstood by the public as a stylistic dispute. It is nothing of the sort. Instead, it is an essential battle call that helps to hold the cult together. My paper triggered the usual responses about humanistic architecture: "dead-end, profoundly anti-urban, anesthetizing, backward-looking, cul-de-sac, a retrenchment, nostalgic, conservative, anti-intellectual, a rabid aversion to progress, etc." And yet people who feel that way are offering to make a deal! (see the previous point F).

Many times before, we have seen false promises of innovation and a bright new future mask the intentions of a cult that is eventually to destroy a nation, continent, or entire civilization. An essential rallying point is the manufactured enemy: something upon which to focus the cult's hatred. This is much more than a turf battle. At this time, Léon Krier's traditional buildings seem to be focusing the wrath of the architectural establishment, even as many of its top practitioners are quietly making money from building traditional commissions. But the young followers have been fanaticized to attack. They are the profession's cannon fodder.

Respondents to my article kept coming back to their battle cry: that the architecture my friends and I propose leaves little room for architecture as an art. This, of course, is an outrageous lie, but it is a very powerful weapon to use against us. It triggers an angry, visceral response from every aspiring architecture student. Out of delicacy, I do not wish to quote here propaganda and lies that were used to systematically justify attacks against victim groups in the past.

We can understand deconstruction's opposition to traditional architecture because of ideological competition, but the vehemence of its hatred is a pure cult phenomenon. Once the cult starts attacking a target, it has no other recourse but to destroy it completely. For pulling back is tantamount to an admission of error — instead of a noble purification campaign, the annihilatory attack is revealed as a criminal act against an innocent entity. The original characterizations of perpetrator and target become switched. Not only are participants exposed as mindless followers implicated in a hideous crime, but all their sacrifices have been in vain.

Glimpsing the target's humanity (in this case, the life-supporting qualities of traditional buildings) is a profoundly disturbing experience, which translates into even more hostility towards the target. Rob Annable, in criticizing my article, unwittingly gave us a poignant cinematic characterization: "Anybody who's seen *"Night of the Living Dead"* has seen deconstruction in action" (Annable, 2004).

It is very telling that respondents assumed automatically that my architectural work is neo-traditionalist. Since no one other than my design associates has ever seen my actual sketches for buildings, this is merely an assumption without any basis. The manufactured enemy (I'm talking now of a group of people instead of buildings) has to be both faceless and abstract. Anyone who questions the cult's dogma is classed a neo-traditionalist, because that is the label for the faceless enemy.

A reader may well ask: why is this reaction specifically a CULT reaction, and not just a normal institutional reaction to criticism? It is true that contemporary architecture represents a very powerful institution. Nevertheless, I think that an institution founded on a healthy philosophical basis would react by appealing to common sense. Instead of falling back on its dogma (point A), it would spell out architectural principles that are simple, profound, and touch our heart directly. If those are easily understood, then they most probably have enduring value. Science, for example, reacts to criticisms from a position of strength coming from the unshakable nature of its arguments.

Clarity and transparency of thought are the enemies of cults. If their basic beliefs require convoluted explanations before one can appreciate them, or are understandable only to initiates, then they are most likely bogus.

In general, an institution will not resort to manipulations and deceits in order to further itself. Those that do are parasitic on society. Here I have raised the possibility that contemporary architecture is lying about its aims, and disguising them by claiming a separate reality (points B, C, and D). This is a complex question to resolve, yet it will doubtlessly be answered by scientific research into human physiological responses to the environment. Institutions do use power plays and make deals as a matter of course, so those are not distinguishing features; yet what clinches the argument in my mind is the hostility of the architectural avant-garde to all other forms of architectural expression (point G). Institutions compete naturally in the marketplace, looking to improve so as to increase market share. Improvement is contingent on recognizing present faults, thus a healthy institution is its own most severe critic.

Here, by contrast, we sense an absolute, moral conviction of right. Architects talk as if there is no possibility of being wrong, so the intensity of their attack makes it more of a religious (i. e. cult) phenomenon. This type of institution rests on irrational dogma and a strong emotional appeal. In the absence of verifiable precepts, the dogma is supported only by the fervor with which followers embrace it. It is a self-feeding cycle leading to fanaticism.

One respondent suggested that the prominent deconstructivist architects don't care what others think of their work, so that criticisms like my own are irrelevant. I am afraid that he is probably correct. If my assessment of deconstructivism is accurate, then it is not worthwhile defending a fundamentally indefensible fashion; the only important thing is to build as many commissions as possible before the fashion shifts to something else.

PART 16

"THE NATURE OF ORDER"

CHRISTOPHER ALEXANDER AND THE NEW ARCHITECTURE
Book review and Interview of Christopher Alexander.

1. REVIEW OF CHRISTOPHER ALEXANDER'S "THE NATURE OF ORDER".

Every few centuries, humankind undergoes a paradigm shift. New ideas revolutionize the way people think and how they confront their world. A set of ideals is taken up and spreads into society. Such movements require that the population be ready to accept them; a large number of people who share the same frustrations are already thinking along similar lines, so that the message resonates with the multitude and is not simply a cry in the wilderness. The shift represents the "tipping point", catalyzing a reaction that has been unable to take off because it was lacking a few essential pieces. Usually, one person conceives the vision as a whole for the first time, and this completed vision moves people to adopt it.

The architect and scientist Christopher Alexander is offering us a potential paradigm shift with his new four-volume work *The Nature of Order* (Alexander, 2002-2005). It outlines a way of understanding and connecting to the universe, and a way of generating the built environment. Cutting past much of twentieth-century aesthetic and ideological dogmas, Alexander suggests that we have lost touch with our most basic human feelings, and proposes methods to reconnect us to ourselves, and to our world. While this work is ostensibly a manual on a "New Architecture", it is really a roadmap of how to appreciate again (for the first time for many readers) both natural and artificially created beauty. It is also a manual on how to be alive to the maximum extent possible by manipulating our surroundings; hence the connection to architecture.

Volume 1, *"The Phenomenon of Life"*, offers straightforward empirical tests that tell us whether any artifact, building, or built environment makes us feel more alive or less. It is a simple matter, therefore, to choose our surroundings so that we always feel alive. These tests are based on both perception and geometry; properties common to all structures that make us feel alive. Amazingly, these geometrical properties are also found in structures that ARE alive, as with biological organisms, and also in the extended sense of inanimate structures formed by nature.

Alexander then shows that these properties were understood intuitively by all the greatest artists, artisans, and architects of the past, who used them subconsciously to create humankind's historic works of art. That is, until the 20th century, when those pursuing innovation started to violate them.

Alexander convinces even the most skeptical reader by giving lengthy discussions in the second volume, *"The Process of Creating Life"*, based on scientific arguments. Anyone with an amateur's interest in popular science can easily follow his explanations, and they serve to overwhelmingly validate the claimed results. This is the wonderful aspect of this work: Alexander alternates between sensory tests that convince us in our heart and viscera that what he says is true; and detailed intellectual arguments that do the same for our rational, thinking mind.

The third book, *"A Vision of a Living World"*, is devoted to the art and science of building and design: everything from the scale of an entire city, to a neighborhood, to a single building, to an individual room, to a tile that will ornament a room and make it "alive". By itself, the existence of living structure on every level of scale will undoubtedly provoke a revolution. For Alexander convincingly argues that we connect to structure on every scale, and that the ideology of "pure form", which eliminated built ornament and coherent substructure on the human scales from the height of a person down to the width of a hair, was fundamentally destructive. Even in the field of architecture, where hagiography is standard practice, and where buildings by star architects are declared to be "miracles", Alexander creates deep anxiety. The worship of star architects is a game played by architectural critics and an entrenched power establishment. Architectural propaganda is meant for the masses, and is not taken seriously by those who are part of the machine. Yet anyone who reads Alexander's new book will be struck by the fact that this is a genuine paradigm shift, and not just another architectural deception intended to promote new faces and a new style. People are used to pretend prophets and cannot face the genuine thing: they tend to become hostile and lose all rationality.

Alexander ultimately and inevitably approaches the religious dimension. He has not shirked his duty, and faces this difficult confrontation head on in the final volume, *"The Luminous Ground"*. He is fully aware of the philosophical and religious implications of his work and devotes considerable thought to analyzing their consequences. When people begin to study this book, and the inevitable war with established architecture breaks out, thoughtful persons will find the truths in the connection to religion a comforting solace until the dust has settled. Then, the world can begin to rebuild itself on human and timeless principles free of a destructive dogma that took it over during the 20th century.

2. INTERVIEW WITH CHRISTOPHER ALEXANDER.

Nikos A. Salingaros: You offer a revolutionary four-volume book to the world. I am worried that people are unprepared for it, simply because it represents such a radical break with what everyone is used to. For example, this book is supposed to be about "The New Architecture", yet many of your architectural examples are not architectural at all. You hit your readers in the stomach by contradicting all they have ever been taught about architecture. Specifically, they expect to see photos of buildings without people, because that's the current conception of architecture — built structure that is validated by formal or ideological arguments. Nothing to do with human beings, since a building's raison d'être is supposed to be purely formal or ideological. Yet your examples of architecture just show people having a good time or coping with life in environments of negligible "architectural" qualities.

Your point is that architecture is not about building style, but is really a state of mind, and that good architecture is any structure, however modest, that generates an identifiable positive state of mind that allows you to be alive to the fullest extent possible. This idea is profound as well as revolutionary, since it stands architecture on its head. You validate our most basic feelings as human beings and insist that the built environment must nurture our inner joy, sadness, vulnerability, unselfconsciousness, and so on. All the formal architectural concerns — and names like Le Corbusier, Ludwig Mies van der Rohe, Frank Gehry, and Daniel Libeskind — are thus thrown out of the window.

Christopher Alexander: Of course, I have never had a rule in my mind telling me that I must participate in the psychotic process that we call architecture today. My allegiance is not to the profession as it is constituted today, but to the Earth, to buildings, and to people. Seeing the fact that most of our contemporary ways of dealing with architecture have been insane, I turned my back on them, and started from scratch. I began that work about forty years ago, and have been gradually approaching an architecture of a true humanity, year by year, ever since then. It has grown, and now may be called a coherent view of what architecture ought to mean.

Many of the people who pay attention to what I say are not architects. They are ordinary family people, engineers, biologists, computer scientists, politicians and political scientists. All these people know that something is wrong, and they know deeply what is wrong, but they have not had a leader who shows them that it is OK to say these things.

NAS: Why are you not afraid of being ignored, or even killed, or of having hatred pushed in your face by other contemporary architects who see that you are undoing what they stand for?

CA: The truth is a powerful thing. It gives people courage. And as the person who is saying these things, I need courage, too. But the fact that what I have to say is true gives me great courage, and the will to go forward, because I know, and other people know it is the truth. And, surprisingly, it gives many young architects courage, because they recognize it as the truth. Many architects today are walking about, knowing deep down, that they are doing something bad, or artificial, or meaningless, but not knowing exactly how to cut this mental cancer out of their systems. When they hear and see what I have done and built, and written, they begin to relax. Why do they relax? Because they hear someone speaking the truth, and many of them decide to follow that truth, because it makes them feel whole within themselves, even just to admit to these problems.

When it turns out that I have real practical solutions as well, and that what I have to say is not only true, but also morally right, and also practical, then they get excited and there is no reason for them to give up. They feel refreshed and renewed.

NAS: *After having dismantled architecture, you come back with overwhelming scientific arguments and show how to put it back together again in a coherent manner. You demonstrate to anyone who has even an amateur's knowledge of popular science that most 20th-century buildings are lifeless and incoherent, and that their place in books of great buildings is simply a mistake. The problem is that many people do not have this minimal scientific background to appreciate your claims, and will be offended by it without being able to verify it for themselves. You are contradicting something that was accepted by our civilization, regardless of whether ordinary people ever felt comfortable with it or not; a credo that became part of our culture and educational system.*

Most people are terrified by revolutions and changes of paradigm, and this is certainly one. People might agree with you on a deep level in their heart and gut, but be too scared to let go of what they have been taught. They will support the established view out of fear. Truth doesn't matter in such occasions — the instinct for survival fights against drastic change because, who knows, maybe your ideas will not stop at architecture, but will turn society itself upside down. Should we fear the collapse of social and economic order as we know it — how can you convince the world that your ideas are not dangerous?

CA: My ideas ARE dangerous. They are dangerous to the established order, which has, unintentionally, created an inhuman world during the last fifty years. The pressure of living in this inhuman world, together with the horrible consequences — drugs, war, mindless jobs, mindless television, broken homes, teenage violence and so on — have brought people to a breaking point. At this time, more and more people are determined to change their world. One reliable estimate is that 60 million people, in America alone, are ready to stop playing along with the artificial and deadening world we have created, and are determined to find new ways of doing things, new ways of thinking, new ways of acting, new ways of building — so that we become reconnected to ourselves.

This is an enormous thing. To all these people all over the Earth — and there are perhaps as many as one billion such people worldwide — to these one billion people these ideas are not dangerous at all. Instead they have a life-saving, healing quality, which can help to place all of us in a new relationship with our planet, with one another, and with our lives and values.

NAS: *Finally, there is the "architect problem": what to do with existing architects. According to your own estimates, there are about half a million architects around the world. The vast majority was taught in schools that turned modernist after the Second World War, and is therefore trained in sterile and formalist methods totally disconnected from life. Younger architects are even worse, because they are trained to deconstruct forms — what's left has no coherence whatsoever. One could say that many of those architects are trained to destroy and prevent rather than to generate living structure, although it never occurs to them that that's what they are doing. What's to become of them? Fine. The star architects have had their moment of glory, and can retire wealthy, but what about the unknown practitioners who worshipped the star architects? It would be easier to re-train them into another profession rather than to make them change their working habits, since their methods have been part of their beliefs and worldview for much of their lives.*

And then, who is going to build the world from now on? If our architects have been trained to be anti-architects, then you obviously need to train fresh people to do the job right. But where are they now? And since universities have the tenure system, how do you get rid of die-hard modernist and deconstructivist professors who run those programs now? Where are young architects going to learn an architecture that promotes life since they cannot do it in a university?

CA: Even half a million architects can easily become obsolete, if they keep on doing things which are superseded by other, better methods and by the efforts and work of others. When the automobile was invented, the horse and buggy lasted a few years, and finally dropped to one side as a minor entertainment, but was simply no longer the main way in which people moved around. The new form of architecture that I am speaking about is beginning to be understood by engineers, by ecologists, by computer scientists, by builders, by artists, by biologists, by economists. Many of these people recognize that architects are simply not dealing with the problem of the environment in a realistic or useful fashion, and that the task of building now falls on their own shoulders. Under the impact of that kind of thinking, people are now developing new ways of banking, new ways of development, new forms of social reconstruction, and new forms of housing, new forms of sustainable settlements.

In many countries, the primary way of conceiving and making buildings and settlements is already people-oriented. It is not recognizable within the existing paradigm as architecture, and architects despise it because it looks low budget, low tech, and is oriented to people's desperate needs — yet all this is, within the perspective of our new architecture, a major contribution to the new, life-based paradigm. All this is only its beginning. These new kinds of professionals, and new social forms, are beginning to develop and propagate new ways of doing things. And what architects now claim is simply being laid aside as the nonsense it really is.

Some young architects will join this new process with enthusiasm, as is already happening. Will the others choose to come along? I believe the remainder of the architects who continue trying to teach nonsensical deconstructivist ideas will, within a few years, simply be forgotten.

The new architecture I propose will ultimately supersede the present views, because it is true, because it is based on common sense and makes sense for ordinary people everywhere, and because it is based on good science. You can fool some of the people some of the time, but you cannot fool all the people all the time.

❦

ENDNOTE TO THE FIRST EDITION
BY LUCIEN STEIL

Nikos Salingaros is poignantly addressing the correct issues of what architecture and urbanism are about, and should be about. The fact that he is a mathematician, like the architects from antiquity and those who built the Hagia Sophia as much as the numerous Renaissance artists, is definitely not an accusation which should diminish his credibility.

If Charles Jencks celebrates the latest deconstructive madness by referring to a poorly digested scientific incubation, and if Peter Eisenman loosely quotes from modern mathematics to illustrate his random experiments of an uninhabitable architecture; well then, mathematics are surely welcome!

Nikos Salingaros, however, is encompassing an understanding of architecture and urbanism rooted in an understanding of mathematics and generally of science. This is intrinsically linked to the definition of complexity, of which life can be understood as the most essential manifestation. Architecture has been since its origin (and until its dismantlement by modernism) the most potent enrichment of nature, and the most articulate support — material, intellectual and spiritual — of the unfolding of mankind's cultures and the most cultivated expressions of life.

Salingaros might be more than prophetic when he identifies the 11th of September 2001 as the tragic end of modernist architecture. One might easily understand ridiculous contemporary schemes as some clownish and grotesque last spasms of a modernist establishment that is sick because of its disdainful ignorance of the wisdom of the universe, as much as of the mathematical laws of beauty and harmony. This establishment ignores the real human purposes of architecture and of science, and pursues its loveless and lifeless attempts to consecrate the disorder of reason as the order of the human environment! It is a documented fact that a large majority of people all over the world prefer to live and work in comfortable, familiar, well-scaled and proportioned buildings and towns. Most architects, however, are trained to practice an architecture without people and without humanity, for the sake of some imposed abstractions of a modernist aesthetic. Those aesthetics are antagonistic to the most common intuitions and feelings.

Architectural education is in a profound crisis, as it continues to educate professionals who are incompetent to articulate a shared culture of the built environment, and to build desirable places and buildings.

The confused and highly unpopular reconstruction schemes proposed by New York's elite and other internationally famed architects celebrates most ostentatiously an incapacity for reconstruction. At the base of this is the unwillingness of architects to contribute to creating a popular, comfortable and beautiful contemporary building culture.

In fact, as Nikos Salingaros suggests, this moral tragedy of the architectural profession is based on theories and an understanding of architectural practice that is rooted in a fundamentalist idealization of discomfort and deconstruction, and is articulated in a variety of grand gestures of built nihilism.

I think it is a reasonable assumption to expect the world's reconstruction to be the most vivid articulation of an architecture that can be loved in an act of commemoration. Within a process of healing, the world can become a place of wholeness and of life, of reinforced identity and of shared values of a humanist civilization.

<hr>

ENDNOTE TO THE SECOND EDITION
BY MICHAEL MEHAFFY

A more charitable report on contemporary architecture — which this volume decidedly was not — might have related the *fait accompli* of industrial economies of scale, and defended its roots in the heroic project to turn that reality to humane ends. It might have excused an increasingly desperate progression of abstract novelties as the inevitable aesthetic adventure demanded of us by a mechanized, abstract age. It might have defended the political necessity of acknowledging the helplessness of art to do anything but speak truth to power through expressive deconstruction.

In this volume Nikos Salingaros was having none of it. For him architecture is no arcane sculptural art, but an act of civic participation and world-shaping of the most public and populist sort. And he is appalled by the way that architects get an artistic *carte blanche* to wander all over the landscape, inserting self-impressive constructions willy-nilly, doing anything, it seems, except leading the larger building culture in something like a sustainable enterprise.

For him architects and planners are instead to be considered more like doctors of the built environment, with a standard of care for the health of their patient, the city. And like any doctor, they shoulder an obligation first, to do no harm. The scientist in Salingaros is also appalled at the pseudoscientific claims, the hocus-pocus, the willful disregard of the evidence of previous failures. In this architectural malpractice the current leadership is simply failing humanity: colossally, abysmally, unforgivably.

So this volume is an unapologetic Jeremiad, a broadside, a wake-up call. It is an indictment of the school of architecture originally called deconstruction — or, for those who have since seen fit to run away from that term, post-structuralist architecture by any other name. But it is also an indictment of architecture as a profession today, and the "anti-architecture" that it has become: self-indulgently provocative to the point of destructiveness.

Not surprisingly, the case Salingaros makes is not welcomed by many architects who would defend the cause of their unfettered artistic adventures. True, its brush is occasionally broad, and as was noted, it is hardly charitable. Yet since its first publication it has attracted its share of admirers, even in the architectural establishment — including a favorable notice in *Architectural Review*. The Prince of Wales has been known to quote admiringly from it, on one occasion to a President of the Royal Institute of British Architects, who was reportedly sympathetic in turn. (It was that same RIBA President who launched a BBC show called *Demolition*, in which members of the public took turns selecting especially hated buildings to blow up — all of them fine recent examples of Salingaros' "anti-architecture".)

As new and fearsome challenges loom on the horizon — the rebuilding of New Orleans after Katrina, the other daunting challenges of climate change, the creation of a sustainable model for the hypertrophic growth of cities around the world — the shortcomings of what Kenneth Frampton recently called "neo-avant-gardist kitsch" (quasi-radical in form but nihilist in content) are becoming painfully evident. Notwithstanding the occasional appended propeller gadgets, the architects are increasingly seen to be fiddling while Rome burns. They are ignoring the underlying pattern of unsustainable technology, and worse, serving as peddlers of it.

It's fair enough to admit now that we all face the same global challenges of commodification and unsustainable development, as Frampton noted. But the first step is surely to re-set the profession's moral compass, to re-assign itself with the leadership of the culture of building as a whole, returning to the ethical ideals of Morris, Gropius or Wright, to use the profession's position of influence, such as it is, to make life better for human beings.

That in turn will require a harsh assessment of the crippling metaphysics of the deconstructivists, who fall into the post-structuralists' self-created trap, trying to solve slippery problems of truth by destroying any effective theory of truth — rather like dealing with a continually leaky boat once and for all by scuttling it. But as physicist Alan Sokal demonstrated some time ago, science becomes an impossible fiasco under this philosophical regime. Whatever our humble uncertainties (and they are many), human health, ecological integrity, and the fate of societies like ours are not much beholden to the nuances of someone's privileged narrative. The epistemological progress of science — the full-bodied, Galilean version, rather than the technological variety — is an important lesson for us all.

Salingaros has expressed one regret about this volume, that it has not treated what can and must be done to address these shortcomings. That will have to follow, and is following, as he, Christopher Alexander, and a small army of allies and collaborators, seek to develop new models of design, development and construction management, new financial processes, and new incremental and generative approaches to planning. Promising new tools are already available, and more are on the way.

But a recognition of the nature of the problem is surely a first necessary step. And surely we can say, three years after its first publication, that this volume has made an important contribution in that regard. It has, in the voice of the small child, pointed out to a growing audience that the architectural Emperor has no clothes, and it's high time for something different.

ENDNOTE TO THE THIRD EDITION
"WHY DO WE HAVE HORRIBLE INHUMAN ARCHITECTURE?"
BY JAMES KALB

Why do we have horrible inhuman architecture? I've claimed that the issues are basically religious: "we want the world we build around us to look like the world we believe in. Otherwise it seems stupid, distracting, phony and aside the point". So if you're a modernist technocrat who makes a religion of the laws of physics, modern industry, and the triumph of the will, you build in the international style. If you're a postmodern who believes in chaos, obfuscation, and the triumph of the arbitrary will, you build like a deconstructionist.

In his book *A Theory of Architecture*, Nikos Salingaros proposes a couple of other thoughts:

1. The international style is cheap to build, and you can churn out big glass boxes without much thought, so it naturally won out. Any excuse is good enough for what makes things easier for the people who run things. Presumably, computer-aided design makes pop post-modernist buildings equally cheap (although not the luxury starchitect constructions that give the style iconic legitimacy). Post-modernist style is international style artificially made "playful", so it seems less boring.

2. Post-1920 architectural styles are viruses in the same sense computer viruses are viruses. They work, in fact, the same way a biological virus works. They are simplified scraps of information that are packaged in a way that enables them to enter a host system (like a human brain or culture) and take over the system so it becomes a machine for replicating and spreading the virus. So, if you encapsulate the extremely simple international style in slogans like "hygiene", "social progress", or whatever, and spread it with the aid of modern means of propaganda like glossy architecture magazines, then institutions and practitioners will pick it up as a quick, easy and prestigious substitute for actual thought and knowledge. The institutions and practitioners become vehicles for its forcible dissemination. Soon it'll be all there is. (Salingaros refers to intellectual viruses as "memes", although I think the term is usually used in a broader sense to include all components of transmitted culture.)

He places much more emphasis on the second line of thought. It's a frightening one because it can be applied to all aspects of human culture. The basic point is that current information networks, which make everything anyone has ever said on any subject whatever instantly available to everyone, are ideal settings for the propagation of intellectual viruses, and thus for the replacement of thought and knowledge by flashy content-free slogans. Thought and knowledge are difficult to build up and defend because the world is subtle and complicated. On such an analysis, the absolute unjustified dominance of empty and destructive architectural theories (forced on the whole world by "experts" whose authority is only increased by their rejection of comprehensibility and common sense) would be matched elsewhere in social life. The Harvard understanding of the humanities I have been complaining about — that they are social constructions that could as easily be reconstructed by whoever is in a position to make his authority good — would become the whole truth.

Salingaros doesn't discuss that line of thought, although in an article published in TELOS that ended up as a chapter in this book he's applied it to the thought of Jacques Derrida. He does however suggest that arbitrary, inhuman, content-free architecture is an educational force that creates arbitrary, inhuman, content-free minds. We can't connect to the built world, so we lose the ability to connect to the world generally. We suppress our natural reactions to our physical surroundings, so we become inhuman and willing to do whatever we are told, no matter how destructive. We become, in fact, tools for those in power with no lives of our own. Sounds like yuppiedom.

A bothersome feature of the Salingaros book I just commented on briefly (*A Theory of Architecture*) is that it's necessary. Basically, he's saying that buildings should look normal to normal people, and fit in with the way normal people normally act and feel. Nobody's ever had to say that before. Up to 80-100 years ago such things could not have become an issue. To make those points in a world in which normality has officially been abolished as oppressive and fraudulent, and everyone's been trained to be clueless, he has to go into complicated stuff involving fractal hierarchies, information content, self-similarity at different levels of scale, Darwinian evolution, and what not else.

That's got to be done, and he does it well, but how far is it going to get us? Suppose he gave a brilliant explanation of why Bertie Wooster is funny that actually communicated something to an audience trained to be humorless. The explanation might help them accept jokes as jokes, and perhaps become more tolerant of uneducated people who continue to laugh at life's oddities, but it's not going to turn them into P. G. Wodehouse. From where I stand, the future of architecture still looks troubled. Theories that show why obvious atrocities are atrocities are good, but far from sufficient.

The following remarks on "The Architecture of Hell" were inspired by the present book. The satanic is rebellion against God. In more abstract and secular terms, it is rebellion against all order that is not a matter of unconstrained human choice. Either way, contemporary intellectual culture often tends toward the satanic. Extreme idealization of human autonomy makes willfulness, transgression, and subversion seem like virtues. They destroy traditional standards, which are felt as shackles, and emancipation is thought to be the highest human good.

A problem with that kind of free-floating emancipation is that no movement that embraces it can be self-sustaining. It will be parasitic, pathological and destructive. Man is not complete in himself but part of something larger. An order we create by our own will can't sustain human life or even itself. It can only exist by setting itself against the remnants of natural and traditional order that are still needed to carry on social functioning. It disrupts the things that make life possible.

When theorists like Bernard Tschumi cite Sade favorably (in his book *"Architecture and Disjunction"*) or emphasize violence and murder (in his book *"The Manhattan Transcripts"*) they offer their adepts hope of meretricious advancement through superiority to conventional standards. Nonetheless, perversions of thought do not make life better for anyone. They are especially likely to make things worse when the theorists are architects, and their theories actually get built.

The principles that order the built environment matter, because man is rational and symbolic. To act in a human way we must identify, classify and interpret experience quickly and consistently. That means applying coherent rational principles. We may be unaware of those principles, just as we may be unaware of the grammar of our own language, but we have them and live by them, and we pick them up from the symbols that surround us. We surround ourselves with things that make sense to us. Conversely, we learn to make sense of life by means of symbolic representations of how things are. We are immersed in a built environment that teaches us the principles that inform it.

What happens then when the City of Man is built not on the principles of utility, beauty and harmony but on those of Pandemonium (the capital of Hell described in *"Paradise Lost"* by John Milton) — when willfulness, transgression and subversion stop being intellectual provocations and acquire credibility as principles of action through incorporation in the built environment?

Presumably, we get oppression, violence and lies. That's supposed to be a good thing. The idea, I suppose, is that there is no God, no given order that transcends human will, so beauty, harmony and perhaps in the end, utility, are fraudulent and oppressive and must be fought. If so, though, where does the "must" come from? And why put up with the oppression of building anything at all? If you want destruction you can get it straightaway.

The intellectual appeal of nihilism comes from the hope it offers of a certain rigorous purity. The hope is deceitful, because we are dependent and constantly find ourselves in complex situations we must deal with somehow. There is no short-cut to intellectual purity. The choice we have is not between acceptance or rejection of an order of things that precedes and sustains us, since we always accept such an order, but among under-standings of what that order is. God cannot be abolished. If He could then the inhabitants of hell would not be so obsessed by Him. Their obsessions mock their claims of freedom.

REFERENCES

QUOTATIONS

JAMES STEVENS CURL (2004) "Review of "Architectures: Modernism and After", *Journal of Urban Design*, **Volume 9 No. 2**, page 253.

DENNIS DUTTON (2003) in: *The New Humanists*, Edited by John Brockman (Barnes & Noble, New York), page 392.

NICOLAS GOMEZ-DAVILA (1992) *Succesivos Escolios a un Texto Implicito* (Bogotá, Colombia). Reprinted by Ediciones Altera, Barcelona, 2002, pages 80 & 152 (In Spanish).

FRIEDRICH HUNDERTWASSER (1997) "Interview for the SPD Bundestag Caucus, 1993", in: *Hundertwasser Architecture* (Taschen, Cologne), page 74.

ROGER SCRUTON (2000) *An Intelligent Person's Guide to Modern Culture* (St. Augustine's press, South Bend, Indiana), page 87.

GENERAL REFERENCES

CEU — COUNCIL FOR EUROPEAN URBANISM (2004) "The Declaration of Viseu: Architectural Education in the 21st Century", available online from <http://ceunet.org/viseu.htm>.

DIEDERIK AERTS, LEO APOSTEL, BART DE MOOR, STAF HELLEMANS, EDEL MAEX, HUBERT VAN BELLE & JAN VAN DER VEKEN (1994) *World Views: From Fragmentation to Integration* (VUB Press, Brussels).

CHRISTOPHER ALEXANDER (1964) *Notes on the Synthesis of Form* (Harvard University Press, Cambridge, Massachusetts).

CHRISTOPHER ALEXANDER (2002-2005) *The Nature of Order: Books 1-4* (Center for Environmental Structure, Berkeley). Book 1: *The Phenomenon of Life*; Book 2: *The Process of Creating Life*; Book 3: *A Vision of a Living World*; Book 4: *The Luminous Ground*.

CHRISTOPHER ALEXANDER (2002) *The Phenomenon of Life: The Nature of Order, Book One* (Center for Environmental Structure, Berkeley).

CHRISTOPHER ALEXANDER (2004) *The Luminous Ground: The Nature of Order, Book Four* (Center for Environmental Structure, Berkeley, California).

CHRISTOPHER ALEXANDER (2005) *A Vision of a Living World: The Nature of Order, Book Three* (Center for Environmental Structure, Berkeley, California).

CHRISTOPHER ALEXANDER & PETER EISENMAN (1983) "Contrasting Concepts of Harmony in Architecture", *Lotus International* **Volume 40**, pages 60-68. Reprinted in Harvard University Graduate School of Design, *Studio Works* **Volume 7** (Princeton Architectural Press, 2000), pages 50-57. Reprinted in *Katarxis* **No. 3** (2004).

CHRISTOPHER ALEXANDER, SARA ISHIKAWA, MURRAY SILVERSTEIN, MAX JACOBSON, INGRID FIKSDAHL-KING & SHLOMO ANGEL (1977) *A Pattern Language* (Oxford University Press, New York).

ROB ANNABLE (2004) "Deconstruction and Tea", *Wolverhampton Linux User Group* (May 5).

BOAZ BEN-MANASSEH (2001) Review of "The Space of Encounter", *The Architectural Review* (June), page 96.

JOHN BRODIE (1991) "Master Philip and the Boys", *Spy,* May Issue, pages 50-58.

PETER BRUNETTE & DAVID WILLS, Editors (1994) *Deconstruction and the Visual Arts* (Cambridge University Press, Cambridge).

ANDREW BULHAK (1996) *Postmodernism Generator,* available online from http://www. elsewhere. org/cgi-bin/postmodern.

CIAR BYRNE (2004) "Libeskind's £70m V&A extension in peril after lottery fund rejection", *The Independent* (22 July), approx. 1 page.

JEFF COLLINS & BILL MAYBLIN (1996) *Introducing Derrida* (Icon Books UK, Cambridge).

JAMES STEVENS CURL (1999) *A Dictionary of Architecture* (Oxford University Press, Oxford). Second Edition, 2006.

RICHARD DAWKINS (1989) *The Selfish Gene,* New Edition (Oxford University Press, Oxford), Chapter 11.

RICHARD DAWKINS (1998) "Postmodernism Disrobed", *Nature* **Volume 394**, pages 141-143.

JACQUES DERRIDA (1991) "58 min 41 sec: Summary of Impromptu Remarks", in: *Anyone,* Edited by Cynthia Davidson (Rizzoli, New York), pages 39-45.

JARED DIAMOND (2003) "Why do some societies make disastrous decisions?", *The Lewis Thomas Prize Lecture,* Rockefeller Institute, New York City, March 2003. *Edge: The Third Culture,* **No. 114**, April, approximately 10 pages.

CONSTANTINE DOXIADES (1972) *Architectural Space in Ancient Greece* (MIT Press, Cambridge Massachusetts).

"ENCARTA WORLD ENGLISH DICTIONARY" (1999), (St. Martin's Press, New York).

MILDRED FRIEDMAN, Editor (1999) *Gehry Talks* (Rizzoli, New York).

RICHARD GABRIEL (1996) *Patterns of Software* (Oxford University Press, New York).

STEPHEN GRABOW (1983) *Christopher Alexander: The Search for a New Paradigm in Architecture* (Oriel Press, Boston).

JOHN HUTH (1998) "Latour's Relativity", in: *A House Built on Sand,* Edited by Noretta Koertge (Oxford University Press, New York), pages 181-192.

CHARLES JENCKS (1988) "Interview of Peter Eisenman", *AD – Architectural Design,* **volume 58 No. 3/4**, pages 49-61.

CHARLES JENCKS (2002a) "The New Paradigm in Architecture", *DATUTOP* **Volume 22**, pages 13-23.

CHARLES JENCKS (2002b) *The New Paradigm in Architecture* (Yale University Press, New Haven).

PHILIP JOHNSON & MARK WIGLEY (1988) *Deconstructivist Architecture* (The Museum of Modern Art, New York).

OWEN JONES (1982) *The Grammar of Ornament* (Van Nostrand Reinhold, New York). Original Edition, 1856.

ROGER KIMBALL (1990) *Tenured Radicals* (Harper & Row, New York).

LÉON KRIER (1998) *Architecture: Choice or Fate* (Andreas Papadakis, Windsor, England).

THOMAS KUHN (1970) *The Structure of Scientific Revolutions,* 2nd. Edition (University of Chicago Press, Chicago).

DAVID LEHMAN (1991) *Signs of the Times: Deconstruction and the Fall of Paul de Man* (Poseidon Press, New York).

HILARY LEWIS & JOHN O'CONNOR (1994) *Philip Johnson: The Architect in His Own Words* (Rizzoli, New York).

DANIEL LIBESKIND (1997) *Fishing From the Pavement* (NAi Publishers, Rotterdam, Holland).

DANIEL LIBESKIND (2001) *The Space of Encounter* (Thames & Hudson, London).

ROBERT LOCKE (2001) "America's Worst Architect is a Marxist", *FrontPage Magazine*, 10 August.

ELENA MARCHETTI & LUISA ROSSI COSTA (2002) "The Fire Tower", *Nexus Network Journal*, **Volume 4 No. 2** (Spring), approx. 12 pages. Figure 4 shows Johannes Itten's *"Composition with Dice"*.

REX MARTIENSSEN (1964) *The Idea of Space in Greek Architecture* (Witwatersrand University Press, Johannesburg).

JOHN MASSENGALE (2004a) "The Thrilla at Manila: The Coup at Viseu", Veritas et Venustas (25 September).

JOHN MASSENGALE (2004b) "Insular Architecture Schools", Veritas et Venustas (19 December).

JOHN MASSENGALE (2005) "Nicolai Ouroussoff: Blinded by Ideology", Veritas et Venustas (28 June).

JOHN MASSENGALE (2007a) "Funny, you don't look Blueish", Veritas et Venustas (8 September).

JOHN MASSENGALE (2007b) "A Sign of the Times", Veritas et Venustas (22 September).

JOHN MASSENGALE (2007c) "It's The Place, Stupid!", Veritas et Venustas (23 November).

IAN MCFADYEN (2000) *Mind Wars* (Allen & Unwin, St. Leonards, NSW, Australia).

MICHAEL W. MEHAFFY AND NIKOS A. SALINGAROS (2001) "The End of the Modern World", *PLANetizen*, approximately 4 pages; reprinted by *Open Democracy*.

MICHAEL W. MEHAFFY & NIKOS A. SALINGAROS (2002) "Geometrical Fundamentalism", *Plan Net Online Architectural Resources* (January). Chapter 9 of *A Theory of Architecture* (Umbau-Verlag, Solingen, 2006).

DEROY MURDOCK (2003) "Shred the Libeskind Blueprints", *National Review Online* (30 June), approx. 3 pages.

HERBERT MUSCHAMP (2002) "Thinking Big: A Plan for Ground Zero and Beyond", *The New York Times Magazine*, September, pages 45-58.

PHILIP NOBEL (2000) "How Bernard Tschumi's Star Status Undermined His First American Building", *Metropolis Magazine*, April Issue.

CHRISTOPHER NORRIS (1989) "Interview of Jacques Derrida", *AD – Architectural Design*, **Volume 59 No. 1/2**, pages 6-11.

NICOLAI OUROUSSOFF (2007) "Where Gods Yearn for Long-Lost Treasures", The New York Times (28 October).

SUSAN PARHAM (2004) "A Synthesis: New Strategies in Education of Architecture and Urbanism", Council for European Urbanism, available from <http://ceunet.org/reportfromviseu.htm>.

CARLO POGGIALI (2002) "How To Really Enjoy Even Geometrical Fundamentalism", *Temi di Stefano Borselli*, **No 119**, 6 February (in Italian).

ROBIN POGREBIN (2004) "The Incredible Shrinking Daniel Libeskind", *The New York Times* (20 June), approx. 6 pages.

CLIFF RADEL (1996) "UC building is pretty, but pretty what?", *The Cincinnati Enquirer* (May 24), approximately 2 pages.

NIKOS A. SALINGAROS (1998) "A Scientific Basis for Creating Architectural Forms", *Journal of Architectural and Planning Research* **Volume 15**, pages 283-293. Chapter 2 of *A Theory of Architecture* (Umbau-Verlag, Solingen, 2006).

NIKOS A. SALINGAROS (2000a) "Hierarchical Cooperation in Architecture, and the Mathematical Necessity for Ornament", *Journal of Architectural and Planning Research* **Volume 17**, pages 221-235. Chapter 3 of *A Theory of Architecture* (Umbau-Verlag, Solingen, 2006).

NIKOS A. SALINGAROS (2000b) "The Structure of Pattern Languages", *Architectural Research Quarterly* **Volume 4**, pages 149-161. Chapter 8 of *Principles of Urban Structure* (Techne Press, Amsterdam, 2005).

NIKOS A. SALINGAROS (2003a) "Pattern Language and Interactive Design", *Poiesis Architecture* (Toulouse) **No. 15**, pages 385-405. Chapter 9 of *Principles of Urban Structure* (Techne Press, Amsterdam, 2005).

NIKOS A. SALINGAROS (2003b) "Two Languages for Architecture", *Plan Net Online Architectural Resources*, (February). Chapter 11 of *A Theory of Architecture* (Umbau-Verlag, Solingen, 2006).

NIKOS A. SALINGAROS (2003c) "The Sensory Value of Ornament", *Communication & Cognition*, **Volume 36, No. 3/4**, pages 331-351. Chapter 4 of *A Theory of Architecture* (Umbau-Verlag, Solingen, Germany, 2006).

NIKOS A. SALINGAROS (2006) *A Theory of Architecture* (Umbau-Verlag, Solingen, Germany).

NIKOS A. SALINGAROS & TERRY M. MIKITEN (2002) "Darwinian Processes and Memes in Architecture: A Memetic Theory of Modernism", *Journal of Memetics — Evolutionary Models of Information Transmission* **Volume 6**, approximately 15 pages. Reprinted in *DATUTOP Journal of Architectural Theory* **Volume 23**, pages 117-139. Chapter 10 of *A Theory of Architecture* (Umbau-Verlag, Solingen, 2006).

NIKOS A. SALINGAROS (2005) "Towards a New Urban Philosophy: The Case of Athens", Chapter 20 of: Shifting Sense — Looking Back to the Future in Spatial Planning, Edited by Edward Hulsbergen, Ina Klaasen & Iwan Kriens (Techne Press, Amsterdam), pages 265-280.

NIKOS A. SALINGAROS & KENNETH G. MASDEN II (2006) "Architecture: Biological Form and Artificial Intelligence", The Structurist, No. 45/46, pages 54-61.

NIKOS A. SALINGAROS & KENNETH G. MASDEN II (2007) "Restructuring 21st Century Architecture Through Human Intelligence", Archnet-IJAR: International Journal of Architectural Research, Volume 1, Issue 1, pages 36-52.

LOUIS A. SASS (1992) *Madness and Modernism* (Harvard University Press, Cambridge, Massachusetts), Chapter 6.

HILLEL SCHOCKEN (2003) "Intimate Anonymity", *INTBAU Essays*, **Volume 1, No. 5**. German version published by *Umbau-Verlag* (2004).

FRANZ SCHULZE (1994) *Philip Johnson: Life and Work* (Alfred A. Knopf, New York).

ROGER SCRUTON (2000) "The Devil's Work", Chapter 12 of *An Intelligent Person's Guide to Modern Culture* (St. Augustine's Press, South Bend, Indiana).

ALAN SOKAL (1996) "Transgressing the Boundaries: Toward a Transformative Hermeneutics of Quantum Gravity", *Social Text* **Volume 46/47**, pages 217-252.

ALAN SOKAL & JEAN BRICMONT (1998) *Fashionable Nonsense* (Picador, New York). European title: *Intellectual Impostures*.

MICHAEL SORKIN (1991) "Where was Philip?" in: *Exquisite Corpse* (Verso, London), pages 307-11. Originally published in: *Spy*, October 1988, pages 138-140.

BERNARD TSCHUMI (1994a) *The Manhattan Transcripts*, New Edition (Academy Editions, London). First Edition, 1981.

BERNARD TSCHUMI (1994b) *Architecture and Disjunction* (MIT Press, Cambridge, Massachusetts).

HANS URS VON BALTHASAR (1982) *The Glory of the Lord*, Volume 1 (Ignatius Press, Ft. Collins, Colorado).

KAZYS VARNELIS (1995) "We Cannot Not Know History", *Journal of Architectural Education* **Volume 49/2**, pages 92-104.

VASSILIS VASSILIKOS (2007) "Cafeteria Tschumi", Eleftherotypia (6 October).

DAVID WATKIN (2000) *A History of Western Architecture*, 3d. Edition (Watson-Guptill, New York).

EDWARD O. WILSON (1984) *Biophilia* (Harvard University Press, Cambridge, Massachusetts).

EDWARD O. WILSON (1998a) "Integrating Science and the Coming Century of the Environment", *Science* **Volume 279**, pages 2048-2049.

EDWARD O. WILSON (1998b) *Consilience: The Unity of Knowledge* (Alfred A. Knopf, New York).

SAMIR YOUNÉS, Editor (2002) *Ara Pacis Counter-Projects* (Alinea Editrice, Florence, Italy).

Index

EXTRACTS FROM REVIEWS OF
"ANTI-ARCHITECTURE AND DECONSTRUCTION".

"In [this] series of learned and moving critical essays, Salingaros and various close associates argue that we understand life in architecture as the background to human community — the preparation for our dwelling place... One day, perhaps, Salingaros will be required reading for architects. If that happens it could just be that a new orthodoxy will emerge, in which humility, order, and public spirit — the virtues which have been chased from the discipline by the starchitects — will be the norm." — Roger Scruton.

"Finally, some clarity on Deconstruction! This book offers a critical analysis of deconstructivist architecture and its underlying philosophy. Many persons — architects as well as non-architects — feel very strongly enough about this topic, and get quite emotional about it. People either hate Deconstructivist buildings, or they think they are wonderful. The problem is that, up until now, there has not been a way of deciding WHY different people react in opposite ways to the same buildings. This series of essays, previously published in a variety of online and paper journals, brings together for the first time the provocative ideas the author has used to understand Deconstruction and its role in shaping the building environment. There is no other book today that is sufficiently analytical so as to make an impact on today's infatuation with this peculiar building style. [It includes] an explosive interview with Christopher Alexander and a review of his monumental four-volume work 'The Nature of Order'. That may well pave the way for a completely different architecture in our lifetimes, whose characteristics negate all the premises of Deconstruction." — Anonymous Reviewer.

"Nikos Salingaros thoroughly eviscerates the nonsense that passes for deconstructionist architectural 'theory', and goes on to explain why it won't just go away and die. With considerable precision and wit he characterizes the deconstructionist meme as 'the Derrida virus' and shows how it propagates within society. This results in the cult that is the contemporary architectural establishment. As obligate intracellular parasites, viruses are extremely hard to deal with." — Sajjad Afzal-Woodward.

"Nikos Salingaros' 'Anti-Architecture and Deconstruction' should ruffle lots of feathers in the building and design world. But I suspect it'll also fascinate many who aren't generally architecture and urbanism fanatics. Puzzled by the prevalence of hideous buildings (and the kind of thinking that justifies and rationalizes such practices), Salingaros applies his powerful mind to such basic questions as: what is a theory? What might the difference be between an art theory and some other kind

of theory? What are the ideas and aims of the current architectural elite? And what might explain why these flawed ideas have such a powerful hold on so many people? This is a stunning and deep book, as interesting for its analyses of psychology and politics as it is for its discussions of architecture. It's guaranteed to get the brain buzzing; what a treat too that it's a real reading pleasure, written in a voice that's both urbane and forceful." — Michael Blowhard.

"I would rank Nikos Salingaros on the same level with people like Stewart Brand who wrote 'How Buildings Learn'. They both are looking from the outside in at the state of architecture today, and can see the problems and explain the problems from a rational point of view so that you find yourself saying 'that's right' as you read their books. I had the same experience while reading Prince Charles's book 'A vision of Britain' in 1989. Salingaros's books, Stewart Brand's book and Prince Charles's book should be read by everyone." — Audun Engh.

"The book 'Anti-Architecture and Deconstruction' comes at the end of many years of studies and debates, and at the beginning of new reflections on the topic of contemporary architecture... Architecture took over the role of representing modernity in its entirety, from social customs to Technology and Science. Nevertheless, criticism is now coming from the very heart of the scientific world... Definitely, the true importance of this text is to remove every support that modern Architecture has ever claimed from Science. This book is indispensable for whoever wishes to deepen their knowledge of the social aspects of contemporary architecture, [and] for graduate courses in Architecture and Urban Design." — Raffaele Giovanelli.

"Dear Nikos: I finished reading your book 'Anti-Architecture and Deconstruction' some time ago, and have been meditating on it ever since. It was quite fascinating! At times heartwarming, at other times frightening. It reads like something from a fictional anti-utopia; say, George Orwell's '1984', or C. S. Lewis's 'That Hideous Strength'. They are very liberated persons, these ultra-moderns — liberated from logic, reason, nature. I think you are exactly right that this is all ideology, but I also think that underlying this ideology are two hidden ruling ideas: absolute freedom as the only value; and absolute despair. In other words, a spiritual crisis, even spiritual death. Your use of the viral metaphor is quite convincing, and also frightening. I am absolutely convinced that the concept of organized complexity provides a conceptual link that bridges science and the religious tradition. For your insight into this link I am profoundly grateful. Perhaps it is this unity of love, order, and complexity that holds the key to the *pattern language* which will eventually defeat the inhuman and destructive madness that you and Christopher Alexander (and others) have so eloquently and convincingly described?" — Paul Grenier.

"Less than twenty pages of text is enough to deprive Deconstruction of the complex scientific arguments that offer its exponents scientific authority and social approval. It is astonishing that while architecture abandons the principles that made civilizations reach the highest building achievements, at the same time scientific knowledge that results from a drastically improved understanding of Nature rediscovers the quality of those traditional principles. Whereas the most celebrated architects abuse the latest technological gadgets in order to produce caricatures of science, mathematicians such as Nikos Salingaros and Christopher Alexander use science to reveal the ability of traditional architectural principles to innovate by creating humane urban environments. We are facing the submission of the architectural profession to a shortsighted socio-economic structure that promotes the manipulation of ways of thinking in order to create controlled mass behaviors that lead to mass consumption. This structure promises the further destruction of the urban environment, exhausting our hopes for a future in humane, urbane cities with the qualities of the urban environments whose loss we so often regret. However, the clarity of vision that characterizes books such as 'Anti-Architecture and Deconstruction' shows that such a future may not be so far away after all." — Nikos Karydis.

"I think that Nikos' ideas are a great advance in the spirit of Newton's three laws. And there are many phenomena from everyday life that Nikos' principles might explain, but especially regarding our "sixth sense" by which we synchronize ourselves with each other (as if dancing) and which uses our environment as a "baseline" that we might tune ourselves to and thereby empathize with others as we size ourselves to various scales. What I think is needed now is a series of theoretical and empirical experiments to test Nikos' ideas and build on them." — Andrius Kulikauskas

"Salingaros … sets forth scientific evidence showing the series of illogical and misleading failures of the Modern and Deconstruction movements. "Anti-Architecture and Deconstruction" exposes the low degree of organized complexity of such projects, and elegantly outlines their destructive and dangerous nature. The practitioners and propagandists of those movements, who force-fed ugly, monstrous and evil architecture (and the pseudo-intellectual theory that accompanied it) upon the public, are themselves proved to be lacking scientific knowledge, and lack an understanding of the human soul. Dr. Salingaros shows once again, with an outstanding level of intellectual clarity and vigor, that relying upon scientific analyses yields incredible results." — Nicola Giacomo Linza

"Deconstruction is an architectural style that in recent years has gained ever-increasing influence among architects and educators, as well as decision and policy makers and developers of prestige projects. Many famous recent projects are examples of the style. More than just visual fashion, it has serious implications for form, function and aesthetics. Characterized by lack of human-scale details, jagged and convoluted

figures, disjointed masses and planes, glittering glass and polished metal surfaces, these buildings stem primarily from a branch of philosophy whose main representative was the late French philosopher Jacques Derrida. Step by step, the reader is taken through Derrida's description of deconstruction as a virus intended to attack and destroy structures, a definition and purpose shared by his architect disciples. Tschumi's descriptions are even harder to digest, expressing his design concepts in terms of schizophrenic thought processes, spiced with a fascination for the violent, the bizarre and the perverse. Johnson's fascination with nihilism and Nazi ideology, and his praise of war ruins and embedded violence as an exciting form of aesthetics, is at least as disconcerting. Architects cannot go on indulging themselves in the misty atmosphere of 'constructive ambiguity', with the logic of cults, the rhetoric of twisted pseudo-philosophy, and the terminology of disciplines they have no understanding of. It is time for architects to realize that an aggressive, self-propelling group has hijacked architecture, its teaching, discussion and raison d'être." — Isaac A. Meir.

"In his forward to this book, James Stevens Curl writes: 'This book should be required reading in every institution concerned with the teaching of architecture, planning, and all other aspects of the built environment'. I will extend that recommendation to every institution of higher learning concerned with effective education in all subject matters, because this book is also about the world we live in. Though it is focused on the practice of Deconstructivist architecture, in fact this book is also, by inference and extension, a description of the end of urbanism when living, work, social life, and a sense of community connected to a place were displaced by national corporations, the separation of work from residence, the growth of suburban sprawl enabled by the car, shopping centers, and grid-locked roads. [It] is the clearest description of the state of architecture and the destructiveness of the Decon movement. We ourselves, and our understanding of basic human needs for peace and comfort, have been stolen by a non-culture." — Konrad Perlman.

"Undoubtedly, this manuscript is a voice of logic and reason against anti-architecture norms, and the destructive attitudes of their followers. I would add my voice to other reviewers of this manuscript: that it must be a mandatory reading in schools of architecture worldwide. Salingaros' call for going against those attitudes and regaining our interest in solutions to human problems needs to be adopted. The manuscript's thrust for re-associating ourselves to the near and distant past — depending on who we are and the cultural context in which we operate — deserves special attention by both academics and practitioners." — Ashraf Salama.

"Nikos Salingaros is a mathematician who's also a brilliant thinker about architecture and urbanism. 'Solid' doesn't begin to hint at his virtues and talents, but isn't it nice when you encounter 'solid' in the world of the arts? Salingaros has

worked closely with Christopher Alexander , and has become a major architecture theorist in his own right.." — Ray Sawhill.

"I, as well as some of my classmates, have had the opportunity to personally follow the studies of this man over the last few years. And, as more than one person can attest, he is making giant steps towards the future of architecture. His texts are very clear and concise and as we come out of the post-modern era in architecture, it is important that we bring architecture back into the hands of the user and not let it fall victim to the celebrity architect. Dr. Salingaros speaks to this. He advocates that design must be driven by the land, the function it serves, and nothing else. The result is architecture that is sustainable, enjoyable and timeless." — Miles Vandewalle

"This is an interesting compilation of some of the important roots and evolutions of modernism and its latest development, the 'Deconstruction' style. This new work is a fascinating exploration of the history and psychology of modernism, post modernism and deconstruction. It is a revealing glimpse behind the curtain of the contemporary high-end architectural establishment, and the underlying human motivations and misapprehensions which have brought us to our present disoriented way-point. A lot of psychology, and some remarkable philosophy can be found here, as should be the case in any kind of good architectural soul searching. There is also a wonderful and thought-provoking thematic presentation of a 'viral metaphor', which has far-reaching implications, not only for architecture but human endeavor in any and all pursuits. To go a step further, one could say that deconstruction — by its very primitive, crystalline, Godless character — marks the end of innocence for the human; the end of the control and dominance of biological and genetically determined order. In the earth's history the Deconstructionist Style may well mark the stark requirement of the beginning of an acknowledgment of human power, and the resulting imperative of responsibility for what we make of ourselves and our world." — Dirk Visser.